This book analyzes wage hierarchy in market and planning theory, and how these theories can be used as a basis for the comparison of wage structures in Western and Soviet-type systems. The author analyzes statistical data from ten countries in both systems at the beginning of the eighties, and attempts to account for wage dispersion by examining such factors as education and training, discrimination against women, and market structure, as well as the influence of systemic factors.

Professor Redor asserts that systemic differences are not the most significant determinants of wage inequality (the Soviet Union is found to be on a par with the United Kingdom for example), and argues that similarities between the two systems in the dispersion of wages are due to similar patterns of work organization and wage policies within firms, and that many determinants of wage inequality are in fact common to both systems.

WAGE INEQUALITIES IN EAST AND WEST

WAGE INEQUALITIES IN EAST AND WEST

Dominique Redor

TRANSLATED BY
ROSEMARIE BOURGAULT

CAMBRIDGE
UNIVERSITY PRESS

CAMBRIDGE UNIVERSITY PRESS
Cambridge, New York, Melbourne, Madrid, Cape Town, Singapore,
São Paulo, Delhi, Dubai, Tokyo

Cambridge University Press
The Edinburgh Building, Cambridge CB2 8RU, UK

Published in the United States of America by Cambridge University Press, New York

www.cambridge.org
Information on this title: www.cambridge.org/9780521134149

Originally published in French as Les Inegalités de Salaire a l'Est et l'Ouest by Economica 1988
English translation 1992
This digitally printed version 2010

A catalogue record for this publication is available from the British Library

Library of Congress Cataloguing in Publication data
Redor, Dominique.
[Inégalités de salaires à l'est et à l'ouest. English]
Wage inequalities in East and West / Dominique Redor: translated
by Rosemarie Bourgault.
p.   cm.
Translation of: Les inégalités de salaires à l'est et à l'ouest.
Includes bibliographical references.
ISBN 0 521 39531 3 (hardback)
1. Income distribution. 2. Wages – Europe, Eastern. 3. Wages –
Soviet Union. 4. Comparative economics. 5. Compensation management. I. Title.
HC79.I5R3713 1992
331.2'947 – dc20 91-30136 CIP

ISBN 978-0-521-39531-1 Hardback
ISBN 978-0-521-13414-9 Paperback

Contents

Preface to the English edition

This book concerns the 1970s and the 1980s, that is to say, the period before the major economic and political upheavals that most countries in Eastern Europe have experienced.

It concerns two subjects: the wage structures and the labor economy where important similarities (and more specifically "isomorphisms") between Western and Soviet-type economies have been underlined. Is it not a bit paradoxical to analyze these isomorphisms when, far from converging toward the Western economic system, the Soviet-type system (STS) has fallen apart in most East European countries? We think that the answer to this question is no.

First of all the theoretical oppositions between centralized and decentralized economy, administrated and private economy, planned and market economy, cannot be applied integrally to the analysis of labor and wage structures. Indeed, the purely administrative assigning of manpower to jobs began to disappear from the Soviet bloc countries during the fifties. This resulted in a certain decentralization of labor exchanges. Financial perks in the form of bonuses, differentiation of wages between firms, regions, and sectors were introduced progressively in different forms from country to country.

In addition, certain elements which constitute the subject of this book are only indirectly related to the factors having brought about the fall of the STS. Moreover, we maintain that our research sheds light on the causes of this fall, from the specific angle of labor and wages.

From this point of view, we will distinguish the factors that explain the economic failure of the STS.

Elements having no role or a minor role in the economic failure of the STS
1 The degree of earnings and individual income inequality.
One of the main empirical results that we found is that there is no systemic difference between the general dispersion of earnings and

income in the two systems. We ranked, for example, the six Western economies and the four Soviet-type economies studied in decreasing order for earnings dispersion (using the Gini coefficient and the coefficient of variation for wage-earners as a whole); this classification resulted in a mixture of economies from both systems (part I, chapter 3). We got the same result when studying the dispersion of income available to households taking into account income from secondary activities in the Soviet type economies (part II, chapter 9).

It appears for example that the Soviet-type economies are no more egalitarian in the eighties than most economies of Northern Europe (Denmark, FRG, the United Kingdom). Thus it appears that the thesis that egalitarianism in the STS is a factor of the low level of labor productivity and of economic inefficiency seems to be disproven.

2 The determinants of the wage structures.
Some of these determinants play a similar role in explaining wage differentiation in both systems. A detailed statistical analysis reveals that gender, skill, and sector of activity of wage-earners are linked with earnings dispersion in the West as well as in the East (part I, chapters 3 and 4).

However in this analysis some "systemic differences" are disclosed. First it shows that in the STS wages in sectors that were defined as "having priority" (mining, steel) remain relatively high given the structure of skills therein. Secondly manual workers are relatively better paid than their Western counterparts when compared with non-manual workers. This difference has political and ideological grounds. At the origination of the STS, the wages of manual workers were increased relative to non-manual workers. It was the same for wages of the industrial sectors relative to the service sectors. These changes were based on an interpretation of the Marxist distinction between productive and unproductive labor which can be criticized (part II, chapter 8).

Nevertheless the study of pay differentiation according to the skills of workers and more specifically between managers and simple employees does not disclose any systemic difference. Indeed these skills must be distinguished as functions of the individuals in the firm organization. In practice, in the STS, white-collar workers working in unproductive functions (commercial, administrative) are placed at the bottom of the wage scale. But the pay level of the managers of the production departments as compared to the pay of manual workers is not different from that of their Western counterparts.

In addition, the relatively high wages of manual workers did not result in a lack of interest in executive positions or higher education. On the contrary, according to sociological surveys carried out in Hungary and Poland as well as certain Soviet monographs, there is a tendency for workers to leave agriculture in favor of white-collar jobs in firms, or to move from industry to the tertiary sector. This phenomenon can be explained by the poor working conditions in production workshops as well as by the payment system (piecework) which makes payment subject to fluctuations. It must be noted that the same tendency is characteristic of many Western economies during the seventies and eighties. The interest in the service sector can be explained by the opportunities it affords to have parallel activities or to benefit from secondary income.

3 Internal management of labor and pay.
In the STS the planning organizations control the "wage fund" of each firm (its wage bill) and in some cases the average wage. This planning relied from the beginning on purely administrative procedures. The economic "reforms" which were applied from the sixties aimed at connecting this fund with different indicators of the efficiency of the firms (for example labor productivity (see part II, chapter 6).

During the same rather brief period, the Administration also attempted to control directly the numbers of workers hired. In fact, despite these administrative constraints which are negotiable between firms and the ministries upon which they depend, there is a fair amount of freedom concerning the internal management of labor and the wage bill. This is why the theory of internal market/external market was applied to Hungarian firms for example (part II, chapter 7). In Soviet-type economies, firms structure wages (within the context of the Administrative constraints which suppress the wage bill) and design promotion channels so as to hold on to manpower and to avoid having to fill vacant positions from outside labor markets which are struck by a shortage of manpower.

Factors directly connected with the fall of the Soviet-type economic system
It must be borne in mind that our purpose is not to work out a general theory but to learn from the particular area that interests us.

1 Communication lines between the planning center and firms. Centralized assigning of manpower supposes *in theory* that the planning center has a mass of relevant information at its disposal, and that it is capable of handling this information rapidly. This question was the central issue in a famous debate between F. A. von Hayek and O. Lange during the inter-war period. The experience of Soviet type economies proves that communication difficulties linked to centralized planning are insurmountable and create increasing sources of inefficiency in modern economies.

As for the example of the planning of the wage fund of each firm, the strategic role of which was defined earlier, the center must determine, on the basis of production objectives, the total employment and its structure by skill, the productivity of labor for each category. However, all of these elements are necessarily uncertain. Moreover, given this procedure, which Western and Eastern economists have analyzed at length, it is in the interest of firms to conceal their information about their production function. These procedures resulted in an irrational assigning of the wage bill and hence of manpower between firms and sectors (as compared to the evolution of the final demand) and an important waste of human resources. This inefficiency which is linked to central planning is even more serious than "X inefficiency"; the analysis thereof shows that firms take advantage of a certain autonomy in the internal management of manpower and in the internal distribution of the wage bill. Even if these two forms of inefficiency are linked, our analysis tends to show that the internal capacities of firms to adapt to change in their environment (move from an administrated economy to a market economy) should not be underestimated, provided the move is gradual.

2 The tremendous rigidity of structures of activity.
First of all, in so far as the system of planning in the STS is designed to realize production objectives, without firms having to bear the real cost of production, firms accumulate "manpower reserves," thus concealing unemployment. This resulted in tremendous hiring difficulties for the new sectors of production. "Labor shortages" were common in all of the Eastern European economies until the end of the eighties (part II, chapter 6).

The "paternalistic" behavior of planning centers exacerbated this phenomenon (Kornai (1980)). Indeed, the planning center made up the deficits of many firms without ever reorienting or restructuring the activities thereof. Therefore, a wider and wider gap grew between production and social demand (many products were not sold, whereas in other sectors there were major shortages of consumer goods). In this way, we can explain the hypertrophy of heavy industry, which had "priority" status from the beginning of the STS to the end of the eighties. Indeed, there was a continual increase in employment in these branches (except in Hungary), despite the change in demand (directed at new materials) and world supply (the emergence in the West of new technologies which reduce manpower needs).

3 The organization of labor.

As for the organization of labor, innovations borrowed from the West were introduced into Soviet bloc firms very late. In addition, the tremendous size of production units, as well as the hierarchical conception of power in firms, favored the adoption of methods of labor organization similar to Taylorism. Eastern economies did not apply, nor were they inspired by new methods of organization which appeared in the West in the seventies and spread in the eighties. These methods leave more room for worker initiatives and provide greater flexibility of labor organization in order to meet quantitative and qualitative changes in demand.

Finally, it is certainly the inability of the STS to adapt to the important changes that occurred in the West in recent years and which touched the East as well – acceleration in technological advances, new aspirations of wage-earners, new models of consumption – which brought about the economic fall of the Soviet system.

Introduction

Are the wage differentials between individuals having different levels of formal education and professional training and experience, between men and women, blue- and white-collar workers, executives and simple employees of the same magnitude in the Western system (WS) as in the Soviet-type system (STS)? Are the factors determining these differentials identical?

These are some of the questions we will attempt to answer in this text. Such a task is rendered all the more complex in so far as we will be comparing economic systems which have different institutions and political and social structures. Nevertheless, we would like to point out in this introductory chapter that:

1 Economists of both systems justify interindividual wage differentials in the same way. This facilitates the definition of a group of common references upon which our comparison is based.
2 The functions and the proportions of the wage-earning classes in the two systems are similar. Thus, it is possible to apply one and the same method to the study of the wage structures.

I THE PROBLEM

What are the criteria for evaluating interindividual wage differentials?

In the WS as in the STS, there is agreement as to the fact that the differentiation in individual wages should satisfy two criteria.

The first is an efficiency criterion. The function of pay is to induce each worker to maximize his efforts. It should lead him to work where he may be the most productive. Generally speaking, this criterion tends to underlie the rule according to which each worker should be paid in accordance with his productivity.

According to the second criterion, that of equality, individuals who do the same job, with the same intensity, should receive the same pay.

Naturally, these two criteria may be mutually contradictory. For example, two individuals doing the same work, with equal intensity, but in two different firms, may, for numerous reasons, be unequally productive. The quality and the regularity of the supplies of raw materials may differ, as well as the regional infrastructure or the technical characteristics of plants. For the purpose of our research, it is important to note that theorists of both market and planned economies have tried to eliminate this contradiction. J. L. Cayatte (54),[1] showed that the convergence of the theory of human capital and the theory of certain Marxists who have influenced Soviet economists, hinges upon the relationship between formal education, professional training, and experience of an individual on the one hand, and his productivity and pay on the other. More precisely, individuals having the same level of formal education, and professional training, and experience are deemed equally productive and therefore receive the same pay. The formula – equal education and training, equal wage – satisfies at one and the same time the criteria of efficiency and of equality. We will refer to this convergence between market and planned economy theorists in making our own comparisons.

From a socio-political standpoint, the officials and leaders of the STS portray in a contradictory manner the magnitude of the wage differentials in their own system as compared to that of the WS.

Firstly, it is often said that pay is excessively egalitarian in the STS. The basis of this analysis is left unclear. Pay is supposed not to be sufficiently differentiated so as to offer appropriate incentives for workers. In other words, the wage system supposedly takes into account more the criterion of equality than that of efficiency.

However, it must be pointed out that Soviet-type Socialism is not, in principle, egalitarian. Marxist analysis is based on the opposition of wage-earners and Capitalists. Once class antagonisms have been eliminated, that is to say, in the Soviet sense, once collective ownership of the means of production has replaced private ownership, fundamental social inequality ceases to exist.

From this standpoint, interindividual earnings differentials, within a given social group, become totally justified, provided that

---

[1] The number in parantheses refers to the bibliography at the end of this work.

they are based on the quantity and the quality of the work supplied by each individual.

Given that there are few comparative, notably statistical, studies on this subject and that the few existing ones take into consideration but a small number of countries, the first important objective of our research is to estimate the dispersion of wages in the economies of each system. Nevertheless, this dispersion may be quite different depending upon whether or not we are considering the group of wage-earners in its entirety, blue-collar or white-collar labor, etc.

In other words, this comparison must be multidimensional, taking into account all those factors which may be linked to wage differences.

Isomorphism and the systemic effect

To what should this comparison lead?

Rather than opposing the analogies and the differences in the wage structures of the two systems, we prefer to use the concepts of "isomorphism" on the one hand, and of "systemic effect" on the other.

We will use the term isomorphism between two structures when it is possible to establish a "bi-univocal" correspondence between the elements of these structures, as well as between the relations that hold these elements together. This term, borrowed from the language of mathematics, has the advantage of being more general than that of identity and more precise than that of analogy.

The study of isomorphic structures is carried out on two levels. The first level concerns the comparison of the elements that constitute each structure. We may take the example of interindividual wage dispersion. This is first estimated and compared by means of statistical indicators. The comparison has to do with the individuals who make up each structure.

The second level consists in comparing the relations which determine this dispersion. Among these, we might note the relation between an individual's wage and his degree of formal education and/or professional training and experience, the sex of the wage-earner, the fact that he has a blue- or white-collar job.

It is possible to conceive that the correspondence may be established for only part of these relations which then enter into our comparison. In this case, it can be said that there is a partial isomorphism between the two structures under study. In so doing, we are taking liberties with the original mathematical notion of isomorphism (Piaget (137), p. 80–90). Such is the price to pay when taking into account the complexity of socio-economic phenomena.

When the relations or the factors structuring the wages of one system or another cannot be made to correspond, we will use the term systemic effect or systemic difference. In other words, the very fact of belonging to a given system is such that the wage structures of the economies that make up that system have specific characteristics that are without equivalents in the other systems.

2 THE METHOD AND THE AREA OF RESEARCH

Are the concepts of wages, their function, and the proportions of the wage-earning classes similar in the two systems and do they justify the use of a single method of analysis? We think that the answer to these questions is yes.

The functions of wages in the two systems

Firstly, for the working population in both systems, the wage rate is a fundamental factor underlying the choice of profession, job mobility, and motivation. In fact, from a macroeconomic standpoint, the assignment by the administration of manpower to workplaces, a widespread practice in both systems during the Second World War and in the Soviet Union under Stalinism, presently plays a small role.

True, according to the principal legal texts of the STS, work is a right as well as an obligation. Failure to work can be sanctioned by virtue of legislation on social parasitical behavior. Nevertheless, at the present time in the STS, administrative control of the distribution of manpower by branch and by firm is weak. Still, it should be noted that, in the Soviet Union, kolkhozniks are obliged to obtain permission from the administration to leave the job which they hold within their kolkhoz.

Secondly, wages are an important element in global economic regulation. In Soviet-type economies (STE), one of the fundamental objectives of planning is to adjust the wages bill to the total amount of available goods on the market. In Western economies (WE), more and more the plans of stabilization and control that are imposed by the State are designed to control the rise in wages.

Nevertheless, there is here an important systemic difference. Whereas in the STS, there is state regulation even down to the level of the industrial firm, in the WS, the latter is free to determine the wages bill of its employees. The instruments of economic policy remain indirect. In this area, it is legitimate to contrast economic policy which prevails in the WS with Administrative regulation in the STS.

We will be obliged to take into account this systemic difference in what follows; however, such a difference in no way invalidates the use of a single method of analysis which is based on the comparison of the functions of wages in both systems.

Thirdly, a major part of household income is socialized in the East as in the West. Indirect wages constituted by family allowances and illness and invalidity benefits are of a comparable level in the two systems. In addition, the degree of free services available to the population (education, health), as compared to the average wage, is not fundamentally different (Kende (94), pp. 114–16; Redor (141) pp. 89 and 107).

Therefore, it would be false to maintain, as have some theorists of the STS, that, given the number of free services and allowances, wage-earners are not as subjected to monetary constraints as they are in the WS. We subscribe to the analysis of Kornai (101) according to whom budgetary constraint on households is as tight in the STS as in the WS.

It is true that the existence of shortages for certain goods might lead one to believe that these can be obtained outside the market and at a price fixed by the administration, well under that of the equilibrium. To uphold such a belief is to forget the existence of illegal markets on which monetary constraint is fully operative.

The problem of "benefits in kind" given the position that an individual occupies in a firm or in society remains to be considered. These are always difficult to evaluate, but appear to be higher in the STS than in the WS. Taking them into account does not give rise to any particular theoretical problems. They can be considered as a form of pay like any other. The principal problem is a statistical one, as in both systems the total value of this kind of pay remains partly or totally unknown. We will have occasion to demonstrate that researchers have been able to deal with this problem using indirect means and that certain Western surveys have been able to make up, at least in part, for the lack of official information concerning benefits in kind in the STE (Morrisson (125) and (126), Ofer and Vinokur (130) and (131)).

On the proportion of the wage-earning classes in the two systems

For the most highly developed economies in each system (the United States, France, the FRG, and the United Kingdom on the one hand, and Hungary, Poland, the GDR, Czechoslovakia, and the USSR on the other hand) the proportion of wage-earners in the total labor force is between 75 percent and 90 percent (D. Redor (141) documents in appendix, pp. 2 to 22). Moreover, in the two systems, the non-salaried workers are primarily farmers (in WE and in certain STE, such as Poland) or co-operators (in the majority of STE).

There is, however, a difference: professionals in the WE are often wage-earners in the STE. It must not be forgotten that these professions, (lawyers, barristers, brokers) with the exception of physicians, are not widely represented in the STE. For this category, there is a real difference in the status between the STE and the WE. However, one must not forget that in certain WE a sizeable proportion of physicians are wage-earners.

In addition, the dispersion of wages in industry will guarantee the homogeneity of the population employed, which is made up of wage-earners in both systems. It will be compared with the dispersion of the wage-earning population as a whole.

Defining the scope of the study

This brief overview of the methodology points to the fact that a comparative study of wage dispersion must be multidimensional. Starting from the economic analysis of wage differentials, the approach leads to the consideration of what Koopmans and Montias ((99), pp. 31–2) refer to as the "total system," that is to say, in the present case, all of the elements that may influence wage dispersion, be they institutions, the political system, the educational system, the norms and cultural representations that prevail in the WE and in the STE.

We have chosen to study highly developed economies in both systems for which we have the most comparable information at our disposal.

We selected Belgium, Denmark, the United States, France, the FRG, and the United Kingdom on the one hand, and Hungary, Poland, the GDR, Czechoslovakia, and the USSR on the other.

In the case of Hungary and Poland, official data on wages are relatively abundant. In depth research was carried out in the West for the other STE, which made our task easier.

In addition to the difficulty of gaining access to statistical information, there were other factors behind our choice. The comparison between the United States and the USSR may be explained by the particular role that each plays in the economies of the WS and the STS. Moreover, the rapprochement of the FRG and the GDR, given the common past of these two countries, is well suited to the study of the possible influence of an economic system on wage structures.

Within the STS, it is interesting to determine whether economic reforms in Hungary, as compared with other countries, have had an impact on wage differentials. Nevertheless, the limited size of this economy obliges us to choose small economies in the WS as well. This factor may influence the dispersion of wages. It is for this reason that we have selected Belgium and Denmark. The latter presents the advantage of being a member of the Scandinavian group, which, we have every reason to believe, plays a particular role in the WS.

The field of research here defined was first marked out in the pioneering works of Bergson (46) (48) (49) on the comparison of the two systems. Bergson is responsible for the establishing the methodology thereof by first comparing the wage dispersions in the United States and the USSR between the two wars, then the growth of production, labor productivity, and the sectoral structure of these economies.

3 OUTLINE

This book is divided into two parts. One is analytical and relies heavily on statistical comparisons, the other is explicative and seeks to account for the isomorphisms and systemic differences that are outlined in part I.

Part I

Starting from a critical analysis of the wage hierarchy according to
the theories of planned and of market economies, we show that these
theories come together on a number of points. They may therefore
be used as a reference for comparison (chapter 1).

Next attention will be given to the notions of wage disparities,
based on the characteristics of individuals (sex, religion, culture), or
of the firms employing these individuals. We will present an overview of the existing comparative studies of wage dispersions in the
WS and in the STS. Then we will define a single method with which
to analyze each system (chapter 2).

The aim of the statistical analysis is to attempt to evaluate, using
the appropriate indicators, the dispersion of wages in the two systems
as well as the factors underlying this dispersion. If, in the two
systems, formal education and professional training and/or experience, as the existing theoretical models would have it, contribute
significantly to the explanation of interindividual pay differentials,
still other factors come into play. There is wage discrimination
against women on the one hand and the heterogeneous demand for
labor on the other hand. Evidence of the latter comes from the
interbranch wage differences (chapters 3 and 4).

During the period from 1950 to 1980, one notes a rather stable
dispersion of wages in the two systems. However, such stability is less
important in the STS where sudden changes in economic policy,
especially in the USSR, weigh heavily (chapter 5).

Part II

First of all, the mixed regulation of wages in the WS will be
contrasted with the Administrative regulation in the STS. In the
former, wage rates are subject to short-term fluctuations of employment as well as to collective bargaining and, in certain countries,
economic policy. In the latter, the evolution of wage rates are
relatively regular and not subject to short-term movements, notably
those of investment cycles. The aim of economic policy is to limit
dysfunctioning in the consumer goods market by maintaining
constant pressure on the evolution of wages (chapter 6).

It is obvious, therefore, that the economic environment in which
firms are placed is radically different. However, we will demonstrate
that the division of labor and power in firms and the constraints

which bear upon wage management are the sources of isomorphisms uncovered by statistical research (chapter 7).

Moreover, the meaning of the relationship between wages and education will be considered. The differences in pay between blue-collar and white-collar workers will be interpreted in light of the organization of labor in firms and in light of the socio-political values inherent in each system (chapter 8).

Next the notion of pay will be broadened to that of income from work which encompasses secondary activities and taxes as well as the benefits in kind which managers in both systems receive (chapter 9).

Finally, we will evaluate the scope and the weight of the isomorphisms underlined in both systems. We will examine to what extent these structures satisfy both the efficiency and equality criteria previously defined (chapter 10) and we will pose the question, in our conclusion, as to the need to go beyond this dichotomy.

The analysis of wage structures in the Western system and in the Soviet-type system

The aim of this first part is to construct a theoretical framework on which to base our comparisons of the two systems. We will show that, according to market theorists, and planning theorists, an individual's position in the pay hierarchy is a function of his level of formal education, professional training, and experience which are deemed to be the principal determinants of his productivity. Consequently, the conceptions of equality and efficiency of the pay scale are largely convergent.

Secondly, the purpose of the statistical analysis is to test for a connection between the degree of education, professional training, and experience and pay in both systems, first in industry and then in the economy as a whole. In so doing, we will evaluate the validity of market and planning theories with reference to differences in wages observed.

Thirdly, we will integrate into our statistical analysis elements which are defined by both theories as "imperfections." By this we mean wage discrimination and the role of the means of production in the structuring of wages.

It is necessary to clarify certain concepts. When using the notion of a wage hierarchy, one is obliged to exclude factors of disparity. In fact, a disparity is defined as the difference in pay between two individuals doing the same work (Cayatte (54), 5).

The premise is that there are homogeneous classes of workers for which the wage rate is the same. This is, therefore, an application of the principle of equivalence in exchange.

Thus, it is first necessary to define n homogeneous categories of workers. The wage hierarchy then is the ordered sequence of n prices corresponding to these n categories of workers. These prices are thus free of wage disparities.

Wage disparities may arise from the inherent characteristics of certain wage-earners. This is the case for wage discrimination that is linked to sex, to culture, to religion, and to age. Wage disparities may also come from the heterogeneous nature of firms. For a given job, pay may be different for reasons having to do with the internal organization of the firm or the position they occupy in the market.

In order to take into consideration wage disparities, it is necessary to introduce the concept of *wage structure*. By this we mean the set of the relations which determine wage differences between individuals and groups of individuals, relations which concern both the wage hierarchy and wage disparities. These relations not only tie wages in with other elements of the economic system, but also with the system as a whole, that is to say with the social structures, and the political, institutional, and even cultural system.

In the pages that follow, starting from the theoretical conceptions of the wage hierarchy, we will work our way to the analysis of the wage structures in the two systems.

CHAPTER I

The wage hierarchy in the market and planning theories

First of all, what exactly do we mean by "the market and planning theories" of wage hierarchy? Why should we compare them?

From our standpoint, what these terms designate is a body of thought, of models, which are essentially normative. The market theory provides a model of the functioning of Western economies. This model is defined as optimal with reference to a criterion such as maximizing well-being in society.

In the same way, current thinking on planning theory provides a body of conceptions and normative models of the functioning of the STE. For example, the aim of planning is to maximize national production, given the available resources both productive and human.

Our task is to explain how, within the framework of these theories, wages are to be fixed so that the general objectives assigned to each system are reached. In what follows, we will begin by presenting an initial framework and an initial group of references designed to analyze first the hierarchy and second the structure of wages in each system.

I THE WAGE HIERARCHY IN THE MARKET THEORY

1 Human capital as the basis for the wage hierarchy

Market theory starts from the principle that the efficiency of an individual, his capacity to produce goods and services, depends first of all on his innate qualities, such as his intelligence, his physical strength, etc. However, investments in human capital increase this capacity (Becker (42), pp. 37–41). These are comprised of expenditures for education and for professional training of all sorts, for health, and, in a general way, of all expenditures for the purchasing of goods and services which may improve the productivity of the

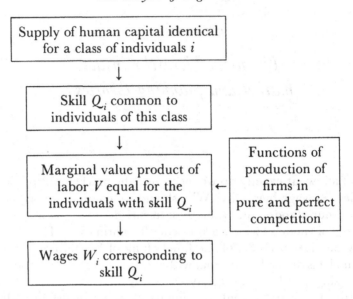

Figure 1.1 Determination of the wage hierarchy in market theory.

worker. With reference to education and vocational training, it is necessary to add the "opportunity cost" which corresponds to the wages that the individual would have earned if he had taken on a job rather than being trained.

It is possible to integrate the theory of human capital into the neo-classical theory of production in the following manner (see figure 1.1):

1 The qualification Q_i of a category of wage-earners is defined by a given level of human capital. The latter is selected on the basis of a calculation of profitability of the same type as that of material investment. Generally speaking, investments in human capital offer decreasing returns given the limits of the intellectual capacities of any individual. Therefore, everyone chooses the level of investment which equals his marginal productivity (decreasing) and the interest rate at which he can borrow (Riboud (145), pp. 143 ff.).

2 The individuals who constitute this class Q_i have the same V, marginal value product, which is calculated using a function of production which brings together production and the different forms of human and material capitals.

3 The wage rate W_i is equal to the marginal value product of individuals having the skill Q_i.

The stock of accumulated human capital is thus the factor which defines each homogeneous class of workers and which determines the wage hierarchy (see figure 1.1).

This theoretical model calls for several remarks; we will limit our comments to the notion of skill and to the problem of the measure of human capital.

2 The limits of the notion of human capital

The question of the evaluation of the stock of human capital is at the heart of the debate. Individuals choose the investments which make up this capital in order to maximize their net income. From this point of view, the value of this capital must be linked to the conceptions of Fisher (75) when he writes:

Capital, in the sense of capital value, is simply future income discounted, in other words, capitalized. The value of any property, or of rights to wealth, is its value *as a source of income*, and is found by discounting that expected income. We may, if we so choose, for logical convenience, include as property the ownership in ourselves (...). I define wealth as consisting of material objects owned by human beings (including, if you please, human beings themselves). (pp. 13–14)

Thus there is a double link between the theory of Fisher and the theory of human capital. First of all, Fisher maintains that human beings may constitute capital in so far as they are the source of income earned in exchange for their labor. Secondly, it is possible to calculate the value of this cpaital, as it is for any capital, by discounting the income of which this capital is the source.

The theory of Fisher makes the notion of human capital coherent. Starting from investments in formal education and in professional training, and the income which is linked thereto, it is possible to calculate the value of capital so accumulated.

However, if it is true that such reasoning makes it possible to calculate the value of the stock of capital, it is also true that it does not take into account the physical measurement of this stock. Thus we are faced with the classical problem of all theories of capital: the measurement and the comparison of heterogeneous capitals. For human capital, it is a question of *measuring abilities and acquired knowledge which determine the level of efficiency in work.* The problem is to come up with a procedure which "homogenizes" different human capitals and which makes it possible to compare and to classify them.[1]

The difficulty lies in the fact that the abilities and acquired knowledge necessary to realize a given job are diverse; they include theoretical knowledge, manual abilities, and the capacity to adapt. Thus it would be necessary to define an almost infinite number of human capitals. If we limit ourselves to theoretical knowledge, the cost of education becomes the relevant criterion for classification. It is obvious that we must distinguish disciplines and sub-disciplines within this classification. Even if we were to compare the degrees awarded for studies of equal duration, it is certain that there are tremendous differences which remain between the knowledge and abilities acquired by individuals.

Finally if the *value of the stock* of capital is clearly defined, the physical measurement of this stock is not, any more so than that of skill. The latter is only an indicator of discounted income from formal education and professional training. The notion of the quality of work is not part of the theory based on Fisher's definition. For a given class of wage-earners, there are heterogeneous abilities and knowledge.

In this approach, the hypothesis of pure and perfect competition is crucial. Indeed, the distinction between the worker's skills and those demanded by the job, a useful distinction in approaches which are based on issues other than a purely competitive labor market, makes no sense here. Each worker has the job for which he is the most productive, his skills are fully employed, and correspond to the skills necessary and sufficient to hold his job.

Firms take a fixed wage rate on the market, and all workers having the same skills are paid the same.

The following criteria are thus satisfied:

1 An efficiency criterion: Individuals select their investments in human capital in order to maximize their net earnings. As firms also behave rationally, wage-earners are allocated to the jobs where they are most efficient.

2 An equality criterion: Two individuals with the same level of formal education and professional training and experience are

---

[1] In what follows, our critical remarks are based on the exposé of Cayatte ((54), pp. 31–9).

paid the same. In addition, their pay corresponds exactly to the marginal contribution of each individual to the production of his society.

Thus, it seems that the contradiction between efficiency and equality has been erased. Nevertheless, there are two remaining, important obstacles to this point of view. The first one is that of the measure of human capital, which has been evoked previously; the second concerns that of wage disparities which refute the hypothesis of free competition.

2 THE WAGE HIERARCHY IN PLANNING THEORY

1 The wage hierarchy based on the labor theory of value

The wage hierarchy as seen by the founders of Marxism
The theoreticians of the STE often refer to the writings of Marx. We will begin by analyzing the elements in Marx which may serve as the basis of the definition of the wage hierarchy in a planned economy.

In *The critique of the Gotha program*, Marx and Engels (122) wrote, concerning the first phase of Communist society:

The producer will receive from society a voucher stating that he has produced so much labor (...) and with this voucher, he will be given consumer goods from the social stocks which cost an equal quantity of labor. He will receive from society in another form the same quantum of labor which he has produced. (p. 30)

How does one compute the "quantum" of labor that each one brings to society? Marx and Engels do not clearly answer this question though they do shed light on the determining factors behind the differentiation of wages (*The critique of the Gotha program* (122)).

But one individual is stronger, physically or morally than another; he produces therefore more work in the same period or he is able to work more. And for labor to be used as a measurement, it is necessary to determine its duration or its intensity, otherwise it would cease to be a unit. This equal right is an unequal right for unequal labor. (p. 31)

If we apply this definition, the wage hierarchy is based on interindividual differences with respect to the duration and the intensity of labor.

Moreover, in his analysis of Capitalist society, Marx hardly analyzed pay for complex (skilled) as opposed to simple (unskilled) labor. It is obvious that Marx concentrated on the conflicts between wage-earners and Capitalists; he did not take an interest in the origin of pay differences within the class of wage-earners.

But above all, Marx refrained from linking labor productivity to wages. Such a link would have negated his theory of exploitation in the Capitalist economy.

Nevertheless, certain Marxists sought to determine what the determining factors behind the wage hierarchy in Capitalist society might be. Engels (74) writes: "In a society of private producers, the cost of the training of the skilled worker is borne by private individuals" (p. 229). He goes on to develop the idea whereby the wage hierarchy is itself based on the fact that workers must get back the cost of their professional training. The wages earned during the course of their professional life are therefore equal to the cost of means of subsistence of the labor force, to which the total cost of formal education and professional training must be added.

The Strumilin school

These are the elements that were available to the first theoreticians of Soviet-type planned economies. They latched on to the few available writings of Marx on the first phase of Communism. The paradox lies in the fact that they also widely used Marx's and his successors' critical analysis of Capitalist society. The Soviet economist, Strumilin, as early as the twenties, tried to base the planned economy, and notably the planning of earnings, on the value of labor. We will first present the principal elements of this approach. Then we will quickly review a second stream of thought with a rather different source of inspiration, that of mathematical planning represented by its main proponent Kantorovitch.

Neither a global conception nor a complete formalization of the wage hierarchy in a planned economy is to be found in the works of Strumilin. Nevertheless, his research on the formation of prices and the theory of value, as well as that on the profitability of the educational system,[2] as well as the works of some of his contemporary followers are such that it is possible to construct what might be the basis for a wage hierarchy in such a theoretical context.

Strumilin's main idea is that Marx's theory of value can be

---

[2] Strumilin (157), (158), (159), and in French the reader may refer to Denis and Lavigne (66) chapter 3, section 1.

applied to the Soviet society. Exchanges are the result of "an active price policy." Strumilin uses this expression to designate planning.

If we consider complex labor, Strumilin uses the labor theory of value, and takes into account the fact that the "production" of skilled labor necessitates labor on the part of teachers and trainers. Skilled labor has therefore more value than unskilled labor, as the value of the labor force, like any other commodity, is determined by the man hours necessary to produce it.

Consequently the pay differentials among workers with different skills may be explained by the labor time it takes to train each skill. The corresponding cost is borne by the workers who get it back in the form of pay earned during their professional life. Certain of these elements can be traced to Marxist analysis of Capitalist society, notably that of Engels which we mentioned previously. But Strumilin goes further adding that formal education and professional training and experience are the determinants of the efficiency of each category of worker.

Putting aside momentarily his theoretical approach, he backs up his proposition with evidence based on numerous empirical studies carried out in sectors or in firms of the Soviet economy. These monographs seek to prove that the level of efficiency of wage-earners, evaluated by average work productivity, is a function of their degree of formal education, professional training, and experience.

In this way, a logical chain linking the level of formal education, professional training, and experience, to average labor productivity and pay is formed. The objectives of equality and efficiency of a planned economy are thus fused. Each individual has the job where he is the most productive (on the average) so as to be paid the most. Each individual is paid proportionately to the quality and the quantity of the work with which he supplies society. All individuals who have the same level of formal education, professional training, and experience and who work with the same intensity are paid the same if the conditions of production are uniform.

The following formula sums up this notion:

The principle of Socialist distribution is proved by the remuneration of labor according to its results and with this the achievement of the highest productivity is stimulated. This principle secures for all workers wages proportionate to the quantity and to the quality of their work, or, in other words, wages proportionate to the value created under uniform conditions, so that each worker gets an identical proportion of the value created by him. (Strumilin (158), p. 96)

Some critical comments on the wage hierarchy in the labor theory of value
The reference to "uniform conditions" of production is an important one. Pay which is proportional to labor productivity does not meet with the equality criterion unless the firms in which workers are distributed have identical technical characteristics. If this is not the case, wage-earners with the same level of formal education, professional training, and experience will not be equally productive and therefore will not be paid the same. This raises the question as to the role of planning in the structuring of plants. Strumilin was aware of the difficulty as he recommended that investments be such that firms be equally fitted with means of production.

Moreover, it must be pointed out that the criterion of efficiency is here based on wages which are proportional to the average productivity of workers. However, it is easy to demonstrate, as did theoreticians of mathematical planning for example, that it is only when individuals are paid at their marginal productivity that national production is maximized. This contradiction ceases only if the marginal labor productivity is constant in all firms.

In addition, Strumilin's analysis on the whole falls within the field of labor value. However, Soviet-type economies have always been monetary exchange economies. Strumilin undeniably tried to set up social accounting and planning based on labor-time, but these endeavors never amounted to anything more than laboratory experiments.

Consequently, workers cannot be paid according to the actual value they create; rather their productivity is evaluated by, for example, a system of production prices which include profit from the technical capital used (Denis and Lavigne (66), pp. 148–58).

2 The wage hierarchy according to the mathematical planning school

Theoreticians of the mathematical planning school are closer to the theory of human capital in so far as they use a marginalist approach of the wage hierarchy.

In one of the presentations of the theoretical model of optimal planning, Kantorovitch ((93), pp. 71ff) seeks to find the linear program of planning that maximizes national production, under the constraints of material and human resources. Workers are grouped by skills according to "the real conditions of production," that is to say by craft, which cannot be substituted one for another, in the production process.

By the duality theorem, "an objectively determined evaluation" (ODE), which corresponds to the marginal productivity of a labor unit is ascribed to each skill of labor.[3]

The wage-earners' pay may differ greatly from the ODE which corresponds to their skills. The purpose of the calculation of the ODE is to distribute the workers by firm and by branch so as to maximize national production.

This is understandable if we consider that the ODE are determined in the concrete conditions of production. In other words, they hinge closely on the volume of production by branch, and above all on the rarity of each skill relative to the needs of the plants. Kantorovich maintains that it would not be in keeping with the Socialist principle of pay according to work if certain wage-earners were generously paid because of deficiencies in the educational and training systems, and, notably, because of temporary shortages of certain categories of labor.

The principal problem is to dissociate the ODE of each of the skills of labor from the corresponding wage. Indeed, under such conditions the question is how should labor be distributed in accordance with the plan? Two solutions are theoretically possible.

The first consists in authoritatively assigning labor according to the directives of the plan. Soviet-type countries have given up these kinds of methods since the end of the Stalinist era. Thus there remains what in Soviet terminology is designated "incentive and motivation" to work. These are steps that are taken so that the production objectives of the plan may be realized by the available labor force. Kantorovitch says nothing about the means to be used, nor does he say anything about the incentives necessary to guarantee that labor is distributed optimally among firms.

Kantorovitch defines wages negatively in the theory of optimal planning. We know that wages differ from the ODE defined for each skill; what we do not know is to what extent they differ. It is perhaps for ideological reasons that Kantorovitch avoids answering this

[3] We refer the reader to Boncoeur ((50), pp. 212–18) for a summary of the question of skills of labor and salary by Kantorovitch.

question. Indeed, it can be argued that the optimum in planning theory on the one hand and in market theory on the other hand are identical. The economic mechanisms which give rise to this optimum are fundamentally different. In one case rational "planning center" controls certain economic variables and perfectly decentralized economic mechanisms are at work in the other.

However, Kantorovitch's ODE by skills is equal to marginal productivity by skills. In a Socialist economic system based on optimum planning, are workers paid according to exactly the same principals as those which govern a market economy where competition is pure and perfect? Kantorovitch would not dare uphold such a view. However, in his theory the problem of the determination of the wage hierarchy is left unresolved.

Finally, Abdel Fadil ((25), p. 44) states that "dual prices and wages" are "the prices of programming which serve only as *indicators of economic choices* so as to achieve the most efficient utilisation of existing resources". But, within the framework of such planning, choices must be put to work. In order to do this, apart from a purely administrative policy of assigning workers to jobs, the "rational" solution consists of bringing the actual wages as close as possible to the "optimum evaluations" of human resources.

In conclusion, it should be pointed out that there are important differences between Strumilin's and Kantorovitch's conception of skills.

For Strumilin, skills are related to the complexity of labor, that is to say that there is a tight correspondence between the skill and the level of formal education, professional training, and experience of a given category of workers.

For Kantorovitch, skill is defined as a class of individuals who have the same "craft." Two individuals who belong to the same class, who perform the same tasks and who have the same functions, may have different levels of formal education, professional training, and experience. Conversely, two individuals who have the same level of formal education and professional training may have two different jobs, and, in practice, be unequally productive.

Kantorovitch's model is more oriented toward the actual search for economic optimum. It is obvious that if as Kantorovitch maintained workers were paid according to their marginal productivity, the criterion of equal pay for equal levels of formal education, professional training, and experience would not have been respected.

3 A COMPARISON OF THE WAGE HIERARCHY IN THE MARKET AND PLANNING THEORIES

1 The convergence between the theories

Strumilin starts with the Marxist theory of value, which he then steers away from its original purpose: the critical analysis of Capitalist society. In a Soviet-type society, wages cover the cost of education and professional training, as certain Soviet interpretors of Capitalist society point out as well. However, the important drift from Marx is that formal education, professional training, and experience are the principal determining factors behind productivity which in turn determines wages for a given skill.

The latter, maintains Strumilin, makes it possible to apply the principle by which each individual receives from society a quantity of goods which corresponds to the quantity and the quality of labor that he supplies.

The market and planning theories with regard to the wage hierarchy undeniably converge. Even though the concepts and the hypotheses underlying the determination of certain variables are sometimes different, the logic behind the two theories is identical. In both, one starts from the premise that the level of formal education, professional training, and experience of a worker determines his productivity and ultimately his pay.

The same criticisms can be applied to both theories. Consequently, the critical analyses converge. In the theory of the stock of human capital, the relation between the hierarchy of the stocks of human capital and the wage hierarchy can be interpreted in either way. Indeed, it is the stock of human capital which an individual accumulates which determines his efficiency and therefore his pay. Still, one can argue that the wage hierarchy is determined, above all, by the demands of firms given their own objectives: maximizing profits or other objectives that are linked to the internal organization of work. From this point of view, the wage hierarchy is an instrument which firms use to urge their employees to improve their skills and to become integrated into a certain organization of labor which is modeled by the firms themselves.

In the planning theory, the link between the level of formal education, professional training, and experience and labor efficiency and wages is justified by the fact that everyone should receive from society a wage equivalent to his contribution. Here too wages are determined by the level of formal education, professional training, and experience. However, given the fact that the cost of education and training is borne, at least in theory, by society, it is unfair that it fall into the hands of individuals.

But the wage hierarchy can also be interpreted as an instrument in the hands of planners and ultimately of firms to orient workers toward those kinds of educational and training programs that are deemed to be the most useful to society or to be "social priorities". In this case it is the wages which determine the level of education and professional training of the workers rather than the contrary.

2 The limits of the two theories

Generally speaking, the two theories fail to take into account the actual *functions* of an individual within an organization. Both theories fail to consider the place that an individual occupies in the power structure of an organization.

In addition, in these two theories, formal education and professional training depend on the workers' choice. The question must be raised as to whether or not firms themselves have a role to play in the training or the retraining (transformation) of the labor force (Vaneecloo (165)). From this perspective, firms are the agents of the structuring of training and hence of wages.

Moreover, the two theories attempt to bring together the principles of efficiency and equality of pay: the criteria which the wage hierarchy are supposed to satisfy are the same.

True it has been proven that these criteria are not satisfied unless restrictive conditions, on the structure of the means of production (in the theory of planned economy) or on the competitive nature of the goods and labor markets (in the theory of market economy) are satisfied.

Nevertheless, these criteria act as norms to which each system tries to conform. They can thus serve as a reference for our comparisons. We will use them to interpret the findings of our own research. It is indeed this method which is followed by Koopmans and Montias (99). First, these two authors point out the common objectives of the economic theories of the East and of the West. Second, these common objectives provide the basis for the evaluation of the results and performances of the two systems.

It is necessary to determine whether the relation, the direction of which has never clearly been identified, between the level of skills, which are largely defined as the level of formal education, professional training, and experience, and wages is empirically verified in both economic systems. If this relation is empirically proven in the two systems, one can expect to find great similarities between the wage hierarchies in both.

However, the limits of these theories lead one to the hypothesis that the wage structures observed in the two systems cannot be explained solely by the differences in the level of formal education, professional training and experience of the labor force. For this, we will first take into account wage disparities and then the role of firms as agents of the structuring of wages.

CHAPTER 2

Constructing a comparative model of wage structures

In market theory, as in planning theory, wage disparities are the consequence of deviations from the rule according to which, for the same level of formal education, professional training, and experience, two individuals, reputed to be equally productive, are paid the same. The differentials can come from wage discrimination against the members of certain social groups. They may also come from the heterogeneous nature of demands for labor from different firms or sectors or from the structure of the markets in which firms operate.

These initial remarks will lead us, by way of existing studies, to incorporate factors which, in the two systems, may be linked to wage structures. It will then be possible to put our comparative method of analysis into shape.

I WAGE DISPARITIES IN THE MARKET AND PLANNING THEORIES

I Wage discrimination

In the theory of market economy
Becker is the initiator of the theory of wage discrimination in a neoclassical framework. He attempted to explain why membership of certain social groups resulted in wage inequalities despite equal skill and productivity.

In order to do so, Becker introduced the concept of "individual discrimination coefficients." Each one of these can be analyzed as a "taste for discrimination" to which a monetary counterpart may be attributed. If an employer should pay wages W corresponding to the marginal productivity of a wage-earner, and if he behaves as if he were confronted by a wage cost $W(1+d_i)$, by definition d_i is the discrimination coefficient against the wage-earner under consideration. The discrimination coefficient is thus subtracted from the wages of the person who is discriminated against. The same analysis may be applied to a white wage-earner who bears a psychological cost when he works with a black wage-earner. This cost is equal to the discrimination coefficient d_i against a black worker and must be offset by an equivalent additional pay.

The market discrimination coefficient does not depend solely on the individual discrimination coefficents. It also depends on the nature of the labor market which may be more or less competitive (the more the structure of a market is monopolistic, the greater the discrimination), on the relative weight of whites to blacks, and on the technical possibility of substituting whites for blacks according to the differences in skills of the two groups.

According to Arrow (34), another cause of discrimination stems from imperfect information available to employers about the labor market. Arrow considers two complementary categories of jobs: skilled and non-skilled. Employers must realize a specific investment in order to hire skilled workers. This investment corresponds to the period of training after which it then becomes possible to be certain that the hired worker is as productive as the skilled worker.

One can hold the hypothesis that an employer cannot know *a priori* if a given worker is skilled or not. However, he does know that the probability that a white worker be skilled is greater than for a black worker. If one assumes that the entrepreneur maximizes the expected value of net earnings realized by hiring a worker of whatever sort, the entrepreneur will necessarily offer a higher wage to a white worker.

In this way, the explanation for discrimination shifts from "a taste for discrimination" toward the consideration of imperfect information available concerning the skill and productivity of workers. These two explanations complement each other in so far as imperfect information is not foreign to beliefs and prejudices.

If we refer to the theory of human capital, wage discrimination is expressed by the fact that workers who are victims thereof are paid wages which are below their marginal productivity. The investment in human capital is therefore less profitable; individuals who are objects of discrimination will have a tendency to demand less human capital than do others. All things being equal, the former will not be as well educated or trained.

This is the case in Western economies where a low level of education and professional training reinforces the effects of wage discrimination.

In addition, there is *segregation* when the proportion of workers N, employed in a firm or a region, differs from that which would result from a random distribution. Segregation concerns the employment of workers by region, by firm, or by sector. One may take into account the category of labor as well, as does Becker ((43), p. 57).

We will be obliged therefore to distinguish segregation in employment and wage discrimination, for, even if the two phenomena are related, they may take on various forms. It is possible to imagine, at least in theory, a situation where a high level of wage discrimination is related to a low level of segregation or the reverse.

Finally, Becker may be understood in terms of the opposition of a collective optimum and an individual one. Discrimination is viewed as an imperfection which disrupts the equality between a worker's marginal productivity and pay, thus making the economy drift away from the collective optimum. From this point of view discrimination should be suppressed.

One should not overlook the fact that it may be in the economic interest of a given firm to practice wage discrimination. For example, a firm which employs on a long-term basis workers who are victims of discrimination and which groups these workers in certain establishments or workshops makes greater profits than a firm which does not practice wage discrimination and employment segregation. Given the fact that our study will be concerned with the existing wage structures in WE, these phenomena must be taken into account.

One must not forget that wage discrimination touches several social classes. Apart from discrimination for reasons of race or culture, there is sex discrimination in Western countries (Sofer (155)). Finally, there is discrimination on the basis of social background when wage differences subsist among the members of different social classes who have achieved the same level of education and professional training. Lévy-Garboua has shown that there is such discrimination in French society (Lévy-Garboua (108), pp. 29–48).

In the planning theory

With reference to wage discrimination, there is an important difference between theoreticians of market and planned economies. Whereas the former have tried to explain the existence of discrimination within the market, the latter have denied the existence thereof in a planned economy. They maintain that suppressing the private ownership of the means of production eliminates wage discrimination and segregation in employment.

Referring to the text by Marx and Engels on the aforementioned *Critique of the Gotha program*, Csikos Nagy ((63), pp. 124–5) maintains that in a STE "workers should not be discriminated against for reasons of sex, age, nationality, race or social background." If the nationalization of the means of production is a necessary condition in order to eliminate exploitation, Csikos Nagy admits that wage discrimination is not automatically suppressed. Still the wage policy, within the framework of a planned economy, should succeed in eliminating them.

However, although there is little statistical information and few studies on wage discrimination in the STS available, it seems, given what information is available (Moroney (124)), that segregation in employment and wage discrimination against women, for example, are high. Such discrimination is supposedly of a level comparable to that of the WS. Naturally, we will attempt to empirically verify this fact and, above all, to explain it.

In conclusion, market economy theoreticians such as Becker have taken the phenomena of wage discrimination into account. They are held to be anomalies or flaws which should be eliminated as they avert the economy from a collective optimum.

In the planning theory, the very existence of discrimination is denied.

It is easy to understand such positions if one considers that discrimination breaks both the rules of equality and of efficiency of pay. Indeed, if there is discrimination, it means that two individuals with the same level of formal education, professional training, and experience are not paid the same wage (violation of the equality principle), and that workers are not directed to those jobs where they are the most productive, but to those where discrimination is the weakest (violation of the efficiency principle).

The purpose of the study of wage structures will be to evaluate the extent to which there is wage discrimination and segregation in employment in both systems. We will therefore evaluate the distance between the objectives and the reality of each system. Finally, we will attempt to explain the origin of the phenomena.

2 Taking into account the structures of the market and of production

It has been shown that market and planning theories, in general and in the absence of discrimination, lead to the conclusion that, for a given level of formal education and professional training, all workers are paid the same. This is true in a situation of pure and perfect competition in a market economy and in one where the plan homogenizes the factors determining labor productivity.

We will study how each of the two theories explains the differences in wage rates, for an equal level of formal education and professional training, between firms and sectors. Then we will turn to empirical evidence so as to make an initial comparison between the production structures and the wage structures of the two systems.

In the market theory

We will indicate, by simply citing the results, how the wage rate for a given skill is arrived at when hypotheses of atomicity on the goods and labor market are not confirmed.

If we take the simplest case where there is a monopoly in the goods market and a labor market where there is pure and perfect competition, the wage rate is fixed according to the rules which were previously explained. However, in the case where the monopoly exercises a sufficiently powerful demand on the labor market so that the supply cannot be infinitely elastic, the wage rate paid out by the monopolist is inferior to that which would result from a situation of pure and perfect competition. The neo-classical authors use the term "exploitation" to designate the situation of these wage-earners.

In addition, the study of the monopsony, where a single firm or a coalition of firms alone demand labor, shows that, here too, the wage rate is inferior to that of a situation of pure and perfect competition. Here too there is "exploitation" of labor.

The effect of Union activity is to maintain the wage rate above the rate of pure and perfect competition, if we ascribe to Unions the role of a monopolist, or if we assume that the Unions are able to impose closed-shop practices (Becker (43), pp. 62–5).

The question is whether or not the "imperfections" in the goods and labor markets influence the wage hierarchy. The answer is affirmative in so far as the existence of monopolies in the goods market concerns certain sectors which may have labor structures which are notably different from that of the rest of the economy. In the same way, the monopsonies in the labor market may concern certain particular skills.

As for Unions, their organization by sector in most WE may lead one to think that they are influential at this level. If the structure of skills is not the same from sector to sector, the wage hierarchy may be affected. All this may then introduce "imperfections" in the hierarchy such as previously defined. From an empirical point of view, this will lead to testing for the existence of an "effect" of sector organization as a determining factor of wage structures in the WS.

Moreover, the firms' capital stock appears to influence the level of the wages which they pay out. Silvestre (153), following a statistical study of workers' wages in French industry, came to the conclusion that high wages are not necessarily the result of a need for highly skilled labor. He coins the term "sector effect" to refer to the fact that the most highly capitalistic sectors are those which pay the highest wages, after eliminating the differences in skill level between sectors. Given this fact, the relationship between wage and productivity does exist, but it reflects the level of technology of the various sectors and not the skill of the labor force. In his commentary on this same study, Silvestre (153) concludes:

The variations of the average labor productivity are responsible for wage differences which benefit workers who happen to be in the most capitalistic or the most productive industries. We have here a situation in which labor productivity is not solely linked to the additional investments undertaken by workers, but where, on the contrary productivity depends essentially on more global factors which can hinge on the product market or the nature of the firms of each sector. (p. 203)

Other structural studies have pointed out that wage differences between sectors are connected with the average size or the degree of concentration of firms (at the sector level) (Jenny and Weber (89)).

The same studies carried out at the firm level have proven that, within a given branch, for a given degree of skill, important wage differences can only be explained by differences in firms' "capacity to pay." The "firm effect," in light of the aforementioned studies, may be explained by the level of technology, the share of the market, or the profitability of the firms (Daubigney, Fizaine, and Silvestre (65)). Studies of the major WE (Turner and Jackson (163) and Weigend (167)) have uncovered similar results. However, if one adheres to the aforementioned empirical studies, the most concentrated branches or those with the highest per capita capital or the highest level of profit, pay out the relatively highest wages.

Nevertheless, this does not lend itself to interpretation in light of the theory of the monopsony in the labor market or of that of a monopoly in the goods market faced with a labor supply which is not infinitely elastic. In these two cases, the equilibrium wage rate is inferior to the pure and perfect competition rate. The wage rate is superior only when the Union has a monopoly on hiring.

It appears necessary, therefore, to reconsider the axioms relative to the behavior of economic agents placed in situations of imperfect competition.

Basing our analysis on a statistical study, we will assess the impact on wages of the structures of production and the structures of the markets. In the second part, we will introduce a theoretical re-interpretation.

Taking into account the structures of production in the planning of wages
Certain arguments that are used to explain wage disparities between different sectors of the WE are not easy to transpose to STE. This is true of the role of Unions in wage bargaining negotiations and also of the positions that firms occupy on the goods or labor markets. However, one might think that other, more technical factors (per capita capital, the length of production lines, linked with the size of firms), play the same role in each system.

In theory, the wage differentials by sector in a STE should only be accounted for by differences in the level of labor skill. However, a number of studies refer to "priority sectors" of the economy and to the wages paid out in these sectors. It is indeed acknowledged that certain sectors of the economy must be developed before others and that, to attract the necessary labor force, it is necessary to pay out higher than average wages in these sectors.

It is obvious, therefore, that there is a contradiction between the principle whereby an individual is paid according to the quantity and quality of work he provides and the practice of paying out higher wages in priority sectors. Borc ((51), pp. 130–1) maintains that this contradiction ceases to be if one accepts the fact that the principles which govern the level of wages must be reconciled with the rapid development of the economy and more specifically with the "maximum satisfaction of the workers' consumption." In other words, wage differentiation from sector to sector must be determined in accordance with the priorities set forth by the production plan. Given the fact that the latter is set up so as to maximize production and consumption of the economy as a whole, workers' well-being will be maximized as well, at least on a long-term basis.

In the empirical study that follows, we will try to identify the priority sectors as well as the economic and social factors behind the determination of these priorities.

From a confrontation point of view the question arises as to whether or not the distribution of the means of production between sectors are similar in the two systems. A factor which might bring the wage structures closer together. The American economist, Pryor (139) who studied the relationship between the concentration of firms and intersector wage structures in six STE and in fifteen WE, is of this opinion.

Pryor's results are important and it will be necessary to explain on what the similarities to which he points are based. In order to do so, we will have to analyze in depth, the factors structuring wages at the firm and sector level.

Finally, all of the studies which have been presented so far have pointed to the necessity of broadening the field of research initially limited by the two theories. The economic analysis of wage dispersion between individuals constitutes a step in this direction.

2 WAGE DISPERSION AND THE ECONOMIC SYSTEM

Beginning with the theories of wage hierarchy, we incorporated progressively into our analysis wage disparities related to certain characteristics of individuals, of production structures, and finally of the markets in which the firms operate. In so doing, we have moved toward a study of a group of phenomena common to the two systems and which determine what we have called the wage structures.

The study of the *dispersion* of individuals' wages provides a link between our initial theoretical approach and the wage structures in the two systems. We use the term wage dispersion to refer to the degree, great or small, of inequality of wages within a given social group or population. We may use different indicators of the deviation from the mean, such as standard deviation, variance or coefficient of variation, to measure this dispersion.

The study of the factors determining pay dispersion can be carried out on two axes.

The first involves theorizing on the origins of wage inequalities and the nature of the statistical distribution of wages that appear in Eastern and Western economies. The second consists of evaluating the wages differentials of individuals and the factors which determine these differentials using statistical procedures such as the analysis of variance. Exploring the two axes will make it possible ultimately to define a method of analysis applicable to the two systems.

1 Elements of the economic analysis of wage dispersion

In theory, wage dispersion is a function of the dispersion of individual performances (labor productivity) and, beyond that, of the level of formal education, professional training, and experience. From this point of view, the question must be raised as to whether or not the statistical distribution of wages can be explained by the distribution of the level of formal education, professional training, and experience of a given population. We shall present first the theoretical studies that have tried to solve this problem.

The authors thereof consider that the factors behind the distribution of wages are more numerous and more diversied than the market and planning theories would lead us to believe. In the empirical study that follows, we will specify which factors are operative in the WS and the STS.

Pareto (133) was among the first theoreticians to study the dispersion of earnings in a given society. By analyzing different populations at different periods of time, he came to the conclusion that the wage dispersion could be formalized by the relation:

$$N = AX^{-a}$$

where N is equal to the number of individuals whose income is higher than a given amount X, A and a are parameters that are specific to each statistical distribution. According to Pareto, a was remarkably stable over time and space since it was always equal to 1.5 approximately. This was the basis for the idea that the dispersion of income was independent of the economy and of the society under study, and that any attempt to reduce individual inequalities of income was a losing battle. Individuals climb or descend the social ladder according to their skills and gifts, following a process of natural selection and elimination which is comparable to that which governs the animal kingdom.

Lange (103), in his analysis of the Western system, maintains that the wage inequalities may be explained by a filtering or screening mechanism throughout the vertical mobility axis which is similar to the selection in the school system. In addition, earnings from private property are supposedly cumulative, a fact which might help to explain the highly unequal nature of Pareto's distribution. Moreover, there is no such distribution in Socialist Poland due to the suppression of private property and the reduction in social inequalities.[1]

Pareto's thesis, which is now considered to be outdated, has nevertheless been revived in a particular area of organization theory, dealing with executives' pay. Indeed, Simon (154) presented the hypothesis that each executive was paid according to the number of individuals working under him. The wage hierarchy thus mathematically formalized makes it possible to show that the wage distribution follows a statistical law of the same type as Pareto's.

It is not an accident that these works are solely concerned with executives. Indeed, the statistical data which have been available since the Second World War have proved that if Pareto's curve fits with the highest income bracket, corresponding to 20 percent of the total population, this was far from the case for the dispersion of the income, especially the wages, of the population as a whole.

Indeed, the statistical distributions of wages and income in all countries are unimodal and leptokurtic. These distributions follow very approximately a lognormal law. In addition, the dispersion coefficients for wages, which are calculated on the basis of these distributions, show that there are very important differences from period to period and from country to country.

In a theoretical article, Kalecki (92) showed that, if y is the product of n independent random variables having a finite variance, the distribution of y tends towards a lognormal distribution when n tends toward infinity, in other words, the logarithm of y follows a Gaussian law.

[1] On the contrary, Lange, using statistical data taken from the year 1955, demonstrates that the income of workers in Poland is very close to a lognormal distribution ((103), p. 67).

The thesis which certain economists, such as Roy (149) have upheld, is that the wage distribution in a given society is the result of the working of a large number of random factors such as the level of formal education, professional training, or experience, health, skill, and punctuality. The distribution of these individual characteristics is a Gaussian one in a given population. However, it operates multiplicatively on the level of wages. For example, poor health reduces the productivity of workers, whatever their skills, by a given proportion, rather than by a given amount.

A great number of empirical works use this same approach. For example, an econometric study applied to a cross section of the American population produced the following results (Taubman (161)). The factors significantly related statistically to the level of individual wages are: education, intelligence, taste for risk, number of hours worked, health, professional experience, attraction to volunteer work (negative relation), religion, social class as defined by socio-professional status.

2 Comparative studies of wage dispersion

In the empirical part of his book, Lydall ((111), chapters 5, 6, and 7) studied the dispersion of wages and the evolution thereof during the course of the twentieth century in twenty-five countries, members of the STS, as well as the WS.

The results of the calculations of the dispersion and the concentration of wages[2] concerns the early sixties and twenty-five countries, three of which are Eastern European: Czechoslovakia, Hun-, gary and Poland. Hungary and Czechoslovakia were classified in the group with the lowest wage dispersion, as were New Zealand and Australia. In the next group, we find, by order of increasing dispersion, the United Kingdom, Poland, and the FRG. Finally, France appears to be a country where the wage dispersion is decidedly higher.

In addition, if we consider the category of manual workers alone, the wage dispersion in Hungary and in Czechoslovakia is the same as in France, and in the United Kingdom. In Hungary and Czechoslovakia it is higher than in the FRG. In Poland, this dispersion is higher than that of the five other countries.

[2] Lydall (111), pp. 153–6; the coefficient of variation and the relationship between different percentiles of the distribution of the pay of male wage-earners are taken into account.

Next, the author sought to uncover the causes of this unequal dispersion of wages. For all of the countries studied, there was an increasing relation between the dispersion of wages and the dispersion of the levels of formal education, professional training, and experience.

Nevertheless, certain economies do not conform to this model which only concerns in fact a sub-group of the countries studied. This is the case for France where the dispersion of levels of education is relatively low compared to that of wages. The opposite is true for the three STE. The dispersion of levels of education is relatively high compared to that of wages.

Then the hypothesis that the inequalities among wages are linked to the proportion of individuals working in agriculture is examined. Such a hypothesis is based on the fact that the transfer of labor from agriculture to industry would increase wages inequalities amidst the population working in industry. Indeed, agricultural workers are often poorly or little trained and wages in agriculture are lower than in industry, which would tend to mean that the newcomers to industry would settle for relatively low wages.

In practice, there is an increasing relation between manpower employed in agriculture and wage dispersion. However, once again, this is true for a sub-group of the countries. Indeed, in countries where there is relatively little agricultural manpower, there are important differences in the dispersion of industrial wages. Lydall hypothesizes that, below a certain threshold, the working population in agriculture no longer influences wage dispersion in industry.

Finally, the suspected decreasing relation between per capita GNP and wage dispersion is not clearly evidenced. For Canada, the United States, and France, wage inequalities are significantly higher than in other countries despite a high level of development. Conversely, the three STE have a low level of wage dispersion compared to their level of development.[3]

What can be learned from Lydall's study?

1 We observe important national differences within the economic systems. In the WS, France occupies a particular position. Wage dispersion in industry is very high, and the author is unable to explain this phenomenon. Within the STS, wage dispersion in

[3] Bergson (49), in a more recent study (1984) of nine principal WE and the USSR, upholds the idea that there is a decreasing relation between the level of development of an economy and the dispersion of the pay of wage-earners.

industry is relatively high in Poland. The fact that there is a significant labor force in agriculture does not suffice to explain this phenomenon.

2 The study of the determining factors of wage dispersion points to the complexity of the contributing factors that must be considered. If it is true that the dispersion of the levels of formal education, professional training, and experience have a role to play, other socio-economic factors must be considered as well, notably the weight of the labor force employed in agriculture and the inequalities of pay between white- and blue-collar workers. Lydall's analysis is necessarily general and does not make it possible to determine whether the factors determining wage dispersion are different in the STS and the WS or to know if their effects are felt less strongly.

At this point, it is necessary to return to the distinction between wage hierarchy and wage structure. We have demonstrated how the market and planning theories, originally born of two opposing schools of thought, ultimately arrived at the same conception of the wage hierarchy based on the level of formal education, professional training, and experience on the one hand and labor productivity on the other.

The two theories are founded on axioms the purpose of which is, in one case, to make the utility theory of value coherent with the wage hierarchy, and, in the other, to make the labor theory of value coherent with the wage hierarchy. However, once we leave behind the world of "pure economics" and once we try to bridge theory and observation, we are obliged to take into account the notion of wage structure which, by definition, allows us to test observable relationships and ultimately to incorporate them into our analysis.

3 A UNIFIED METHOD OF ANALYSIS FOR THE TWO SYSTEMS

1 The area of investigation

In our opinion, the study of the market and planning theories as well as the results of empirical analyses which have been presented, justify the use of a single statistical approach, that is to say the application of the same tests and models to the WE and to the STE.

Indeed, if we accept the market and planning theories, the level of formal education, professional training, and experience of the labor force is a fundamental determining factor of pay in both systems. In addition, the elements of analyses which complement the two theories leads one to test the hypothesis as to whether or not wage discrimination exists in both systems. We will focus our attention on wage discrimination with respect to women. Indeed the question of discrimination based on ethnic group or culture is different in the two systems: there are very few foreign workers in the STE studied here.

Moreover, the connection between the wage structure and the structures of production, notably the concentration and capital stocks of firms should be studied. In truth, the elements which make such a hypothesis plausible have essentially been uncovered in the WE. The test of these same relationships in the STE in no way prejudices that their existence will ultimately be proven.

We will also study the differences in wages between manual and non-manual workers. In their study of the criteria which define the different categories of wage-earners, Marchal and Lecaillon (117) brought out the importance of this distinction which is founded on:

Union membership which is often different in these two categories of workers,

specific forms of pay,

specific working conditions, there are supposedly in all economies particular "constraints" for manual workers,

different life styles.

If the Unions are not comparable in the two systems, we may hold the hypothesis that the other elements which distinguish manual and non-manual workers operate in the same way.

It is remarkable that the market and planning theories ignore this distinction. Here again, in the two theories, the difference in level of education, professional training, and experience accounts for the difference in pay of these two categories of workers. But it is difficult to compare the level of formal education and professional training of manual and non-manual workers. Furthermore, if we take into consideration the organization of the work of manual workers, their productivity may vary depending upon the degree to which their jobs are fragmented, diversified, or automated. The interest of this approach goes beyond the Sociology of organizations. The efficiency and the profit-making of firms is also a function of the pay of manual as opposed to non-manual workers, of the division of labor between them, and the degree of supervision of manual workers by non-manual workers which varies from country to country.

2 The logic behind the statistical study

Two kinds of analyses will be carried out.

The first will attempt to characterize the wage distribution of each of the economies under study as compared to the standard distribution (the lognormal distribution previously studied). Next, the wage dispersion will be evaluated using several indicators (coefficient of variation, GINI coefficient, the ratio of the ninth to the first decile) so as to get the most reliable results.

Then we will attempt to estimate the impact of the following factors: category of worker (manual or non-manual), sex, level of formal education, professional training, and experience on the total pay dispersion.

The second will consider the relation between the demand for labor and the pay structure using the analysis of intersector wage differences. A single econometric model of the determination of intersector wages will be tested for those economies for which we have sufficient information. Certain factors of the preceding analysis, such as sex and the level of formal education and professional training will be included once again, which will make it possible to do cross-comparisons. We will also introduce the notions of concentration of activites by sector and the amount of capital stock per worker, so as to bring out the eventual role of the means of production in the wage structure.

At the end of this first part, it will thus be possible to evaluate the differences in both systems, between the structure of wages observed and the theoretical models of market and planning. We will explain these differences in the second part.

CHAPTER 3

A statistical analysis of wage dispersion

There are many important methodological difficulties involved in any international-scale comparison. In the present study, these difficulties are all the greater as we are comparing economies which belong to different economic systems. In a number of ways, these economic systems are based on different principles.

In addition, each system has its particularities. As far as the WE are concerned, it is important to note the work of the Statistical Office of the European Communities (SOEC) which has sought to make statistical systems uniform. We were able to use uniform data on wages for France, the FRG, Denmark, Belgium, and, to a lesser degree, the United Kingdom.[1] But the American and to a certain extent the British data,[2] are very different from the aforementioned on questions of classification as well as methodology.

As for the Soviet type economies, the availability of data varies and the classifications used are far from being uniform. While statistics on wages are relatively abundant for Hungary and Poland, they are much less so for Czechoslovakia and above all the USSR. For the latter, we essentially used data, patiently reconstructed by Western researchers based on the few existing Soviet studies (McAuley (112), Wiles and Markowski (170)).

I A STUDY OF THE STATISTICAL DISTRIBUTIONS OF WAGES IN THE TWO SYSTEMS

1 Testing the hypothesis of lognormality of the distributions

For numerous reasons, it is important to be familiar with the statistical distributions of the wages of the countries under study.

---

[1] See pp. 202–3.
[2] Given the incomplete nature of the data published by the SOEC on the United Kingdom, we used data from the New Earnings Survey to complete our study.

First, such knowledge may be a preliminary to econometric analyses where one assumes that certain hypotheses concerning the statistical distributions are satisfied. Second, such knowledge makes it possible to confront and compare the statistical distributions of wages in the STS and the WE.

We have selected the test of lognormality for both its theoretical and empirical implications. It has been shown that a great number of authors subscribe to this hypothesis. They maintain that the wage distribution is determined by several factors whose distribution in the population of wage-earners follows a normal curve and which act multiplicatively on the level of wages.

We will seek to verify this hypothesis for all of the WE under study and for the STE as well. If this hypothesis is not rejected, then a whole area of study of wage determination will be opened to us.

In addition, referring to one statistical law will facilitate statistical comparisons on an international scale. The in-pairs comparison of the empirical distributions would indeed have been laborious and difficult to interpret.

The notion of pay considered

It is necessary to specify several points: first, the kind of pay to be considered, second the groups and sub-groups of the individuals concerned.

Pay is constituted by the gross monthly earnings[3] before taxes. This definition encompasses social welfare contributions paid by the wage-earners and the bonuses and pay for overtime of a monthly or infra-monthly nature and does not encompass benefits in kind.

We are necessarily dependent on the available statistical sources and we have chosen a definition which has the greatest number of elements in common with the national sources at our disposal (for more details, see pp. 202–3).

As for the periodicity of certain bonuses, it is obvious that one had best opt for the longest possible period so as to include certain annual bonuses. It would have been ideal to use annual earnings; unfortunately, these data are only available for France, the FRG, and the United States.

In addition, in so far as we are attempting to uncover the factors determining the interindividual dispersion of pay, it would have

---

[3] With the exception of the United States for which only data concerning annual earnings were available.

been appropriate to use net wages rather than gross wages. However, our choice was dictated by the statistical sources available. Indeed, Western surveys use the notion of earnings and not of net wages. However, given the fact that social welfare expenditures, which constitute the essential difference between the two notions, are usually proportional to net wages, this choice has but little effect on the analysis of the dispersion of pay (CERC (56), p. 27–41).

Our choice to exclude benefits in kind and to include direct taxes was also motivated by statistical sources; this choice is standard practice in the majority of studies on this subject. The analysis presented in this chapter is solely based on official statistics. In the second part however, we will incorporate the influence of benefits in kind, the impact of taxes, and that of second jobs on the dispersion of pay.

For Poland and Czechoslovakia, net wages are used in the absence of gross earnings. Given that the wage-earner is only minimally charged with national insurance contribution in these countries, we have reason to believe that any statistical bias is negligible.

Defining the wage-earning population
The wage-earning population is defined as comprising all those individuals who are full-time employees and who are paid in full, whatever their age. This definition excludes apprentices and home workers.

This definition seeks to encompass, as precisely as possible, pay for work really accomplished, and to exclude biases that might come from the absence of the wage-earner whatever the cause (wage-earner not paid in full), or from part-time jobs.

Within the wage-earning population as a whole, it is necessary to define, once and for all, two sub-groups, which will be the object of a specific study. In accordance with the definitions of SOEC and INSEE, (the French Institute of Statistics) the category of manual workers includes workers whatever type of pay they might receive, drivers and machinery operators, as well as team leaders when they are directly involved in production. Non-manual workers are all those not included in the category of manual workers.

The very wording of these definitions proves that they are not devoid of ambiguity. Indeed the notion of a wage-earner directly involved in production is not easy to apply concretely when it has to do with workers who have certain managerial responsibilities. The intermediate category of head of teamworkers is a good example. Given the margin of interpretation of the SOEC definition, there is no guarantee that French and German statistics are rigorously comparable with respect to this point. The same uncertainty is true for the STE. It must be pointed out that, in the majority of the countries under study, foremen are classified as non-manual workers.[4]

Statistical methods

The statistical methods used depend upon the data available. Analyzing individual data is out of the question given the cost in time and in computation of such an operation. In addition, it would have been difficult in the WE and impossible in the STE to surmount the obstacle of the confidential nature of individual data.

The distributions by earnings brackets, published in surveys and national censuses, were used. The number of brackets varies from fifteen to thirty depending upon the country. In the following section, we will indicate the problems encountered given the uncertain nature of the data used.

The test of lognorality of the earnings distribution was carried out by comparing the distribution of the logarithm of earnings to the normal distribution. Given the data available, the Chi squared test was applied to earnings distributions in industry in Belgium, Denmark, France, the FRG, Hungary, Poland, and the USSR. The same test was applied to wage-earners in all activities in the United States, the United Kingdom, Hungary, Poland, Czechoslovakia, and the USSR.[5]

Finally, the calculations which we will present are as close as possible, given the data available, to the year that we selected as a point of reference: 1980.

2 *The results of the statistical analysis of wage distributions*

Table 3.1 gives the results of the fitting of the different empirical distributions to the theoretical distribution (lognormal) and of the Chi square test.

---

[4] Excepting the United States and the United Kingdom where the distinction between manual and non-manual workers is unapplicable.
[5] No data were available for the GDR.

Economies for which the hypothesis of lognormality is accepted
The results are significantly different depending upon the economies under consideration. The hypothesis of lognormality for the earnings distributions is accepted (level of significance 0.05) for the FRG, Hungary, Poland, the USSR (industry), the United Kingdom, and Czechoslovakia (all activities).

For these countries, the differentials between the observed distribution and the theoretical distribution are small whatever the earnings bracket considered. It is important to note that this is true for the extremes of the distributions (lowest and highest earnings brackets) for which alternative theoretical models were proposed.[6]

However, for all the other countries, the differences between the distribution of observed earnings and the lognormal distribution are sizeable.

The wages of the extremes of the distribution
For France, it may be noted that there are fewer individuals in the lowest earnings bracket (less than 2,000 francs a month in 1978) than in the expected theoretical distribution. This is due to the influence of a minimum wage which in 1978 was just slightly under 2,000 francs a month. This confirms, therefore, the impact of the minimum wage legislation upon the earnings structure in France and it explains the "abnormally" small number (in reference to the theoretical distribution) of wage-earners with very low earnings.[7] As for the earnings brackets above 2,000 francs a month, the number of individuals observed is significantly above the theoretical expectations. We find, in these brackets, a great number of wage-earners who would be in the lower classes if the distribution were lognormal.

At the other end of the distribution, there are far more individuals whose earnings are high (superior to 15,000 francs a month) than in the lognormal distribution. This may be explained by the particularly high level of earnings of the executive class in France as compared to other countries.

For Belgium, there are significantly fewer wage-earners at the low extreme of the distribution than the theoretical distribution pre-

---

[6] Notably Pareto's model for the upper extreme of the distribution: see chapter 2 of this volume.
[7] This phenomenon has been analyzed in a number of studies on this theme, notably by Depardieu and Payen ((67), p. 23–5) who maintain that the earnings distribution in France, unlike that of the FRG, is not lognormal.

Table 3.1. *Results of the test of lognormality of the statistical distributions*

Country	Number of earnings brackets	Number of degrees of freedom	Deviation between the theoretical and the empirical distribution	Hypothesis that the distribution follows a lognormal law ($P \leqslant 0.05$)
Industry: all full-time employees paid fully				
Belgium (1978)	17	14	86	refused
Denmark (1978)	16	13	108	refused
France (1978)	19	16	186	refused
FRG (1978)	23	20	17.3	accepted
Hungary (1980)	16	13	8.3	accepted
Poland (1980)	18	15	8.1	accepted
USSR (1964)	13	10	16.5	accepted
In the economy as a whole, all full-time employees paid fully				
US (1979)	16	13	65	refused
UK (1980)	29	26	6.9	accepted
Hungary (1980)	17	14	10.2	accepted
Poland (1980)	12	9	7.8	accepted
Czechoslovakia (1979)	19	16	6.6	accepted
USSR (1964)	13	10	21.3	refused

Sources: Belgium (3), tables 124 and 223
Denmark (4), tables 124 and 223
France (5), tables 124 and 223
FRG (12), pp. 24–25, 53–60
Hungary (19), pp. 230–1
Poland (102), p. 19 and (21), p. 166
US (7), 1981, p. 269
Czechoslovakia (23), 1980, p. 209
USSR: A. McAuley (112), pp. 220 and 224
UK (18), pp. A–36, A–37

dicted. It appears that the introduction of an intersector minimum wage in 1975, not by way of legislation as in France, but through collective bargaining (Dancet (64), p. 47) is responsible for the differentials observed at the low end of the distribution. A sort of spill-over effect operates upon the next brackets, notably on the mode of the distribution (bracket having the greatest number of individuals) which is significantly higher in the observed as opposed to the theoretical distribution.

The case of Denmark is similar to that of Belgium. The number of individuals in the lower brackets of the distribution is "abnormally" low compared to the theoretical distribution. In this country, there has been an "egalitarian" wage policy since the fifties coming from Union pressure on collective bargaining. The upshot thereof has been important measures in favor of the wage-earners at the lowest end of the distribution. Hence certain wage raises were distributed equally among wage-earners instead of the usual multiplicative raises ("in percentage"). In addition, in 1977, again within the framework of collective bargaining, a guaranteed minimum wage was introduced, which, according to certain Danish analysts (Hansen (86)), had a considerable influence on the evolution of the wages of non-skilled workers. It is not unlikely that these measures taken as a whole explain the low number of workers in the classes that constitute the bottom of the wage pyramid compared to the theoretical, lognormal model.

In the United States, the situation is the exact opposite of that in several European countries. Indeed, there is an "abnormally" high number of individuals with very low earnings. This is possible in light of the lack of general regulation of minimum wage, either through legislation or through collective bargaining. This is, however, a necessary, but not a sufficient condition. Indeed, in the FRG and in the United Kingdom there is no such regulation, yet there is not a particularly high number of wage-earners with very low earnings.

One is tempted to wonder whether or not the low earnings groups in the United States are made up of racial minorities who might thus be the victims of wage discrimination. Moreover, the United States is the only country for which wage distributions by race are available.[8] The Chi squared test was thus applied first to the wage distributions of white workers, then to those of black workers. The results are close to those concerning wage-earners as a whole. Neither of these distributions is lognormal, and the number of wage-earners in the lowest brackets is decidedly higher than that expected in the theoretical distribution. The median earnings of whites as opposed to blacks was 1.35 in 1979.

In fact, a careful analysis of American data shows that the difference in earnings between men and women plays a much greater role in the determination of the general wage distribution

---

[8] US Department of Commerce, p. 269–70.

than do the inequalities between whites and blacks. Indeed, the ratio of the median earnings of men to women was 1.68 in 1979.

The study of the wage distribution for men, on the one hand and for women on the other shows nevertheless that the number of wage-earners with "abnormally" low earnings is high whatever the sex of the individuals. Given that this phenomenon touches upon the class of wage-earners as a whole, one must look to a particular characteristic of the American labor market, the existence of regions or branches where wages are particularly low, as an explanation.

However, the study of the earnings distributions for men and for women provides interesting information. Indeed, the very great difference in earnings of these two groups explains why the American distribution is bi-modal. The first mode corresponds to that of the earnings distribution for women (between 10,000 and 12,500 dollars per year in 1979) and the second to that of the earnings of men (between 15,000 and 17,500 dollars per year in 1979). This explains in part why the earnings distribution observed is significantly different from the lognormal distribution.

As for the USSR, it must first be pointed out that the results for industry and for the economy as a whole are not as different as a simple overview of table 3.1 might lead one to believe. Indeed the measure of the distance between the empirical distribution and the theoretical distribution for industry (16.5) is just under the critical level where the hypothesis of lognormality is rejected (18.3 given that the level of significance is 0.05). The same measure for the earnings distribution of the economy as a whole (21.3) is just above this level. It is pointless to interpret this difference. Indeed, given the level of significance selected, it is unlikely that the earnings distributions in the USSR are lognormal, at least as far as the most recent year for which calculations have been done is concerned (1964).

However, a number of Soviet publications[9] devoted to the study of the lognormality of the earnings distributions may very usefully complete the rare statistical data which we used. A number of diagrams, for which there is no unity on the X nor on the Y axis, so as to preclude any estimation of parameters, systematically compare the distribution observed for the earnings of wage-earners in the whole economy to the lognormal distribution.

Generally speaking, it appears that increases in the minimum

9 Rimachevskaja and Rabkina (146) and (147).

wage, which happen at very infrequent intervals, but which are quite massive (for instance the nominal minimum wage increased by 42 percent in 1970 compared to 1965), have a considerable influence on the earnings distribution.

In 1946 and 1956, the observed curves were close to the theoretical ones. In 1961, however, the curve of observed frequencies was bi-modal. This may be explained, according to Rimachevskaja and Rabkina ((147), p. 92), by the increase in the minimum wage in industry in 1960, whereas, in services, it remained the same. In 1964, the results presented in the graph ((147), p. 94) by these same authors are similar to our own (a synthetic measure of the distance between two curves is given in table 3.1). As far as the low earnings brackets are concerned, the number of individuals observed is close to the theoretical estimate. As for the mode of the distribution, the number observed is inferior to the theoretical distribution. The opposite is true for the upper brackets but for the highest earnings (more than 140 roubles) there are fewer individuals than expected. In more recent years, 1968 and 1978, important raises of the minimum wage between 1965 and 1970 have greatly influenced the distributions. There are few individuals in the category of low earnings compared to the theoretical estimates.

We might add that in the other STE either there is no legal minimum wage or it has almost no impact due to its low level.

3 What is learned from the study of the distributions

The causes of the deviations from the lognormal distribution
It must not be forgotten that the hypothesis of the lognormality of the distribution of earnings was not rejected (at the level of significance of 0.05) for the STE (with a restriction for the USSR), the FRG, and the United Kingdom.

Among the factors that may make the observed distributions different from the theoretical ones, there is, first of all a minimum wage applicable to all categories of workers in all sectors of the economy. It is significant that the regulation of minimum wage (on a legal or conventional basis) plays an important role in all these economies where there are fewer wage-earners at the bottom of the observed distribution than is predicted by the theoretical distribution.

The influence of wage discrimination on the earnings distribution varies considerably from one economy to another. If we consider the most significant discrimination, that against women, there seems to be little impact on the earnings distribution in the FRG, the United Kingdom, Poland, or Czechoslovakia. However, it seems that this discrimination may account, completely or partly, for the lack of lognormality in the American distribution. It will be shown that the earnings differentials between men and women in this country are particularly high.

Nevertheless, leaving aside the two phenomena which we have just studied, the earnings distribution is decidedly lognormal. This result remains to be explained.

Two isomorphic models of the wage differentiation in the East and West
Given the general properties of the lognormal function, we think that the earnings distributions in the economies under study are the result, according to a multiplicative model, of a combination of random factors such as the level of formal education, professional training, experience, seniority and age.

We may explain the fact that these factors operate multiplicatively by the method of calculating pay or more specifically the progression of wages within the pay scales of the firms and organizations of the economies under study. Indeed, individual pay differences are based on the application of percentages of variation and not on uniform amounts. For example, seniority may make an individual eligible for bonuses which are calculated by applying a multiplicative coefficient to the wages of a "new" worker who does not have seniority. In the same way, in order to go from one professional category to another, a mulitplicative coefficient is applied to the original category. This is true for all wage increases from the lowest to the highest level.

Moreover, we are of the opinion that potential interregional or interfirm differences also conform to a multiplicative model. Let us imagine that two firms or two regions, with exactly the same skill structure, pay out a different average wage. We go from the first to the second not by adding or subtracting a fixed sum, whatever the category of wages under consideration (additive model), but by applying a multiplicative coefficient to each category. This explains why, as far as wages are concerned, the lognormality of distributions is not affected by the existence of "sector effects" or "firm effects."

If our explanation is correct, it means that the earnings distribution within each firm, each sector, each economy is lognormal. The same is true of each category of wage-earner, such as men or women, manual or non-manual workers, etc. In economies that have been studied extensively, such as the FRG (Depardieu and Payen (67)), the hypothesis has been confirmed empirically.

This theoretical analysis is all the more important, since, according to our estimations, it is applicable to both WE and STE.

This analysis points to the fact that despite economic, institutional, and social structures that are decidedly different in the two systems, the pay differentiation clearly is based on an identical model. There is, therefore, a first link between the wage structures of the two systems.

One might raise the question as to whether or not the multiplicative model fits the wage structures of the STE better than the WE. Indeed, among the STE, the USSR is the only country where, in some years, the earnings distribution differs significantly from the lognormal distribution, a difference due to an important increase in the minimum wage.

Given the small number of STE under consideration, it is not possible to answer this question with any degree of certitude. A great number of factors, however, might explain the fact that the STE come closer to the theoretical distribution. First of all, the application of a minimum wage, whose role in many WE has been pointed out, has a much weaker impact in the STE. Indeed, it is only in the USSR where the distribution is not rigorously lognormal, that the minimum wage plays an important role.[10]

It is also possible that the single wage scale, centrally defined and which is detailed at the sector and ultimately at the firm level, has a tendency to homogenize the wage structures. One must be prudent, however, in considering this last argument as the study of the wage determination in the firms of the STE discloses that the Directors benefit from a rather considerable degree of autonomy as regards the internal managing of the labor force and the distribution of the wage fund which is allocated to them.

---

[10] In Hungary and Poland, there is a minimum wage, but it is fixed at a very low level and very few wage-earners are paid this rate.

2 EVALUATING THE EARNINGS DISPERSION

Our aim is to measure the earnings dispersion in each of the economies under study as precisely as possible. In this way, we hope to contribute to the on-going debate over the inequality of earnings in the STS as opposed to the WS. In addition, we will examine those factors which determine this dispersion.

1 Statistical indicators

We will begin by a descriptive approach to the earnings dispersion. There are a great number of indicators of dispersion from which to choose, many of which have been analyzed in the classic work by Atkinson (37) on the economy of inequality.

There are two kinds of indicators: those that provide a synthetic measure of the individual wage differentials and those that concern certain parts of the distribution.

In the way of synthetic indicators, we will use the coefficient of variation (ratio of standard deviation to the mean) and the Gini coefficient.[11] These indicators, however, are not appropriate to describe earnings inequalities that are located at the extremes, top or bottom, of the distribution. Two distributions, with an identical Gini coefficient, may have very different extremes.

In order to compensate for the faults of the synthetic indicators, we have used indicators which concern different parts of the wage distribution. The first is the ratio of the ninth to the first decile. The first decile corresponds to the wages of that individual who has the tenth rank starting from the bottom of the distribution when wages are arranged in increasing order and the group consists of 100 individuals. The ninth decile corresponds to the wages of the ninetieth individual in the distribution. Finally, the estimation of the function of Lorenz (the relationship between the cumulative percentage of wage-earners and the cumulative percentage of the whole wage) made it possible to evaluate the part of the wages paid to wage-earners in the top 10 percent of the distribution and to those in the bottom 10 percent of the distribution. Finally, five indicators of

---

[11] In reality only the coefficient of variation is an indicator of dispersion. The Gini coefficient is an indicator of concentration. However, this distinction is not operational for our study and we will always ascribe to the term "dispersion," the general meaning of which is outlined at the beginning of this section. Such an approach is in keeping with many previous studies, notably that of the CERC (56), pp. 28–30 and (57), pp. 26–7.

the pay dispersion were calculated (tables 3.2 and 3.3). This relatively high number has two objectives. First of all, no one indicator is perfect and each provides different information. For example, deciles are given in terms of monetary data which makes any international comparison impossible. It is for this reason that we have calculated the ratio between two deciles (the first and the ninth). However, in so doing, we have been unable to disassociate inequality at the bottom and the top of the distribution. Another reason is that, for some economies, above all among the STE, very few studies and publications are available, and, when they are, often only one indicator is used. The latter is included in our five, making indispensable cross-comparisons possible.

Concretely, the calculations were carried out following the hypothesis that the average earnings of each bracket correspond to the center of this bracket.[12] However, given the fact that the classes at the bottom of the distribution and at the top were open, we chose to cut them according to a uniform threshold for all countries using a graphic method.

Close attention must be paid to errors that might interfere with such calculations.

On the one hand, there is the error which results from the regrouping of the observations to the center of each bracket of earnings, and on the other hand, the sampling error. In order to evaluate the first kind of error, whenever possible, we compared our results with those calculations carried out on individual data. This kind of error was proven minimal in light of such comparisons. It was always inferior, in absolute value, to 5/1,000 on the estimation of the mean, 3/100 on the coefficient of variation, 6/100 on the variance, and 3/100 on the Gini coefficient.

The random error resulting from the wage sample surveys has also been evaluated (see pp. 202–3 on statistical sources). First of all, for STE it is non-existent since the data used are based on exhaustive census undertaken in firms. For the European Community economies (with the exception of the United Kingdom), the level of sampling ratio is high and the error therefore is very low (at most 2/1,000 on the mean, 1/100 on the coefficient of variation). For the United States and the United Kingdom where there were far fewer indivi-

---

[12] For more details on this method as well as the calculation of the errors on the estimation of the dispersion coefficients of earnings see Redor (142), appendix, pp. 88–94.

duals surveyed, the random error is a bit higher (5/1,000 at most on the mean, 17/1,000 on the coefficient of variation).

2 A description of the earnings dispersion

We will begin by analyzing the synthetic indicators of all categories of employees, then the particular cases of the wage-earners at the extremes of the distribution.

The global results

If we consider industry (table 3.2) the coefficient of variation and the Gini coefficient are higher for France than for other countries, followed by the USSR, Poland, and Belgium. The FRG and Hungary come next and are very close and cannot be disassociated; this is also true for the three aforementioned countries, given the uncertainty of the calculation of these indicators. Finally, Denmark is by far the country with the lowest earnings dispersion.

As for the economy as a whole (table 3.3), we only have data on the WS for the United States and the United Kingdom, making it impossible to compare, at the present time, these data with the preceding ones.

The United States comes first by far, followed by the United Kingdom, the USSR, and Poland, so close that it is impossible to separate them given the error on indicators. Finally, Hungary and Czechoslovakia are the two countries where the earnings dispersion is the lowest.

Generally speaking, Atkinson shows ((37), p. 32) that if the Lorenz curves of several countries overlap (which is true of France and the STE if we look at table 3.2), it is not possible to classify them according to their degree of inequality without advancing hypotheses as to the weight which is given to each part of the wage distribution.

It must be pointed out that the data concerning the United Kingdom are not rigorously comparable to that of other countries. They do not include men under 21 and women under 18. The pay dispersion is therefore underestimated (see Marsden and Saunders (119), pp. 17–23 on this point).

From this point of view, it is not possible to determine which system is more egalitarian.

It is possible to regroup the two sets of synthetic indicators (having

Table 3.2. *Study of the dispersion of earnings in industry*

Country	Category of wage-earners	Coefficient of variation	Coefficient of Gini	Share of total earnings paid to the bottom 10% of wage-earners in the distribution	Share of total earnings paid to the top 10% of wage-earners in the distribution	Ninth decile / First decile
Belgium (1978)	all categories	0.41	0.20	0.072	0.17	2.6
	manual workers	0.25	0.14	0.066	0.14	2.0
	non-manual workers	0.45	0.23	0.067	0.19	3.0
Denmark (1978)	all categories	0.29	0.16	0.060	0.15	2.0
	manual workers	0.21	0.12	0.073	0.13	1.7
	non-manual workers	0.33	0.18	0.073	0.16	2.1
France (1978)	all categories	0.53	0.25	0.078	0.20	3.4
	manual workers	0.27	0.15	0.071	0.15	2.0
	non-manual workers	0.53	0.26	0.070	0.20	3.6
FRG (1978)	all categories	0.35	0.19	0.065	0.16	2.3
	manual workers	0.27	0.15	0.062	0.14	1.9
	non-manual workers	0.37	0.20	0.059	0.16	2.5
Hungary (1980)	all categories	0.37	0.20	0.062	0.17	2.5
	manual workers	0.35	0(.19	0.061	0.16	2.4
	non-manual workers	0.40	0.22	0.061	0.17	2.8
Poland (1980)	all categories	0.41	0.22	0.057	0.17	2.8
	manual workers	0.40	0.22	0.058	0.18	2.5
	non-manual workers	0.43	0.23	0.059	0.18	2.9
USSR (1964)	all categories	0.44	0.24	0.054	0.18	3.0
USSR (1961)	manual workers	0.40	n.a.	n.a.	n.a.	3.1

Note: n.a.: not available

Sources: Belgium (3), tables 124 and 223
Denmark (4), tables 124 and 223
France (5), tables 124 and 223
FRG (12), pp. 24–25, 53–60

Hungary (19), pp. 230–1
Poland (102), p. 19 and (21) 1981, p. 269
USSR: A. McAuley (112), pp. 224 and 225

Table 3.3. *Study of the dispersion of earnings in the economy as a whole*

Country	Category of wage-earners	Coefficient of variation	Coefficient of Gini	Share of the total earnings paid to the bottom 10% of wage-earners in the distribution	Share of the total earnings paid to the top 10% of the wage-earners in the distribution	Ninth decile – First decile
United States (1989)	all categories	0.67	0.33	0.037	0.22	4.3
United Kingdom (1989)	all categories	0.44	0.23	0.054	0.18	2.75
Hungary (1980)	all categories	0.38	0.21	0.057	0.17	2.5
	manual workers	0.36	0.20	0.053	0.16	2.5
	non-manual workers	0.40	0.22	0.053	0.16	2.7
Poland (1980)	all categories	0.43	0.23	0.054	0.18	3.0
	manual workers	0.42	0.23	0.051	0.18	2.8
	non-manual workers	0.42	0.23	0.058	0.18	3.1
Czechoslovakia (1979)	all categories	0.37	0.20	0.052	0.16	2.4
USSR (1964)	all categories	0.44	0.24	0.045	0.18	3.3
USSR (1981)	all categories	n.a.	n.a.	n.a.	n.a.	3.0

Note: n.a.: not available

Sources: US (7), 1981, p. 269
UK (18), pp. A–36, A–37
Hungary (19), pp. 230–1
Poland (21), 1981, pp. 166–7
Czechoslovakia (23), 1980, p. 209
USSR: A. McAuley, pp. 220–1 and E. Aleksandrovna and E. Fedorovskaja (30), p. 21

to do with industry on the one hand, and the economy as a whole on the other) by giving an equal weight to all the parts of the distribution of wages (this corresponds to a value o of the parameter E in Atkinson's inequality indicator). One must speculate as to the place that Belgium, Denmark, France, and the FRG would occupy, if we had at our disposal data on the economy as a whole.

The example of Poland, the USSR, and Hungary tends to point to the fact that the earnings dispersion in all of the economy is slightly higher (but not always to a significant degree) than that of industry. Such a result is logical if one considers the tremendous diversity of activities which are taken into account. Such regularity leads one to extend the results of industry to the economy as a whole.

If we were to execute this transposition for Belgium, Denmark, France, and the FRG, it is clear that France would find itself between the United States on the one hand, and the United Kingdom, the USSR, and Poland on the other. Belgium would be part of this group. The FRG would be closer to Hungary and Czechoslovakia and Denmark would come last.

Thus it is possible to represent the classification of the earnings dispersion of the economies under study by decreasing order for the years 1978–80.

1 The United States
2 France
3 The United Kingdom
  USSR
  Poland
  Belgium
7 Hungary
  FRG
9 Czechoslovakia
10 Denmark

This classification does not highlight any clear difference between the two systems. Although it is true that the United States and France are at the head, the FRG is in the next to the last group and Denmark comes last of all.

The position of the United States may be explained partly by the size, the geographical diversity, and the social and racial diversity of the population. Given this fact, one might well have expected the earnings dispersion in the USSR to be higher than that of Poland. It is also remarkable that within the WS the earnings dispersion of the

FRG is inferior to that of Belgium. One must be careful, therefore, even within a given system, not to adhere too rigorously to a correspondence with the size of an economy, the diversity of its regions and its activities, and the pay dispersion. Obviously, other socio-economic factors come into play.

What we learn from this initial overview is that the intrasystemic differences in the earnings dispersion are great, whereas there is no clear intersystemic difference.

The position of wage-earners at the top and bottom of the distribution
The study of the portion of the whole earnings that is allocated to the wage-earners at the top and the bottom of the distribution, as well as the relationship between the first and the ninth decile will help us to grasp more fully the origin of the earnings dispersion in the economies under consideration.

First the importance of the regulation of minimum wage (studied previously during the Chi squared test) in Belgium, Denmark, and France must be mentioned. In the latter, it is surprising that, despite the high general earnings dispersion, the share of the total earnings which is allocated to wage-earners at the bottom of the distribution is relatively high.

On the contrary, for the other countries, notably the STE, this share is much lower. The United States is by far the country where the wage-earners at the bottom of the distribution are in the most unfavorable position (compared to other categories of employees).

If we look at the top of the distribution, we see that the United States and France are particular cases. The share of the total earnings which is allocated to wage-earners (10 percent of the top of the distribution) is very high and may explain to a large extent the rank of the two countries in our classification.

For other countries, however, this share is relatively weak; this is the case for Denmark, first of all, and also of the FRG, Czechoslovakia, Hungary, and Poland.

These observations are confirmed by the analysis of the ratio between the ninth and the first decile. Compared with synthetic indicators, this ratio is small in France and in Belgium by virtue of the guaranteed minimum wage. Its high level in the United States is a function of the particular characteristics of the two extremes of the distribution. In the USSR, because so little goes to the wage-earners at the bottom of the distribution, the ratio between these two deciles is relatively high, especially in 1964. There are, however, important fluctuations from year to year depending upon the minimum wage regulation.

Wage inequalities among manual workers and among non-manual workers
It was only possible to study the earnings dispersion of manual and non-manual workers in a few countries. Indeed, some do not correspond to the aforementioned SOEC definition by which the category of manual workers is reserved for workers and wage-earners directly involved in production.

The study, on a harmonized basis, of the earnings dispersion of manual workers in industry (table 3.2) points to a classification that is quite different from that of all categories of workers. Indeed, the dispersion is decidedly higher in the STE studied (Hungary, Poland, the USSR) than in the Western economies. Within the latter group, Belgium, France, and the FRG are very close and Denmark is far behind.

If we consider non-manual workers, France comes first. This position, which numerous international, comparative studies have pointed to, may be explained by the level of earnings of managers. Belgium and Poland come next, followed by Hungary and the FRG and finally Denmark.

All of these observations are fragments of the mosaic that we have just uncovered and which we will seek now to put together.

3 Initial interpretations

There is no systemic difference in the earnings dispersion for the wage-earners as a whole
First of all, some of our results concerning the Western system match those of several studies carried out on this subject. For example, if we take the earnings dispersion of the wage-earning population as a whole, our ranking is the same as that established by the CERC ((57), p. 116) for the beginning of the seventies. First came the United States, followed by France, then the United Kingdom and finally the FRG. However, the earnings dispersion of non-manual workers was highest in France.

As for the STE, there are very few statistical studies available. Nevertheless, Lydall (111) has provided evidence of a high earnings dispersion in Poland. Likewise, Askanas and Levcik (35) rank

Poland and the USSR first among the STS for earnings dispersion, followed by Hungary and Czechoslovakia, using the ratio between the ninth and the first decile.

However, the most important finding of our study concerns the comparison between the STE and the WE. There appears to be no systemic difference between the earnings dispersions of wage-earners as a whole. Although at the beginning of the eighties the United States is the country with the highest earnings dispersion, both the WE and the STE occupy the ranks that follow.

The fact that there is no systemic difference between the earnings dispersion is of significant importance, and goes against the two concepts of the relation between the economic system and the pay dispersion which were described in the introduction to this study.

According to the first concept, Soviet-type societies are egalitarian in so far as they have always been supported by the lowest working classes. Many economists of the STS insist on minimal differentiation in pay, which they deem an insufficient incentive for work.

In the second concept, a high wage dispersion is perfectly justified provided it corresponds to an important dispersion in the quantity and quality of work that individuals supply. From this point of view, it is conceivable that the dispersion of pay be higher in the STS than in the WS.

In actual fact, looking at these initial results, it appears that the relationship between the earnings dispersion and the economic system is complex. The most important thing to note is that this dispersion varies tremendously within economic systems and especially within the WS. Consequently, in order to explain national differences or possible systemic differences, it is necessary to adopt a finer analysis than that we have been using up until now.

In order to provide a more in depth analysis of these results, we will evaluate the impact of different factors, such as the sex of the wage-earners, the nature of their work (manual or non-manual), and the level of their formal education, on the earnings dispersion as a whole. In so doing, we will evaluate the average earnings of each category of wage-earner and we will analyze the variance of the earnings as a whole. However, the more our study progresses, the fewer countries will be taken into account. The fact is that this kind of statistical study (analysis of variance) necessitates more and more detailed information that is often lacking for many economies,

Table 3.4. *Ratio of average earnings of manual and non-manual workers in industry*

Belgium (1978)	Denmark (1978)	France (1978)	FRG (1978)	UK (1978)	Hungary (1980)	Poland (1980)	GDR (1980)	USSR (1980)
1.49	1.30	1.70	1.38	1.18	1.13	1.05	1.05	1.05

Sources: Belgium (3), tables 124 and 223
       Denmark (4), tables 124 and 223
       France (5), tables 124 and 223
       FRG (12), pp. 24–25, 53–60
       UK (6), tables 124 and 223
       Hungary (19), pp. 230–1
       Poland (21), 1981, p. 269
       GDR (22), 1982, p. 118
       USSR (23), 1980, p. 365

especially STE. For this reason, we have eliminated from our analysis certain important factors, notably the age of wage-earners, their seniority, and the characteristics of the firms (size, capital stock) which may influence the earnings dispersion. Some of these factors, however, will be included in the analysis of intersector earnings differences, which close our statistical study (chapter 6).

3 FACTORS AFFECTING EARNINGS DISPERSION

1 Differences in earnings according to category of workers (manual–non-manual)

Manual workers are comparatively better paid than non-manual workers in the STE

The ratio between the earnings of non-manual and manual workers (table 3.4) points to a rift between the WE and the STE. The difference between the two categories of workers is much higher in the former than in the latter. It must be noted that the United States is not included in this classification as the distinction between manual and non-manual workers in this country does not correspond to our own definition.

Nevertheless, if we were to consider American statistics, made to conform to ours, there would be little change. In a study by the

CERC (57) on the early seventies, the United States came between France and the FRG for this classification.

It is remarkable that in the STE the average wage of a manual worker is scarcely different from that of a non-manual worker. At this point in our study, it is too early to thoroughly interpret this fact. To do so, we must compare the wage structures on the one hand, and the organization and the division of labor between the two categories of workers on the other for each system.

It is particularly difficult to interpret the difference in earnings between manual and non-manual workers. Indeed, neither market nor planning theory incorporate this distinction easily. It is hard to analyze in terms of skills given the fact that it is often impossible to compare the skills of manual and non-manual workers. It is not surprising therefore that the most satisfactory analyses in this domain are sociological. This is the case for the comparison between France and the FRG conducted by the research team of the LEST (Maurice, Sellier, and Silvestre (123)).

A synthetic analysis of the pay of manual and non-manual workers
A second point needs to be taken into account. Whereas the total earnings dispersion in the STE is of the same magnitude as in the WE, the difference in earnings between manual and non-manual workers is notably less. We might be tempted to interpret this as a paradox unless the earnings dispersion within one category or the other (or both) is higher than in Western countries. Indeed, this fact has been proven for manual workers. This latter phenomenon balances out, in a sense, the former.

In this case, the formula for breaking down the sum of squared deviations (SSD) relative to the average earnings is the following: SSD of earnings of all wage-earners = SSD within the category of manual workers + SSD within the category of non-manual workers + SSD of average earnings of manual and non-manual workers.

The ratio of the SSD of the average earnings for manual, on the one hand, and non-manual workers, on the other, to the total SSD corresponds to the determination coefficient $R2$. The intra-modality SSD (within each category of worker) represents the part of the total SSD which "the model does not explain."

The computations were carried out on the SSD of the logarithm of the earnings (table 3.5). Apart from the fact that the break down formula may be applied under any circumstances, one may consider

Table 3.5. *Study of the difference in earnings between manual and non-manual workers in industry*

	France (1978)	FRG (1978)	Hungary (1980)	Poland (1980)
(1) SSD from the mean of the logarithm of earnings of manual and non-manual workers	0.0087	0.0035	0.0004	0.00001
(2) SSD of the logarithm of earnings of wage	0.028	0.021	0.023	0.028
$R^2 = \dfrac{(1)}{(2)}$	0.30	0.17	0.02	0.002
Degrees of freedom corresponding to (1)	1	1	1	1
Degrees of freedom corresponding to (2)	36	44	32	20
F	16.0	8.9	0.5*	0.4*

Note: *Difference between the logarithm of earnings of manual and non-manual workers not significant ($P \leqslant 0.05$)

Sources: France (5), tables 124 and 223
FRG (12), pp. 24–25, 53–60
Hungary (19), pp. 230, 231
Poland (21), 1981, p. 269

that the distribution of the logarithm of earnings is approximately normal (see the commentary on the lognormality of the earnings distribution: section 1 herein). The Fisher test, therefore, may be applied.

For France, category of worker represents 0.30 of the total variability (SSD), which is high. In the FRG, it is 0.17. However, in Hungary and Poland, this factor is a very small part of the variability of earnings.

All of these analyses confirm the hypotheses presented at the beginning of this section. If we refer to the category of worker, in the STE, the earnings dispersion of wage-earners as a whole may be explained essentially by the earnings dispersion within and not between each category. This is not the case for the WE. In the FRG, and to a large extent in France, the difference in earnings between manual and non-manual workers accounts for a large part of the dispersion.

We will now turn our attention to other factors which might explain the pay dispersion in the two systems. First we will look at the gender of the wage-earner, which, as we have previously noted, has been widely pointed out in studies of WE. On the contrary, this factor has not been widely studied in the STE due to a lack of available statistics. Indeed, not one Eastern European country has published general statistics on the wages of women! We used the distributions by brackets of women's earnings which can be found in certain statistical yearbooks (Hungary, Poland, Czechoslovakia) to compute the mean and the dispersion of wages for women. In so doing, we have come up with original information.

2 Differences in pay on the basis of the gender of wage-earners

In most countries, men's wages are 50 percent higher than women's
The average earnings for men are about 50 percent higher than those for women whatever the country and the economic system.

The only exceptions to this rule are Denmark where the ratio of earnings between men and women is relatively low (27 percent in favor of men) and the United States where it is particularly high (77 percent).

Although general statistics on women's earnings have never been published for the USSR, using certain monographs bearing upon earnings in firms, it is possible to affirm that the ratio of men's earnings to women's is similar to that of other STE studied here.[13]

The results of our computations are all the more interesting in so far as the data concerning women's earnings are not published in the STE (table 3.6).

In fact, the earnings differentials between men and women are very close to those of Western countries. In theory, these differentials may be explained in several ways.

First of all, this might be the result of individual differences such as the level of formal education, professional training, and experience, or seniority, qualities which in both planning and market theories, are thought to determine the efficiency of the worker and therefore his pay.

Second, it might be that women are victims of wage discrimination, which means that, for an equal level of skill, seniority, and experience, they are paid less.

[13] Using data from many monographs of this type, McAuley (113) estimates at 2/3 the ratio of women's earnings to men's in the Soviet economy. This corresponds to a difference of 50 percent in favor of men's earnings over women's.

Table 3.6. *Ratio of male and female earnings*

Denmark	Belgium	France	FRG	UK	US	Hungary	Poland	Czech.
1	1	1	1	1	1	2	2	2
(1978)	(1978)	(1978)	(1978)	(1980)	(1979)	(1980)	(1961)	(1970)
1.27	1.47	1.47	1.47	1.58	1.77	1.45	1.54	1.50

Notes: 1 Industry
2 Economy as a whole
Sources: Belgium (3), tables 124 and 223
Denmark (4), tables 124 and 223
France (5), tables pp. 124 and 223
FRG (12), pp. 25–25, 53–60
UK (18), pp. A36–A37
US (7), 1981, p. 269
Hungary (189), pp. 398–9
Poland (21), pp. 398–9
Czechoslovakia (23), 1971, p. 146

It is not possible to provide a definitive answer to this question at this point in our study. Nevertheless, we can draw some initial conclusions based on our previous analyses.

First of all, the fact that the differences in earnings between men and women are as high in the STE as in the WE is a social and economic phenomenon of primary importance. Indeed, either women are the objects of wage discrimination or their social promotion is decidedly less than that of men given, for example, inferior level of formal education and professional training.

In order to go further in our research, it is necessary to study the level of formal education and professional training as a factor of earnings dispersion (section 4 following).

The relation between the difference in pay between men and women and the total earnings dispersion
When we break down the SSD of the logarithm of earnings, distinguishing men's earnings from women's (table 3.7), we observe that the corresponding differential explains an important and significant part of the total earnings dispersion in all of the economies under study.

At first glance, it might appear surprising that the United States and Denmark are on the same level. However, one must not forget (section 2 previously) that the total earnings dispersion is high in the

Table 3.7. *Study of the difference in earnings between men and women*

	SSD from the mean of the logarithm of earnings of men and women (1)	SSD of the logarithm of earnings of all employees (2)	$R_2 = (1)/(2)$	Degree of freedom corresponding to (1)	Degree of freedom corresponding to (2)	F of Fisher
Belgium 1 (1978)	0.0044	0.021	0.21	1	41	10.9
Denmark 1 (1978)	0.0017	0.013	0.13	1	39	5.9
France 1 (1978)	0.0043	0.028	0.15	1	30	5.4
FRG 1 (1978)	0.0050	0.021	0.25	1	40	12.5
UK 1 (1980)	0.0080	0.031	0.26	1	52	18.1
US 1 (1979)	0.0108	0.077	0.14	1	32	5.2
Hungary 1 (1980)	0.0057	0.024	0.25	1	26	8.1
Poland 2 (1961)	0.0053	0.038	0.14	1	48	7.8
Czechoslovakia 2 (1970)	0.0071	0.023	0.30	1	36	16.1

Notes: 1 Industry

2 Economy as a whole

Sources: Belgium (3), tables 124–223

Denmark (4), tables 124–223

France (5), tables 124–223

FRG (112), pp. 24–25, 53–60

UK (18), pp. A–36, A–37

US (7), 1981, p. 269

Hungary (19), pp. 230–1

Poland (21), pp. 398–9

Czechoslovakia (23), 1971, p. 146

United States and low in Denmark. In this context, the part of the total variability of earnings explained by the difference in pay between men and women is similar. In other words, gender is an almost identical factor behind the earnings dispersion in the two countries, though the wage inequalities are much higher in one than in the other.

Among the economies where the differences in earnings between men and women play a particularly important role compared to the total earnings dispersion, one notes Czechoslovakia, the United Kingdom, Hungary, and the FRG. Here too there is no systemic difference.

We are well aware of the limits of the preceding study. The fact that women have less formal education and professional training might well explain the level of their earnings. The distributions of men and women in manual and non-manual jobs might well also influence the inequalities in pay between men and women, given the fact that, in the WS above all, manual workers earn far less than non-manual.

By "crossing" several factors, we are able to obtain a more in-depth statistical analysis. Given the limited nature of the information available, we will limit our crosses to the category of worker (manual and non-manual) and gender, then gender and level of formal education and professional training.

3 Pay given the workers' category and gender

Pay differentials between men and women are high whatever their category
Table 3.8 shows that the earnings differentials between men and women are high in all countries whatever the category. We might add that the differential is slightly higher for non-manual workers.

As was previously stated, women's low level of pay may be a function of wage discrimination or, on the average, of an inferior level of formal education and professional training as compared to men.

Whatever the explanation, it is applicable to both manual and non-manual workers. The analysis of earnings in terms of the level of formal education and professional training, on the one hand and gender on the other, is of primary importance in defending our argument as to wage discrimination against women.

Table 3.8. *Ratio of earnings of men and women given the category of labor
(manual workers non-manual workers)*

	Belgium I (1978)	Denmark I (1978)	France I (1978)	FRG I (1978)	Hungary I 1980)	Poland 2 (1961)
Average earnings of male manual workers ———————————————— Average earnings of female manual workers	1.39	1.20	1.34	1.34	1.47	1.59
Average earnings of male non-manual workers ———————————————— Average earnings of female non-manual workers	1.59	1.46	1.65	1.59	1.58	1.77
Average earnings of men ———————————————— Average earnings of women	1.47	1.27	1.47	1.47	1.47	1.45

Notes: 1 industry
  2 the economy as a whole
Sources: Belgium (3), tables 122–4
  Denmark (4), tables 122–4
  France (5), tables 124–233
  FRG (12), pp. 24–25, 53–60
  Hungary (19), pp. 230.1
  Poland (21), 1962, pp. 230–1

4 Pay on the basis of level of formal education and professional training and gender

A harmonized definition of level of formal education and professional training of wage-earners

We are faced with two major difficulties in our task. The first concerns the available statistical data for the STE which are very sketchy with regard to level of formal education and professional training. In addition, the definitions of these different levels are often different from those in the EC. This is also the case for the United Kingdom (at least when referring to the New Earnings survey) and for the United States.

We will begin by testing the hypothesis that there is a relation between wages, on the one hand and the level of formal education (school and ultimately university), professional training, and experience on the other. This definition has its flaws obviously. It is always difficult to compare different types of formal education and professional training. However, for the purpose of empirical studies, this definition can be translated into a common standard such as the number of years of education or training necessary to hold a certain job or occupy a certain position.

By studying this relationship, we will necessarily distinguish manual from non-manual workers. This distinction is justified in so far as these two categories have different, and scarcely comparable, levels of formal education and professional training.

We have broken up the class of manual workers into three, using the three classes of manual workers adopted in the FRG (Jurisse (90)) and the French distinction between skilled, semi-skilled, and non-skilled workers. The Hungarian yearbook of employment uses the French classification.

The definition given for the three classes in the FRG is the following: workers in category 1 are defined by the level of their vocational-technical diploma, the duration of training, and the experience necessary to occupy such a job, and the level of responsibility. Workers in category 2 are said to have been trained for a period of several months in order to hold their jobs. Finally, category 3 is made up of laborers and workers having simple tasks requiring no specific training.

These definitions are undoubtedly vague and, if we were able to break them down more carefully, we might be able to analyze more closely the relationship between wages and formal education and professional training. Nevertheless, given the fact that the structure of workers' employment according to our calculations is similar in the three countries under study (table 3.9), we assume, though we are not absolutely certain, that our comparison is well founded.

Pay of workers on the basis of skills and of managers
The ratio of male workers' earnings to female for an equal level of vocational training (table 3.9) remains important. Even for workers who have the highest level of formal education and professional training (category 1 workers), this ratio is close to the ratio of the average pay of male and female workers.

This fact adds weight to the argument that women are victims of wage discrimination in both systems. It is shown that the level of this discrimination is very similar in the two.

Our definition of the level of formal education and professional

The analysis of wage structures

Table 3.9. *Ratio of workers earnings by sex (1978)*

Industry	Belgium	France	FRG	Hungary
Earnings of male workers category 1 Earnings of female workers category 1	1.47	1.31	1.37	1.34
Earnings of male workers category 2 Earnings of female workers category 2	1.40	1.20	1.37	1.32
Earnings of male workers category 3 Earnings of female workers category 3	1.25	1.14	1.32	1.31
Average earnings of male workers Average earnings of female workers	1.39	1.33	1.46	1.43

Sources: Belgium (3), table T 122
France (5), tables T 102 and 124
FRG (12), pp. 24–5
Hungary (19), pp. 46 and 193

training is not flawless. It is true that, within each level, formal education and professional training are not totally identical for men and women. It is also possible that certain factors are at work in favor of men. For example, if the female labor force is more unstable (higher interfirm turnover, more frequent periods of work stoppage),[14] then experience and seniority are inferior to that of the male labor force and therefore pay is lower.

Even if this is the case, one must not forget the essential point. However imperfect our statistical classification might be, it nevertheless matches, in theory, the principal factor behind the earnings dispersion. Taking this factor into account does little to reduce the inequalities in pay between male and female manual workers. Therefore, our argument that there is discrimination against women is reinforced.

As for non-manual workers, the statistical analysis was particularly difficult. The fact is that nomenclature is often vague and categories difficult to compare from one country to the next.

We have tried very roughly to distinguish non-manual workers with a high level of formal education and professional training from the rest.

For Hungary, the distinction between directors, department heads, engineers, and technicians whose jobs necessitate a high level

[14] These elements are partly excluded, however, as we only took into account full-time wage-earners paid in full, that is to say, present throughout the entire reference period.

Table 3.10. *Managers' earnings in industry*

	Belgium (1978)	France (1978)	FRG (1978)	UK (1978)	Hungary (1980)	Czechoslovakia (1984)
Average earnings of employees with higher education/ training (managers) Average earnings of all wage-earners	1.84	2.36	1.42	1.64	1.50	1.30
Proportion of managers among the wage-earners (in %)	5.8	6.3	10.3	8.1	8.8	8.2

Sources: Belgium (3), table T 214
France (5), table T 214
FRG (12), pp. 33–6
UK (18), table T 214
Hungary (19), p. 196
Czechoslovakia, V. Zvolensky (172)

of formal education and vocational training on the one hand and all other categories of employees on the other hand is explicit. For France, we use the INSEE classification for lack of anything better. Indeed the category "managers" also refers to a high degree of formal education (University) and professional training.[15] For the FRG and all the other EC countries, we used the definition of Jurisse (90) of "non-manual workers of categories 1 and 2," characterized by their knowledge of the technical or commercial fields on the one hand, and by their level of responsibilities on the other.

The results in table 3.10 do not prove that the level of formal education and professional training and experience are a more significant factor in the earnings dispersion in the WS. The fundamental difference, which we have already pointed out, is that the non-manual workers as compared to manual workers are paid more than in the STE. Consequently, the result of the international comparison of the position of managers depends largely on the

[15] INSEE (10), p. 281. Managers are defined as having a level "defined by a university degree or the equivalent thereof acquired through professional training."

The analysis of wage structures

Table 3.11. *Relative earnings of workers by level of training (1978)*

Earnings in industry	France	FRG	Hungary
Male workers belonging to category 1 Male workers belonging to category 3	1.36	1.19	1.33
Male workers belonging to category 1 Male workers belonging to category 2	1.22	1.11	1.13
Female workers belonging to category 1 Female workers belonging to category 3	1.18	1.14	1.30
Female workers belonging to category 1 Female workers belonging to category 2	1.12	1.12	1.11

Sources: France (5), tables T 102, T 12
FRG (12), pp. 24–5
Hungary (19), pp. 46 and 193

earnings of the category of wage-earners (manual workers, non-manual, workers as a whole), by which the earnings of managers are divided (Redor (142), p.335).

In addition, the study of the earnings of workers according to their training level does not reveal any systemic difference (table 3.11).

In conclusion, we may sum up the findings of this chapter as follows.

Areas where no systemic difference was found
First of all, there is no difference between the WE and the STE as far as the countries of both systems are ranked according to the earnings dispersion of wage-earners as a whole.

Second, the level of pay differentials between men and women is comparable for the WS and the STS on the whole, but is lower in Denmark. The latter result is a consequence of the low dispersion of pay in this country. On the contrary, these differentials are relatively high in the United States where there is great dispersion in wages as a whole.

Moreover, when the level of formal education and vocational training for men, on the one hand, and women, on the other, is taken into account, it appears that a great part of the difference in pay is due to wage discrimination against women. For an equal level of formal education and vocational training and experience, men's earnings exceed women's in both systems.

Areas where a systemic difference may be found

Whereas the pay differentials between manual and non-manual workers are low in the STS and account for only a small part of the earnings dispersion, in the WS they account for a large part.

In addition, the earnings dispersion within the category of manual workers is higher in the STS than in the WS.

Before beginning to explain these observations in the second part of this study, it is necessary to perfect the statistical approach. Up until now, only certain individual characteristics of wage-earners have been taken into account. We have not yet made explicit the role of firms and groups of firms in the structuring of wages. In the absence of more appropriate statistical classifications, we will rely on a statistical breakdown by sector.

CHAPTER 4

Analyzing intersector earnings differences

We selected three sector variables: the concentration of establishments (or firms), the capital stock, and work time. These variables cover certain features of sectors, and the firms which constitute them. We show how they play a role in the structuring of wages.

At the same time, we selected the percentage of women in employment and the level of formal education and professional training of the labor force as variables to explain the intersector pay differences. In this way, it was possible to do cross-comparisons with the previous results. In addition, we took into account the influence of these variables on the differentiation in sector earnings and, in so doing, we were better able to bring out possible "sector effects" or "firm effects" with regard to wages.

We will propose a linear regression model for the intersector earnings differences in the economies as a whole. Once we have defined a uniform classification of activities, we will set up a comparison of the factors which structure sector earnings. Moreover, we will attempt to evaluate the degree of proximity between the different wage structures of the economies under study.

I SPECIFYING A MODEL FOR ANALYZING AND RESEARCHING EXPLANATORY FACTORS

1 The analysis model

Given our previous analyses, the necessary model is the following:

$$W = \prod_{i=1}^{N} F_i^{a_i}$$

or:

$$\text{Log } W = \sum_{i=1}^{N} a'_i \text{ Log } F_i \quad (\text{MODEL } 1)$$

where log W is the logarithm of the ratio of sector earnings to the average earnings of the sectors as a whole; the a_i are the regression coefficients to be calculated. They may also be interpreted as the elasticity of sector earnings as compared to each of the factors under consideration. Log F_i designates the logarithm of each of the factors of the differentiation in sector earnings. There are N factors, and they are divided by the corresponding mean of all the sectors.

The specification of this model is based on the hypothesis that the factors which determine the structure of sector earnings operate "multiplicatively." This hypothesis was analyzed in depth and confirmed for the general distribution of earnings for the majority of the economies under consideration. For the remaining cases we were able to justify deviations from the multiplicative model.

In this light, the most plausible hypothesis is that sector earnings themselves follow a lognormal distribution. First of all, the arguments in favor of a lognormal distribution of earnings within firms are based on the pattern of wage progression. When there is a promotion, an increased coefficient is applied to the earnings of the wage-earner being promoted. Such a practice is particularly widespread for taking into account experience, seniority, or the level of formal education and professional training.

The same reasoning may be applied to the study of sector earnings.

One must consider that each sector is characterized, for example, by a certain level of formal education and professional training of its labor force. Since earnings, given this level, are calculated multiplicatively in all firms, their intersector distribution is necessarily lognormal. In addition, if the general distribution of earnings is lognormal as well as that of each sector, then the distribution of the average earnings by sector is lognormal as well.[1]

We are less affirmative with regard to the distribution of the factors of the differentiation in sector earnings. The fact is that, in

---

[1] This comes from the expression which links the sum of square deviations (SSD), compared to the mean of the logarithm of the general distribution, to the SSD of the logarithm of the interbranch earnings, and to the SSD of the logarithm of the intrabranch earnings (see chapter 3, section 1).

theory, a random variable has a lognormal distribution if it is the product of a large number of independent variables which have no particular distribution. If there are few factors, a random variable is considered lognormal if it is the product of variables which are distributed lognormally.

In this way, we can assume that the distribution of the factors of the differentiation in sector earnings is not lognormal, but normal, for example.

Thus, we can imagine a second model whose specification would be

$$W = \prod_{i=1}^{x} e^{b_i G_i}$$

That is to say:

$$\text{Log } W = \sum_{i=1}^{x} b_i G_i \text{ (Model 2)}$$

where the logarithm of the ratio of sector earnings to the average earnings is a linear function of the factors (G_i) of the differentiation in earnings.

The multiplicative form of the model of earnings is maintained, as they are determined by the product of the exponential of each of the factors.

2 Choosing classifications and variables

The first step was to make the classifications of economic activities uniform. In order to do so, we refered to the methodological works of Ehrlich, Kramarics, and Tüü (73). These authors have achieved uniform statistical data concerning the size of establishments and firms in the major WE and STE by industrial sector.

The uniformization of classifications was carried out at a relatively aggregate level. We were, nevertheless, able to distinguish nineteen comparable industrial sectors, among which there were mining, construction and civil engineering, and wholesale and retail trade.

It might come as a surprise that we included wholesale and retail trade. Indeed, it is commonly maintained that the determining factors behind wage structures differ in industry and services.

This distinction is based on the fact that the nature of work in industry and in services is different, and on the fact that the "skills" of blue-collar workers in industry and white-collar employees in trade are not comparable. However, if we accept the fact that the determining factors behind wage structures are complex, and that the female labor force on the one hand and the concentration of establishments and firms on the other must be taken into account, then there is no reason to leave out trade. Other services, however, such as banks and insurance companies, are not included in the comparison, as their development and their roles are very different in the two economic systems.

We were obliged to leave out the United States, Czechoslovakia, and the USSR as it was impossible to make their national classifications conform to the rest.

We selected our variables on the basis of theoretical studies presented in the preceding chapters.

First of all, we used the gender of employees and their level of formal education and professional training so as to check and complete the results of the analysis of the dispersion of individual earnings. Next we tested the existence of a possible "sector effect" on the level of earnings (chapter 2, section 1). It must be remembered that the presence of this sector effect would be linked to the position occupied by large firms on the goods market which would pay relatively higher wages to their labor force. The size of these firms as well as their position on the goods market would give them the incentive to and the possibility of developing their organization, by controlling, for example, the mobility of the labor force by means of appropriate pay. The sector variables used include the concentration of firms, capital stocks, and work time.

We were not able to gather all of these data for all countries. However, the only real difficulty concerns the level of formal education and professional training for the labor force, for which it was not always possible to make the variables uniform. Most of the time, the number of workers in category 1 was compared to the category of manual workers as a whole, and the number of managers, engineers, and technicians to the category of wage-earners as a whole. For Poland and the GDR, countries where the classification of jobs cannot be said to correspond to the level of formal education and professional training, we used data on the number of degree holders from higher education and vocational technical training.

Finally, the per capita stock for each sector was calculated directly for Hungary, Poland, and the GDR using national statistical yearbooks. For the WE, no such indicator was available in the sector classification used. We computed, therefore, the per capita investment over a three year period, so as to eliminate the short-term variations in investment. For the purpose of comparison, a similar computation was carried out for Poland.

As for statistical sources, the same publications as those previously mentioned were used; they concern the years 1978 or 1980. For the GDR, we used the most recent yearbook (1967) which contains sufficiently detailed information so as to be included in our analysis. Given the decreasing volume of data available in the statistical publications in the GDR, it was not possible to bridge this gap between the GDR and the other countries.

2 NATIONAL MODELS OF DIFFERENTIATION OF SECTOR EARNINGS

1 The most important factors behind the differentiation of sector earnings

For each country, we tested models (1) and (2) designed previously. The variable to be explained is the logarithm of sector earnings divided by the average earnings, which is linked to the presence of women, to an indicator of the concentration of firms, to the per capita capital stock, to the level of formal education and professional training of workers, and to the weekly work time.

Whenever possible, we used two indicators of the level of formal education and professional training so as to compensate for any individual shortcomings.

We showed that there was no theoretical reason to opt for the specification (1) rather than the model of earnings differentiation (2). Therefore, the choice was empirical, based on the best econometric estimation.

The leading role of the employment of women, of the concentration of firms, and of the per capita capital stock
First of all, we used the STEPWISE procedure, a software research tool. For each model, this procedure selects one by one the most significant variables using the Fisher test, and stops at a predetermined level of significance.

For the majority of countries, the first two variables selected were the percentage of female wage-earners per sector (decreasing relation with the logarithm of the sector earnings) and the concentration of firms or the per capita capital stock (increasing relation). There is only one exception to this, and that is the Danish model where the percentage of women employed is not taken into account.

One phenomenon deserves particular attention. In theory, one might think that the variables which reflect the level of formal education and professional training of the labor force by sector would be selected first. This is not the case, however; whether the indicators are directly (Poland) or indirectly (all other countries) concerned with the level of formal education and professional training, these variables explain only a very small part of the variance of earnings. They are sometimes correlated with others (the correlation with the employment of women is negative), and are therefore excluded from the model. The GDR is an exception, since, in keeping with planning theory, the percentage of graduates from higher education has been selected. As we have previously mentioned, it is certain that the indicators of the level of formal education and professional training are heterogeneous and influenced by the nature of the institutions themselves. However, the strong determination coefficient associated with the employment of women in each sector or with the concentration of firms or with per capita capital stock are proof that the level of formal education and professional training is not the only, nor even the principal determining factor behind sector earnings. In order to be so one would have to argue that the sectors where there are the greatest numbers of women are those where the labor force is the least educated and trained, and that the sectors where there is the greatest concentration and the greatest capital stock are those where the level of training is the highest. There is no empirical evidence to support these statements, especially the second.

The negative relation between sector earnings and the employment of women must be seen in light of our previous remarks about wage discrimination. Our results show that this discrimination is coupled with segregation in the employment of women.

Whether we consider market or planning theory, we did not expect to find a positive relation between the concentration of firms and capital stock on the one hand, and branch earnings on the other. Usually, according to both of these theories, the concentration of firms is uniform, and, for the same level of skill, two individuals who are equally productive are paid the same. One can argue, however, that an unequal distribution of capital stock by sector means that labor is not equally efficient and is therefore paid differently. These are the "imperfections" that both market and planning theories take into account.

Incorporating the concentration of firms (or establishments) into the explanatory schema is the most difficult task. Indeed, if we accept the fact that this concentration reflects the oligopolistic position of firms on the goods market, and possibly their role as an oligopsony on the labor market, the relation between earnings and concentration is either non-existent (oligopoly on the goods market) or is negative (oligopsone on the labor market). In order to explain the difference between our observations and the theories, the analysis that follows will focus on the way the labor force is managed in firms of both systems.

2 Models selected

National models with nineteen sectors

Very often, we eliminated variables which reflect the level of formal education and professional training of the labor force as they were not significant. In national models, at best only one indicator of the level of formal education and professional training of wage-earners, one specification,[2] has been maintained. No such indicator was maintained for the FRG, Hungary, or Poland.

However, it is certain that the employment of women (except for Denmark) is highly significant in explaining differentiation in sector earnings, as are the concentration of firms, and (or) the per capita capital stock (table 4.1).

Moreover, the test of comparison of the value of the regression coefficients shows that there is no significant difference ($P < 0.1$) for certain countries. This is the case for the regression coefficient which corresponds to the employment of women in the GDR, Poland, and the United Kingdom. Similarly, the effect of the concentration of firms on earnings is not significantly different in Belgium, France, or the FRG.

---

[2] Indeed, for each country, several indicators of the level of formal education and professional training of the labor force were tested (see table 4.1).

In light of the test of congruence of the different models, the Danish model is by far the least satisfactory. The analysis of the residuals of this model provides no evidence of aberrant sectors which would account for this poor result. This leads us to conclude that sector earnings in Denmark follow decidedly different rules than those at work in other countries.

It must be pointed out, first of all, that the intersector earnings deviations in this country are notably lower than elsewhere. The coefficient of variation of the logarithm of these earnings is in fact 0.096 in Denmark, as opposed to 0.163 in Belgium, 0.146 in the United Kingdom, 0.138 in France, 0.127 in Hungary, 0.813 in Poland, and 0.106 in the GDR. In addition, it must not be forgotten that the differences in earnings between men and women, between manual and non-manual employees, between the highly trained and the untrained people are lower than in other countries. This explains, to a great extent, why the results of the estimation of our model are not satisfactory.

This shows that the distinction between the WS and the STS, in matters of wages, is not as strong as might have been initially imagined. If we were to consider "a Scandinavian system" as a distinct entity, we might find greater differences within the WS than between the WS and the STS.

The results of the estimation of the Hungarian and Polish models are inferior to those of the WE, from an econometric point of view. Nevertheless, close examination of the residuals of these models might well explain a great deal of this phenomenon. The fact is that the earnings in the mining industry, particularly in Poland and Hungary, are exceptionally higher than those predicted by the model. This comes as no surprise because the mining industry has "priority" (as does the steel industry) and should, according to Soviet type planning theory, benefit from more abundant resources and (or) pay better than other sectors.

Particularities of the mining sector in the STE
It appears that the earnings differentials in mining as compared to national models are extremely high in Poland and in Hungary, and to a lesser degree in the GDR. In this industry, earnings are related to neither the gender of the employees nor to the concentration of firms; rather they conform to a different logic. Therefore, one can then form national models. Moreover, taking this into account

Table 4.1. Differentiation of sector earnings: models used (19 sectors)

Country	Model	Variable	Variable	Variable	Variable	Constant	R^2	R^2 adjusted	F
Belgium	2	Wo −0.0098 (−6.1)	INV/CAP 0.00043 (4.95)	MANAGERS 0.0010 (3.1)	ESTAB. 0.007 (2.9)	4.4 (84.1)	0.91	0.88	35.5
Denmark	1	INV/CAP 0.051 (2.7)	o1 0.029 (2.7)	ESTAB. 0.014 (1.4)		3.9 (25.7)	0.62	0.55	8.4
France	2	MANAGERS 0.0018 (8.4)	ESTAB. 0.0008 (3.7)	Wo −0.0008 (−4.3)	—	4.4 (101.5)	0.92	0.90	57.5
FRG	2	Wo −0.0012 (−6.2)	ESTAB. 0.0007 (2.5)	—		4.64 (115.0)	0.82	0.80	37.9
UK	2	Wo −0.0022 (−6.5)	ESTAB. 0.0011 (4.2)	MANAGERS 0.00042 (1.7)		4.5 (85.5)	0.87	0.85	35.6
Hungary	1	Wo −0.22 (−5.1)	K/CAP 0.037 (1.9)	—		5.4 (23.2)	0.72	0.68	20.5
Poland	2	Wo −0.002 (−3.3)	ESTAB. 0.002 (3.4)	—		4.5 (44.7)	0.76	0.73	26.8
GDR	2	Wo −0.0018 (6.3)	HIGHER EDUC. 0.0002 (1.6)	—		4.7 (123.1)	0.88	0.87	44.1

Notes: Model 1: $\text{Log } W = \sum_{i=1}^{n} a_i \text{ Log } F_i$

Model 2: $\text{Log } W = \sum_{i=1}^{n} b_i G_i$

The numbers between parentheses are student's t. All regression coefficients are significant at $P \leqslant 0.1$ except coefficients corresponding to the percentage of people with higher education/training in the GDR, to the concentration of establishments in Denmark and to the presence of managers in the UK, which are significant at $P \leqslant 0.2$.

Wo = % of women among wage-earners

MANAGERS = % of managers among wage-earners

01 = % of workers in category 1 (having received theoretical and practical training over several years)

HIGHER EDUC. = % of graduates of higher education among wage-earners

ESTAB. = % of wage-earners employed in establishments of more than either 500 or 1,000 people

INV/CAP = investment per capita

K/CAP = capital per capita

Sources: Belgium (3), T 002, 004, 102, 106, 122, 202, 214, 302, 314 and Eurostat (2), pp. 58–61

Denmark (4), T 002, 004, 102, 106, 122, 202, 214, 302, 314 and Eurostat (2), pp. 92–5

France (5), T 002, 004, 102, 106, 122, 202, 214, 302, 314, Investment per capita (9), 1983, leaflet 3, p. 154

FRG (13), pp. 90–122, vol. 1, pp. 124–61, vol. 1, pp. 58–120, vol. 2 and (15), p. 269

UK (6), T 002, 004, 102, 106, 122, 202, 214, 302, 314, and Eurostat (2), pp. 72–6

Hungary (20), 1980, pp. 54, 140, 184–9, 206, 209, 234

Poland (21), 1981, pp. 68, 72, 193, 197, 246, 250–4, 261

GDR (22), 1968, pp. 58, 66, 93–7, 142, 357, 463

Table 4.2. *Differentiation of sector earnings: models used, after the exclusion of mining (18 sectors)*

Country	Model used	Variable 1	Variable 2	Variable 3	4	Constant	R^2	R^2 adjusted	F
Belgium	2	Wo −0.00092 (−6.3)	INV/CAP 0.00051 (6.1)	MANAGERS 0.0013 (4.2)	ESTAB. 0.00056 (2.3)	4.4 (92.5)	0.93	0.91	45.2
Denmark	1	INV/CAP 0.045 (2.2)	o1 0.075 (2.4)	ESTAB. 0.018 (1.6)		4.0 (24.9)	0.64	0.56	8.3
France	2	MANAGERS 0.0018 (7.8)	ESTAB. 0.00080 (3.7)	Wo −0.00085 (−4.3)		4.4 (98.7)	0.92	0.90	55.7
FRG	2	Wo −0.0012 (−6.8)	ESTAB. 0.00092 (3.2)	—		4.6 (122.6)	0.85	0.83	43.6
UK	2	Wo −0.0021 (−6.1)	ESTAB. 0.0011 (3.7)	MANAGERS 0.00047 (1.7)		4.5 (82.6)	0.85	0.82	27.8
Hungary	1	Wo −0.13 (−4.7)	K/CAP 0.047 (4.2)	—		4.9 (32.2)	0.80	0.77	30.7
Poland	2	Wo −0.0018 (−4.2)	ESTAB. 0.0018 (0.0013) (3.0)	—		4.6 (64.2)	0.78	0.74	25.9
GDR	2	Wo −0.0018 (−8.7)	HIGHER EDUC. 0.00026 (2.6)	—		4.7 (159.8)	0.89	0.87	62.5

Notes: Model 1: $\text{Log } W = \sum_{i=1}^{n} = a_i \text{Log } F_i$

Model 2: $\text{Log } W = \sum_{i=1}^{n} = b_i G_i$

The numbers between parentheses are student's t. All regression coefficients are significant at $P \leqslant 0.1$ except the concentration of establishments in Denmark, which is significant at $P \leqslant 0.15$

See also table 4.1.

Sources: see sources for table 4.1.

might well explain the relatively poor performances of the Polish and Hungarian models.

Models based on eighteen sectors, with the exception of mining, were tested.

The quality of the models (table 4.2) of countries where earnings in the mining industry are "abnormally" high improved. These countries are the following: Belgium, Hungary, Poland, and the GDR. The model of the FRG improved for the opposite reason: earnings in the mining industry are relatively low.

We used the same variables in the eighteen sector model as in the nineteen. We checked that no variable which had been previously eliminated became significant in the new estimations. There is no cause, therefore, to modify our previous remarks.

Given the available comparable statistical information, we are confident of having arrived at the best possible specification of the intersector differentiation of earnings, using a uniform model for all countries. Thanks to this model, we will be able to compare in detail the intersector structure of earnings in the economies under study.

3 A COMPARISON BETWEEN THE SECTOR STRUCTURE OF EARNINGS IN THE TWO SYSTEMS

We will begin by comparing the sectors which differ the most from the estimated models, and we will go on to analyze the degree of proximity between the intersector earnings structures of the economies under consideration.

1 The sectors that differ most from the estimated models

When we examine the residuals of the eighteen sector models, there is a net rift between the WE and the STE.

Indeed, for the latter, earnings in the sector dealing with the processing of ferrous and non-ferrous metals (notably in the steel industry) are relatively higher than the values predicted by the models as opposed to the results observed for the FRG and Denmark. In France, this sector follows the model rather closely. This result is all the more suprising given that the characteristics of the sector in all five countries are rather similar: low percentage of women, an averagely skilled labor force, and a high concentration of establishments.

It appears therefore that in the STE the "priority sectors," on which traditional heavy industry is based, always benefit from relatively high earnings as compared to those predicted by the model for the rest of the economy. The same is true for the mining industries: there is a noticeable difference between the two economic systems.

There are certain similarities, however. Compared to national models, the energy branch is always underprivileged in France, Hungary, and the GDR. This might come as a surprise if we consider that in France this branch is among those with the highest earnings. The logarithm of earnings predicted by the model (4.90) is not only far superior to the average earnings (4.60) but also to the observed earnings (4.83). There are few women. There are many workers from category 1 as well as many executives. The concentration of firms (or establishments) is high as well as the capital stock.

One should remain critical of the statistical indicators used as far as France is concerned. These might be biased given the monopolistic or oligopolostic position of the firms in this sector. The particularly great number of category 1 workers and executives is perhaps an indication of the fact that the firms in this sector practice wage over-scaling. Our statistical indicators are not immune to this phenomenon.

Building and civil engineering (BCE) and trade do not differ significantly from national models except for BCE in the GDR and trade in the United Kingdom, which is worth pointing out.

These two sectors, the functions of which are in fact different from those of manufacturing industry, are studied separately most of the time. The fact that national models include essentially the percentage of women and the concentration of firms (or establishments) might explain why they can be integrated into our analyses. Indeed it is easy to transpose these factors from industry to other areas of activity. In all countries studied, the earnings in BCE are close to the mean in industry. Given the estimated models, two factors act in opposite directions. A low percentage of women increases earnings, but the small concentrations of establishments offsets the preceding effect. As for trade, the fact that the average earnings are inferior to those of industry may be explained, given the models proposed for all countries, by the large proportion of women and the small size of these establishments.

2 The proximity between the intersector earnings structures of the economies under study

Pair-wise comparisons of the earnings structures
We have regressed the sector earnings of each country one on the sector (table 4.3 gives the corresponding coefficients of determination R^2). This consists in pairwise-comparisons, for two given countries, of the earnings of each branch. The results vary considerably depending upon whether or not the mining sector is included in the comparisons. When included, there are intersystemic differences. The interbranch earnings structures in the WE are strongly linked to each other, whereas in the STE, they are less so. The United Kingdom, however, is an exception to the rule as it is not closer to the WE than to the STE.

If we exclude the mining industries (table 4.4), the picture is quite different. The earnings structures of Belgium, Denmark, France, and the FRG are more closely correlated with each other than with other countries. However, the United Kingdom is as close to the STE as to the WE, and Hungary is as close to the WE as to the STE. The sector earnings of the GDR are as close to those of the United Kingdom and the FRG as to those of Hungary and Poland.

It appears that the essential difference between the WE and the STE resides in the fact that in the latter, two sectors have priority, namely the mining and iron and steel industries.

The isomorphism of intersector earnings structures and the sources thereof
We have yet to explain what is meant by the term isomorphism of the wage structures under study, the term which appears in our introduction.

As we stated previously, two structures are isomorphic if it is possible to establish a bi-univocal correspondence between the elements of these structures and between the relations which connect them. Up until now, we have not used this concept, for we have found that there were no systemic differences between many characteristics of the wage structures, but we have been unable to find grounds for comparison between the determining factors of these structures.

First of all, the correspondence that may be established between the different intersector earnings structures is a linear relation, the estimates of which are given in table 4.4.

Table 4.3. *Coefficient of determination R^2 between the logarithms of the sector earnings of each country (19 sectors)*

	Belgium	Denmark	France	FRG	UK	Hungary	Poland	GDR
Belgium	1	0.582	0.863	0.788	0.668	0.428	0.224	0.520
Denmark	0.582	1	0.758	0.548	0.417	0.220	0.041	0.174
France	0.863	0.758	1	0.794	0.618	0.215	0.092	0.367
FRG	0.788	0.548	0.794	1	0.798	0.363	0.226	0.630
UK	0.668	0.417	0.618	0.798	1	0.656	0.502	0.767
Hungary	0.428	0.220	0.215	0.363	0(.656	1	0.850	0.618
Poland	0.224	0.041	0.092	0.226	0.502	0.850	1	0.636
GDR	0.520	0.174	0.367	0.630	0.767	0.618	0.636	1

Sources: see sources for table 4.1

Table 4.4. *Coefficient of determination R^2 between the logarithms of the sector earnings of each country (18 sectors)*

	Belgium	Denmark	France	FRG	UK	Hungary	Poland	GDR
Belgium	1	0.602	0.886	0.781	0.660	0.561	0.207	0.497
Denmark	0.602	1	0.758	0.558	0.475	0.452	0.066	0.194
France	0.886	0.758	1	0.807	0.687	0.535	0.195	0.419
FRG	0.781	0.558	0.807	1	0.825	0.623	0.306	0.644
UK	0.660	0.475	0.687	0.825	1	0.713	0.441	0.727
Hungary	0.561	0.452	0.535	0.623	0.713	1	0.586	0.691
Poland	0.207	0.066	0.195	0.306	0.441	0.586	1	0.710
GDR	0.497	0.194	0.419	0.644	0.727	0.691	0.710	1

Sources: see sources for table 4.1

Second, the correspondence which exists between the relations that structure sector earnings for each economy comes from previously estimated models (table 4.1 and 4.2). At this level, the isomorphism results from the multiplicative nature of pay models in all of the economies under study, and from the fact that the factors behind the differentiation of intersector earnings are the same.

The origin of this isomorphism remains to be found. It is based primarily on the fact that the determining factors of the intersector earnings structures are distributed in the same way between the different sectors of industry whatever the economy.

Indeed, in all economies, the sectors having the highest concentration of firms (or establishments) are: mining, energy, processing of ferrous and non-ferrous metals, manufacturing of materials for transport, the electricity and electronics industry, and the chemical industry. Likewise, in all countries, the highest percentages of female workers are to be found in: electricity and electronics, instrument engineering, textiles, printing, clothing, the leather industry, food, and trade. In all economies, the capital stock per worker is the highest in the production of energy, the processing of ferrous and non-ferrous metals, the chemical industry, and the manufacturing of construction materials and of paper.

These results are an important link in the logic of our research. They explain the isomorphism between the intersector earnings structures that we have evidenced. Furthermore, such results prod us to seek the causes of such an isomorphism.

At this point, it is possible to outline the general line of research of the second part, without going into detail. In both systems, the degree of concentration of firms must be linked to conceptions of technical progress and the organization of labor. This means that in both systems the market for certain products is dominated by a small number of producers. It will be necessary to study the power of these producers to structure wages in the two systems with very different institutional frameworks.

A high percentage of female workers in certain sectors, and an absence thereof in others, may be explained by the working conditions. However, in so far as there is heavy wage discrimination against women, it will be necessary to look at the types of wage management and, beyond that, at the management of the labor force in firms of both systems.

However, before moving on to fundamental explanations, we must attempt to profit from our statistical analyses by questioning the validity of these results if we give up our static point of view in favor of a dynamic one.

CHAPTER 5

Stability and adaptation of wage structures

We will begin by linking the study of the intersector earnings differences to that of the individual earnings dispersion. Indeed, we will try to provide a synthesis for these two types of investigation.

Next, we will shed light on the evolution of earnings dispersion in the two systems starting with the end of the Second World War. We will take into account socio-economic changes in the two systems during this period. The stability of the WS will be contrasted with the upheavals in the STS due to the arrival of Soviet-type Socialism. The latter have had a tremendous impact on the evolution of earnings dispersion.

I WHAT THE STATISTICAL ANALYSIS OF THE WAGE STRUCTURES TEACHES

1 The area where there is no systemic difference

The two statistical approaches provide convergent evidence. First of all, earnings differences between men and women account for an important part of the individual earnings dispersion, as well as the intersector differentials. Such convergence is important in so far as it was impossible to carry out a direct study of women's earnings in the GDR, on the one hand, and possible in Poland only for the far distant year of 1961.

It is certain, therefore, that the differences in earnings between men and women are as great in the STE as in the WE. The study of the relation between the level of formal education and professional training and the gender of workers, as regards both the analysis of earnings dispersion and sector earnings, proves that the women's low earnings cannot be explained solely by an inferior level of formal education and professional training. Even if this is a factor, women are nevertheless victims of segregation and discrimination in so far as they are in all countries to be found working in those sectors where, for a given level of formal education and professional training, earnings are relatively low.

In our analyses, the level of formal education and professional training appeared as one of many factors behind the individual earnings dispersion as well as sector earnings. It must not be forgotten that the statistical indicators tested were far from perfect. Taking into account the initial level of formal education and professional training, as well as training acquired on the job and which is indispensable for doing a job poses a problem. Statistical indicators do not adequately represent the latter training, especially when these indicators refer solely to a level of formal education, be it primary, secondary, or university.

However, in order to override this problem, we used several indicators for each country. It is possible that the relatively weak influence of the variable taking into account the level of formal education and professional training is partly due to the poor quality of the indicators. But the strength of other factors, such as the presence of women and the size of firms, gives proof that the level of formal education and professional training alone cannot explain the intersector or interindividual earnings difference.

In order to understand this phenomenon which touches both the WS and the STS, one must recognize the central role played by the demand for labor, that is to say by firms. In fact, the hypothesis that should be held is the following: firms model earnings structures in accordance with their own strategies and logic. In this sense, firms are what F. Perroux (136) calls "active units." In the second part of this study, we will explain these strategies and show how they can be compared in the two systems.

There is therefore a rather large area where there is no inter-systemic difference. We mean that it is not possible to establish a significant difference between the economies of each system taken as a whole for the variables studied.

In other words, we can posit that within this area wage structures in the two systems are isomorphic. However, the conditions necessary to define structures as being isomorphic are only partially fulfilled given that this isomorphism concerns only certain elements which make up the wage structures of both systems. Therefore, it can be said that these structures are partially isomorphic.

Next, we will look at the systemic differences which appear in light
of our statistical analyses.

2 *The area of systemic differences in wage structures*

As stated previously, the difference in earnings between manual and
non-manual workers is higher in the WE than in the STE. In
addition, it appears, in light of the analysis of intersector earnings,
that two important industrial sectors in the STE, the mining and
processing of metals industries pay exceptionally well, if we refer to
national models. Thus, sectors which were defined as "having
priority" during the period of extensive industrialization in the STE
have held until the present time their particular position.

It is not possible to explain the position of these sectors by the need
for a particular kind of labor force during the years 1970–80. The
number of workers in these two sectors evolved very differently in
the course of this period in the different countries.

The source of the particularly high wages in priority sectors, at the
end of the seventies, comes from a normative conception of the role
that the mining and steel industries play in the economic development and transformation of society. One has reason to think that,
even if the administrative authorities sought to lower pay in these
branches, there would be tremendous opposition on the part of
wage-earners to such a plan.

The importance of earnings in "priority branches" necessarily
leads us to reconsider our judgment of the total earnings dispersion
in the STE. The question needs to be posed as to whether or not the
interindividual earnings dispersion, which is relatively great in
Hungary and in Poland, might not be explained, at least partly, by
the existence of priority sectors. Unfortunately, given the lack of
data, it is not possible to conduct a statistical analysis that would
take into account the level of formal education and professional
training, gender, and the sector effect. Therefore, we simply calculated the sum of the squared deviations (SSD) of sector earnings
weighted by the number of individuals and divided it by the total
SSD of earnings in industry.

Whereas the intersector earnings dispersion constitutes a small
part of the dispersion as a whole in France and the FRG, in Hungary
and especially in Poland this part is substantially greater. This result

Table 5.1. *Ratio of SSD of intersector earnings to earnings in industry*

	France	FRG	Hungary	Poland
Earnings	0.055	0.074	0.186	0.307
Logarithm of earnings	0.113	0.096	0.172	0.268

Sources: see sources for tables 3.2 and 6.1 above

Table 5.2. *Coefficient of variation of earnings*

	France 0.528	FRG 0.350	Poland 0.410
All industrial sectors except mining	0.529	0.353	0.371

Sources: France (5), tables T 124 & 223
FRG (12), pp. 24–25–53–60
Poland (102), p. 19.

was expected, and reflects the particular role played by mining and the metal processing industries in certain STE. This is particularly true of Poland where in mining earnings are high and the number of wage-earners great. It is not at all certain that the same results would appear for countries, such as the GDR, where the intersector earnings dispersion, is much lower.

We are led to believe therefore that the sector factor plays a more important role in the earnings dispersion in Poland, and to a lesser degree in Hungary, than in France or the FRG. In the absence of precise statistical data, we compared the coefficient of variation of earnings in France, the FRG, and Poland, leaving aside the mining sector.[1]

The coefficient of variation of earnings in Poland is considerably lower, but remains superior to that of the FRG.

We must exercise caution in interpreting tables 5.1 and 5.2. If we were to carry out a statistical analysis of the earnings disperison by crossing industrial sectors, the level of formal education and professional training of the labor force and gender, we might find that the sector plays a relatively small role in the differentiation in

[1] The necessary data are not available for Hungary.

individual pay, because the sectors that pay the most are those with the best educated and trained labor force, those with the fewest women, and those with the highest concentration of forms.

However, although we were unable to carry out all the computations, it is extremely likely, given the impact of priority sectors on the general dispersion of earnings (see table 5.2), that the total earnings dispersion, is all things being equal, greater in the STE than in the WE.

Finally, it is possible to analyze our statistical results in light of the considerations outlined in chapter 1: to evaluate these results according to the criteria of equality and efficiency which are common to the market and planning theories.

3 Interpreting our statistical results in light of the equality and efficiency criteria

Can it be said that in the two systems two individuals who do the same job, which requires the same level of formal education, professional training, and experience are paid the same wage? Are these same individuals paid on the basis of their productivity?

It is doubtlessly too early to be able to answer these questions completely given that the relation between wage and productivity is not explicit (see part II, chapter 6), and that wage management has not been specified in either system. However, already the following remarks can be made.

The relatively weak link between the level of formal education and professional training and wages can serve as a guideline for our exposé.

First of all, wage discrimination against women points to the fact that the equality criterion remains unsatisfied in both systems.

Certain elements from the study of sector wages lead one to the same conclusion. Indeed, capital stock or concentration of firms, at the same time as the level of formal education and professional training of the labor force determine sector wages. The equality criterion is not respected. It is indeed difficult to accept that sectors where the concentration of firms are the greatest or which have the highest per capita capital are those where the intensity of labor is the greatest. In fact, only if these conditions were met would the criterion of equality be satisfied.

The relation between wages and the concentration of firms is ambiguous. It is conceivable that economies of scale are the root of high labor productivity. However, we cannot be assured that the high wages in highly concentrated establishments and firms are the result of their position as oligopolies or monopolies on the goods markets. Given this hypothesis, the efficiency criterion is not met as the theory of imperfect competition demonstrates. Only a closer analysis of the management of wages in firms can clear up this point (see part II, chapter 7).

Finally, some of our results are difficult to interpret in light of the two criteria. This is the case, for example, for the differential between the wages of manual and non-manual workers. These two categories of workers have very different formal education and professional training. The efficiency of each depends on the division of labor, and of power between them. It is necessary, therefore, to analyze these phenomena.

However, before undertaking such a task and in order to conclude our analytical study, we would like to present the broad lines of the wage dispersion in the two systems since the Second World War.

2 THE DYNAMICS OF THE WAGE STRUCTURES

Up until now our statistical study has been static: we have evaluated the earnings dispersion as a whole, or the structuring of sector earnings at the end of the seventies or the beginning of the eighties. Nevertheless, a complete analysis of the dynamics of the wage structures in the economies under study will not be provided. In trying to compute all the necessary indicators, we would come up against the obstacle of a lack of data published at regular intervals. For the European Community countries, for example, the last survey on earnings structure goes back to 1978, and the previous one to 1972. We will limit ourselves, therefore, to using the data appearing in the few studies published on the evolution of the earnings dispersion in the WS and the STS. We will interpret these data in light of theoretical conclusions coming from our own research.

1 Factors behind the dynamics of wage structures

The principal determining factors behind the wage structures – the level of formal education, professional training and experience, discrimination against women, concentration of firms, and per capita capital stock – are slow to evolve.

Indeed some of these factors are sociological such as the condition of women and their place in society. In addition, the structure of the wage-earning population by level of formal education and professional training evolves in accordance with the democratization of the educational system, and the replacement of one generation of workers by another. As for the structures of the means of production, they hinge, to a large extent, on technical changes which mature slowly.

We are thus led to hold the hypothesis that the evolution of the wage structures in the two systems is slow and its effects noticeable only in the long term.

One should by no means underestimate the impact of economic policy or wage negotiations. The impact of the minimum wage, legal or contractual, has been evidenced in many WE. Without a doubt, this is an important factor behind the pay at the bottom of the wage scale.

In the STS, economic policy plays a decisive role. In addition to the role of the minimum wage, previously analyzed for certain countries (e.g., the USSR), the State has the power to control the pay structure down to the level of the firm. During "reforms," this right sparked a debate as to the necessary degree of decentralization and autonomy of firms in wage setting. For the moment, we will simply put forth the principal statistical results that we were able to glean. The latter, as well as previously mentioned results, will serve as the basis for our final theoretical analysis.

2 Observed evolutions

A very slow evolution in the earnings dispersion in the WS since the beginning of the fifties
We selected the ratio of the ninth to the first decile for several reasons.

First of all, this is the only indicator which is published regularly for the STE and notably for the USSR. Second, the estimation thereof, on the basis of the earnings distributions, is relatively reliable. Indeed this indicator can be evaluated by means of a simple interpolation without knowing the pay of wage-earners above the ninth or below the first decile.

It is certain that a broader analysis, based on a greater number of indicators, as in chapter 3, would have been preferable. It appears,

Table 5.3. *Evolution of the dispersion of earnings in different countries for the economy as a whole: ratio of the ninth to the first decile*

Year	US	France	FRG
Male wage-earners			
1949	3.2		
1951			2.3
1954		3.4	
1957			2.1
1959	3.4		
1962			2.05
1963		4.1	
1966			2.1
1967		4.1	
1969	3.8	3.8	
1972		3.9	2.05

Year	France (1)	US (2)	UK (3)	Hungary (4)	Poland (5)	Czech. (6)	USSR (7)
All wage-earners							
1946							7.24
1954	3.5						
1956							4.44
1960	3.8			2.59	3.24		
1961	3.8					2.5	4.02
1964	3.9		3.5				3.69
1966	4.2			2.59		2.4	3.26
1968	3.8			2.64		2.4	2.83
1972	3.7	4.5			2.83		3.10
1975	3.5		2.8			2.42	
1976	3.5	4.2		2.64	3.11		3.35
1978	3.4				3.13		
1979	3.3	4.3				2.44	
1980	3.3		2.75	2.51	2.93		3.0
1982	3.2						
1984	3.3	4.9		2.61			

Sources: CERC (57), p. 127
  (1) Lebeaupin (8), 95, and INSEE M 113 (11), p. 95
  (2) Bergson (49), p. 1063 and calculations from (7), 1985, p. 269
  (3) Bergson (49), p. 1063 and calculations from (18), pp. A36–A37
  (4) Askanas and Levcik (35), p. 205 and Flakiersky (76), p. 51
  (5) Askanas and Levcik (35), p. 206 and Flakiersky (76), p. 60
  (6) Askanas and Levcik (35), p. 204.
  (7) Bergson (49), p. 1077

nevertheless, that the limited information available has little consequence as to the validity of our results. In this way, the classification
by decreasing degrees of wage dispersion for the end of the seventies
(tables 3.2 and 3.3) remains valid based on the ratio of the ninth or
the first decile (table 5.3). We find the United States first, followed
by France, the USSR, and Poland, the United Kingdom, Hungary,
and Czechoslovakia.[2]

The United States was the only country to witness a rise in
earnings dispersion during the post-war period. This phenomenon is
pointed out by the CERC (57) which indicates that the differentials
between socio-professional categories grew wider from 1949 to 1970.
It is true that the level for the year 1949 is low, following the war
years when earnings dispersion narrowed. However, it is important
to note that in 1959 earnings dispersion was relatively high and that
since this time it has had a tendency to rise. Such evolutions are
difficult to interpret.

First, they contradict the notion according to which there is a
decreasing relation between a country's level of development and
pay dispersion. From this point of view, the economic development
of this period should have gone hand in hand with a narrowing of
the dispersion of the levels of formal education and professional
training of the wage-earners. In theory, this would have reduced the
pay range. The decline of traditional industry in recent years, where
wages are low, would have had the same effect.

Other elements may oppose these factors. In order to explain
them, it is necessary to bear in mind the high ratio of the ninth to the
first decile results in the United States from both the particularly
poor position of wage-earners at the bottom of the distribution, and
the strong position of those at the top of the distribution in
comparison with the other countries (see table 3.3).

First of all, the important increase in female labor was certainly a
contributing factor in lowering the wages of the first decile, in a
country where women are particularly poorly paid.

Second, the United States remains a country of immigrants, even
if the arrival of new immigrants has slowed down in the past years.
The existence and the arrival of an under qualified manpower, often
subject to wage discrimination, may have broadened pay dispersion.

As for the high wages, the egalitarian ideology which has deve-

---

[2] On the statistical field covered by "the economy as a whole," see pp. 202–3 and the CERC
(57), p. 114.

loped in the majority of Western European countries, and naturally in the STS, seems not to have reached the United States. The way in which top managers and executives are paid, that is to say the fact that their wages often hinge on the profits of the firms, may explain the high level reached in this country (Bergson (49)).

In France, the end of the growth period of pay dispersion comes in 1966–7. The Grenelle agreements of 1968 seem to mark the reverse trend. In the years that follow, there is a correlation between the increase in the minimum wage, highest in 1974, and the decrease in wage dispersion (CERC (58), pp. 65–6 and 75–6).

Nevertheless, one must remain wary of this correlation. It may well be the result of the sensitivity of the indicator used to variations in the pay of the poorest wage-earners. Had a synthetic indicator been used (coefficient of variation, Gini coefficient), such a correlation might not have been found.

A recent study by the CERC ((58), pp. 83–92), however, shows that wage differentials among socio-professional categories have narrowed, as well as the dispersion within each category (with the exception of top management). Thus, it appears that the hypothesis of a general narrowing of pay in the French economy has been verified. This phenomenon may be the result of a decrease in the dispersion of the levels of formal education and professional training, with the arrival on the labor market of new, post-war generations at the end of the sixties.

This tendency has been stronger than the opposite effect of the increase of the female labor force. This is perhaps the manifestation, at a dynamic level, of the statistical results previously obtained for the year 1978, that is to say that the earnings differentials between men and women in France constitute a relatively small part of the total earnings dispersion.

In the United Kingdom, there was a strong decrease in the earnings dispersion during the period 1965–75. According to a comparative study by the CERC ((57) pp. 127), the fluctuation was similar to that in France. The rise in the ratio of the ninth to the first decile between 1950 and 1965, was followed by a net decline in the total earnings dispersion. There was also a considerable reduction in the differentials among socio-professional categories, and within categories. It is possible that the same factors as in France were at work here, with the exception of minimum wage.

The particular case of the Soviet Union

The Soviet Union is decidedly different from other countries, Western or Eastern. Indeed the decrease in earnings dispersion was great from the beginning of the fifties to the next decade. Even if the indicator used is linked to fluctuations in the minimum wage, the changes are sufficiently clear so as to demand particular attention.

Soviet authors analyze the evolution of the earnings dispersion in their country as a necessity linked to the development of Socialism. Initially, the changes in society, and the disappearance of the Bourgeois intelligentsia would result in an important decrease in wage inequalities. This period corresponds to the years 1918–30 for the USSR (Rimachevskaja and Rabkina (147), pp. 89–92).

In the second stage, economic development would result in the birth of a class of highly qualified specialists. In addition, the need to increase production and labor productivity would explain the important increase in wage differentiation. In the USSR, this was the case from 1930 to the beginning of the fifties. Finally, in the mature stage, the population of wage-earners as a whole would reach a relatively high level of formal education and professional training, which would bring earnings closer together.

We think that the purpose of this statement is to justify changes in the economic policy of the USSR rather than to explain a general phenomenon of Soviet type Socialism, for the following two reasons;

1 In the other STE, there is no such evolution. It is a fact that the arrival of Communist regimes at the end of the forties brought about a drastic reduction in wage inequalities. In addition, ten to fifteen years later, the level of wage dispersion was relatively low especially in Hungary and Czechoslovakia; this might well correspond to the first aforementioned period. However, there was no increase in the following years from 1960 to 1980, rather wage dispersion was stable.

2 The Soviet evolution reflects Stalin's conception of pay and work incentives, which was put into practice in the thirties and remained until the fifties (Bergson (46)). Soviet authorities instituted a global policy of wage differentiation. This policy was based notably on the generalization of piece-work wages for manual workers. Labor norms were calculated in theory so that each worker might maximize his individual productivity. At the end of the Stalinist period, wage dispersion was higher in the USSR than in the United States.

Pavlevski (134) has shown how, after the Second World War, and above all after the Stalinist period, leaders applied a policy of important wage and income increases for all workers. This tendency was reinforced by the wage reform of 1958 which allowed the center of planning better control over the evolution and the structure of wages. The Stalinist system was based in practice on non-uniform norms which resulted in an anarchic wage dispersion. The fact that wages paid out came closer to wages defined by the planning center, and that the general level of formal education and professional training rose, together with substantial increases in minimum wage, explain to a large degree the evolution from the end of the fifties.

The Other STE
Czechoslovakia, Hungary, and Poland are characterized by a certain stability of wage dispersion. Flakiersky ((76), p. 46–52) questioned the impact of the 1968 reform on earnings dispersion in Hungary. This reform consisted in giving firms partial control over the wage bill. It seems that initially this reform led to an increase in wage dispersion. However, as early as 1972, the authorities took a step back, given the increase of the interfirm wage differentials which were not justified by the criteria of economic rationality purported by the reform.

Indeed, the same author showed that in Poland during the period when Gierek governed (1970–9), a net increase in earnings dispersion was recorded. However, the observed differentials were often anarchic. As early as 1980, the trade union Solidarity criticized these differentials and a sizeable reduction followed.

3 Conclusion of the study of the wage dynamics

The chronological analysis of earnings dispersion from the fifties on did not uncover any fundamental changes, with the exception of the USSR for which the end of the Stalinist period marked an important change.

Were we to classify earnings dispersion for the year 1960, it would be identical to that of 1980, with one exception: the USSR would perhaps come before France.

In light of this analysis, there are two points on which the two systems contrast.

1 The weight of economic policy is heavier in the STE, especially

the USSR, than in the WE. This remains to be confirmed by the study of institutions in part II.

2 There was a tremendous decrease in earnings dispersion in the STE at the end of the forties (Poland, Czechoslovakia, Hungary) or the fifties (USSR) and since then the situation has remained stable. On the contrary, in the WE there was a much slower, gradual decrease (except in the United States). The "radicalism" of the initial period of Soviet type Socialism contrasts with the "reformism" of Western countries.

Nevertheless, at the end of the seventies and at the beginning of the eighties, the paths of evolution of earnings dispersion in the two systems converge. We were able to study this period of convergence with the help of various statistical indicators (tables 3.2 and 3.3).

These conclusions encourage us to believe that on the whole the results that we obtained with our statistical analyses are valid. Indeed, our "static" analyses from the end of the seventies to the beginning of the eighties are, in all probability, valid for a relatively long period, that is from 1960 to 1980. Similarly, the principal factors behind wage differentiation at work during the end of the seventies, had very progressive influences during the preceding decades.

Therefore, part II, which is essentially explanatory, will be based on the numerous results of the present period, but will also be based on older results, without the risk of error. Indeed, during the period from 1960 to 1980 there were no important political or social changes in either system.

This is not the case for the economy. There were important changes in institutions (numerous "reforms" in the STE), breaks in economic growth, a rise in the evolution of technology. It will be necessary to explain the stability of wage structures when compared to these changes.

Part II will be organized as follows:

1 We will evaluate the role of economic policy and of institutions in wage regulation in the two systems. We will analyze the influence of the State and of legislation as a whole on the wage structure down to the firm level.

2 We will explain the influences of sectors and of large firms on earnings differentiation in the light of the statistical analyses of part I.

3 We will reconsider the link between the level of formal education

and professional training of workers, on the one hand and the pay and division of labor in firms on the other, analyzing the behavior of organizations.

4 We will look at the question of "incentives" in the two systems as they relate to the pay systems. In so doing, it will be possible to incorporate new elements into our discussion: the non-monetary aspects of pay, the second job, hidden pay, taxation of wage income.

5 Finally, we will bring up the question of a "systemic effect" on wages and of the extent of the differences between the WE and the STE.

PART II

Why are the wage structures
in both systems so similar?

The fundamental question posed in part II is a direct result of the preceding part. How can we explain the isomorphism, however partial, of the wage structures of the WE and the STE? What role do the economic institutions and social relations play in determining the wage structures in both systems? Are there isomorphisms between the institutions, the objectives and the means of economic policy with regard to wages? If the answer to this last question is no, on what can we base the explanation that we are seeking?

Taking into account the levels of formal education and professional training of wage-earners and beyond that, the role of the educational system in the structuring of pay in the two systems constitutes a first axis of research.

However, there are two arguments in favor of going even further.

1 Statistical results show that the relation between the level of formal education and professional training and wages is not as clear as the market and planning theories might have one believe. It is necessary to take into account numerous factors such as wage discrimination, the "sector effect," that is to say the inequalities in wages from sector to sector, which can be found even if we rule out the differences in the level of formal education and professional training of workers.

2 In market and planning theories, there are opposite adjustment mechanisms. In the first case, the wage rate for a given skill is determined by the supply and demand for labor. This complete decentralization of the means of adjustment is the very opposite of the centralization theorized by the STS economists. Theoretically, the planning center controls the productive efficiency of firms and ultimately the productivity of labor and wages by way of investment.

We maintain, however, that the dichotomy between centralized and decentralized adjustments needs to be reconsidered. Indeed, we cannot fail to consider, for example for the WE, collective wage bargaining or possible State intervention by means of economic policy. Conversely, the question must be raised as to whether or not the STE conform to the conception of a totally centralized economy the mechanisms of which conform to the rules of a planner. Here too research can take many roads. How does the State, through economic policy and interventions down to the level of the firms manage to direct the labor force according to the plan? In this framework, what role do wage incentives, on the one hand, and motivations, rules, and administrative constraints, on the other, play?

CHAPTER 6

Two different types of wage regulation

The use of the concept "regulation" is a way of approaching and developing our field of research.

The notion of regulation is linked to that of conserving the structure of a system. It refers to all the transformations which a structure or a system uses in order to react to an exterior disturbance. Regulation is therefore a process of adaptation.[1] From these definitions, it follows that the notion of regulation can be applied to a wide area of research in economics. Indeed, an economist studies how an economic system reacts to an exterior disturbance. It can be said that an economy with pure and perfect competition, where adjustments are made possible by the flexibility of prices, is "regulated by prices." Conversely, in a purely planned economy, regulation comes from a planning center, by way of orders and injunctions that have to do with the quantities to be produced.

In addition, it must be said that the notion of regulation, in our framework, is all encompassing. More specifically, it takes into account all of the elements of the social system which interconnect with the economic system. This means that the principal actors behind the dynamics of the system are taken into account. This includes the State first of all, but also all social groups vying for a share in national income.

From this point of view, the analysis is partly institutional in so far as the institutions and the State do not figure as "exogenous" parameters, but on the contrary are studied in interaction with economic variables.

We might add that the notion of regulation does not assume that the adjustments and adaptations inherent to each system are automatic, or even possible. Regulation crises necessitate changes in

---

[1] According to the conception of Benassy, Boyer, and Gelpi (45), see also Boyer (52), pp. 33–45.

régulation itself, when the system is faced with changes in the social and economic relations.

There are two purposes for analyzing the determinants of the short-term wage rate in the two systems.

First of all, we will reconsider the relation between the level of formal education and professional training, labor productivity, and wages, on which our initial questioning was based. We will have to explain the fact that the relation between the wage rate and labor productivity is not confirmed in either sytem, at least on an annual basis.

Second, given this fact, we will outline two theories: the theory of disequilibrium and the theory of shortage which claim to account for wage regulation in the two systems. The State, collective labor relations, the specific behavior of firms, are all explicitly encompassed in our analysis.

1 On the relation between wage and labor productivity

In the WE, if we look at industry for a given period (1960–80), most of the time we observe no relation between the wage rate on the one hand and average apparent labor productivity on the other hand, even if the analysis centers on the pay of manual workers. This was shown for France, the FRG, and the United Kingdom (Redor (141), pp. 133–44, 160–85).

These results are in accordance with many other studies carried out on this theme, as well as with the principal macroeconomic models.[2]

This was also the case for industrial sectors: there was no relation between the wage rate and apparent labor productivity at the sector level over a given period for any of the economies under study. For the STE, we arrived at a similar conclusion for the same period.

More precisely, the relation between the industrial wage rate in Poland and apparent industrial labor productivity was low, based to a large extent on the existence of a particular cycle during the

---

[2] See the Atlas model of Cellier, LeBerre, and Miquieu (55) which concerns the major Western economies.

decade 1970–80. In Hungary, this relation, also weak, was observed only for manual workers and not for industrial wage-earners as a whole. Finally, this relation did not exist in the GDR (Redor (141), pp. 212–18).

Moreover, for all the STE studied, no relation between sector wage rates and sector labor productivity was found for the period studied.

The question is how can one explain the differences between the traditional theories of market and planning economies and these empirical facts.

For Western economies

1 In theory, the real wage rate is equal to marginal labor productivity. In statistical studies, an indicator of average labor productivity is used, the only one available. In so doing, we introduce a bias because, in theory, in a short-term analysis, marginal productivity and average labor productivity are different.

2 The wage rate and marginal labor productivity are equal at the firm level if the conditions of pure and perfect competition are met. This rate, for a given skill, is the same in all firms. At the macroeconomic level, the same relation is confirmed because the aggregation of individual data is, therefore, free of bias. But, if the competition on the labor market is imperfect, then the equality between the wage rate and the marginal productivity of labor is broken. This distortion is felt on the macroeconomic level when aggregating individual data.

3 For the three WE which we studied in depth (France, the FRG, and the United Kingdom), but also for others, notably the United States (Kerr (96), pp. 172–78), there is a strong correlation between the evolution of average labor productivity and the evolution of production prices, as well as of value added prices. The correlations between these variables is negative.

It is possible to interpret this phenomenon as the result of the effect of labor costs on prices. For example when labor productivity increases, if wages do not change, labor costs fall. It may also be linked to the characteristics of the economic cycle in the WE since the Second World War. Indeed, during periods where the economy slows down, growth in labor productivity slows down as labor is not used to full capacity. Contrary to the pre-war times, periods of recession have often seen a rise in inflation. In oligopolistic economies, firms try to face the rise in wage costs and to maintain their profits by increasing their prices. In so far as nominal wage rates are *de facto* or *de juro*, linked to the evolution of prices, the relation between wage rates and labor productivity is considerably weakened. The direct test of the relation between the wage rate and labor productivity in real terms, which seeks to eliminate the correlation between productivity and prices, proved to be negative.

4 The fact is that the level at which the relation between the wage rate and labor productivity is proven remains uncertain. Labor productivity evolves very differently from one industrial sector to another. The diffusion of technical progress is not uniform, nor is the evolution of demand for goods on markets. On the contrary, sector wages evolve in a quite parallel manner, for reasons of competition between sectors in the labor market, but above all because all wages follow the fluctuations in prices and are subject to the effects of collective wage bargaining.

These analyses taken as a whole are not in contradiction with the fact that, in the long term, increases in wage rates and in labor productivity tend to come together in the WS. This takes us away from the short-term analysis to that of the relations between the accumulation of capital and the distribution of income, which, for the moment, lies beyond our scope.

In Soviet-type economies
The study using the same model as for the WE (variations of nominal wage rate on the one hand and variations of labor productivity in volume and prices on the other hand) also points to an absence of any relation between pay and productivity on a short-term basis (between 1960 and 1980 for Hungary, Poland, and the GDR) (Redor (141), pp. 212–18 and additional documents, pp. 48–56).

1 Whereas there are great differences in the evolution of sector labor productivity, sector wages are closely correlated. A certain competition which exists between sectors to attract labor may serve to explain this correlation, as may the action of the State in an effort to maintain equal and regular growth in sector wages as a whole.

2 If we look at all industry, or the entire economy, during the economic cycle, the variations in average labor productivity are very

marked. They contrast heavily with the regular evolution of the wage rate. Here too one must invoke the role of the State which tries to keep the buying power of the population from fluctuating too much. Fluctuations might have negative effects on the consumer goods market and on social stability.

3 At this point the "imperfections" of planning must be brought forth. It must be remembered that according to the Strumilin school the conditions of production are uniform. If the objective of making the efficiency of investments in all the sectors of the economy equal is realized, paying workers on the basis of their productivity corresponds to the rule of equality: "For equal work, equal pay." It is questionable whether workers who are classified on the basis of level of formal education and professional training are in fact equally efficient whatever the firm and whatever the sector to which they belong.

These doubts are reinforced by the results of the economic analysis of intersector wage differences (see part 1, chapter 4). In practice sectors and firms are unequally endowed with capital goods which determines very different levels of labor productivity among sectors and among firms.

The planning center is faced with the following dilemma. First, it can try to link wages and labor productivity more closely, but in so doing the differences in pay between workers with the same level of formal education and professional training grow wider, which in turn runs the risk of greatly upsetting the distribution of the labor force (uncontrolled mobility). In addition, the "inequitable" nature of this policy can lead to demands on the part of the most disadvantaged groups. Secondly, the planning center may also disconnect pay from labor productivity. The aforementioned statistical results tend to show that it is the second option that was chosen. However, complete wage equality among workers with the same level of formal education and professional training was still by no means achieved. The anlysis of the intersector pay differences clearly attested to this (part 1, chapter 4).

In light of these remarks, the principal theoretical task becomes that of integrating into a short-term analysis the lack of a relation between the wage rate and labor productivity in the two systems. To carry out this task we will present a rapid overview of disequilibrium theory which seems to provide a model of the forms of regulation in the WE and in the STE, and of the "shortage theory" which is applicable only to the STE.

In so doing, we will compare two different approaches to the principal disfunctionings in the WE and the STE. For theoreticians of disequilibrium, the problem is to find a measure of economic policy which reduces the disfunctionings of the labor market and of the goods market in both systems. The wage rate thus becomes an instrument, indeed a stake in economic policy.

The shortage theory opens up the field of study to encompass institutions and the specific planning procedures in the STE. Deviations from the theoretical models for determining the wage rate are not taken as imperfections, but as fundamental elements in the functioning of the STE.

2 Theoretical considerations on the evolution of the short-term wage rate in the two systems

The wage rate in the disequilibrium theory

If we consider the goods and labor markets, we may encounter two kinds of disequilibrium: "Keynesian unemployment" or "classical unemployment."[3]

In the case of Keynesian unemployment, there is an excess supply in the goods and labor markets. The level of employment is dependent on effective demand. Any increase in demand, in the form of a rise in real wages, or in any other component of the demand, loosens the constraints that bind the employment levels.

Thus, the relation between wages and labor productivity becomes broken and the wage rate can be used as an instrument of economic policy, for example when there is a state controlled minimum wage.

In the case of classical unemployment, there is an excess of supply on the labor market and of demand on the consumer goods market. Households are constrained on both markets and firms on neither.

The relation between wages and labor productivity is not broken, and the previously mentioned objections are not answered. However, over a relatively long period, it is possible to imagine that the

---

[3] These terms were coined by Malinvaud (115), pp. 69f.; see also Benassy (44), pp. 58f., and Barro and Grossman (39), pp. 69f.

two kinds of unemployment alternate, which would thus weaken the relation between wages and labor productivity.

In the hypothetical case of repressed inflation, there is an excess of demand both on the labor market and on the consumer goods market (Barro and Grossman (39), p. 49).

Certain Western theoreticians[4] maintain that the STE are in a state of repressed inflation. This analysis is based, first of all, on institutional considerations. Indeed, these authors start from the fact that prices and the wage rate are administered by a central planner. According to these authors, there is a great degree of rationing of consumer goods in these economies. Finally, firms are limited in their demand for employees; they have difficulties in recruiting labor although the activity rates are high.

Economic agents hold back their supply of labor according to their rationing on the consumer goods market.

The wage rate is inferior to labor productivity. A rise in the wage rate increases employment, but this rise alone never suffices to restore full employment, as long as there is rationing on the goods market.

Research based on disequilibrium theory can be criticized on two grounds. The first concerns the aggregate level of the models studied as well as their microeconomic foundation. The second concerns the application of the theory to the STE which fails to take into account, to a large extent, the institutional context.

Indeed it must be upheld that the "labor market" and "the consumer goods market" are themselves the result of the aggregation of n consumer goods submarkets and m labor submarkets which correspond to m categories of workers. There are possible "frictions" which introduce biases in the aggregation procedures in the case where, in certain submarkets, demand is rationed and, in others, the supply.

From a different perspective, disequilibrium theory can be countered by schools of thought which maintain that economic agents behave differently, even formally, according to their social or economic system. They are strongly circumscribed by the institutional framework in which they operate.

In WE, for example, one must not forget the role of collective bargaining on the one hand and management practices in firms on the other.

---

[4] Notably Howard (87) (88) in his analysis of the Soviet Union rationing of consumer goods.

For the STE, Kornai, in his shortage theory, seeks to take into account the institutional framework.

The wage rate in the shortage theory
In his book *Economics of Shortage*, Kornai (101) analyzes in detail the "shortage" which is widespread in the STE, and argues against the idea that these economies conform to the model of repressed inflation.

In order to explain his position, it is first necessary to introduce the concept of shortage which can take the following four forms in the STE:

1 There is "vertical shortage" when a productive resource, a consumer good, or a service is allocated by the administration and when the demand thereof is greater than the quantity available to the administration in charge of the distribution.

2 There is "horizontal shortage" if a resource, good, or service is exchanged for currency and the supply of the seller does not satisfy the initial individual demand. The initial demand results from the intentions of the buyer (household) or from a plan (firm). This is the case of excess demand studied by Barro and Grossman.

3 A firm or an administration lacks the necessary input to realize its plan. There is a shortage within a micro-organization, with constraints placed upon resources.

4 The capacity of the economy to produce is used to a high degree. This is defined by the ratio: $K = x/\hat{x}$, where x is the total production realized, $\hat{x}$ is the maximum theoretical capacity. There is a shortage of production capacity when a growth in activity would bring about a sudden rise in social, marginal costs.

Looking at firms, the cost of productive resources used, notably of the labor force, has very little influence on management decisions. Indeed, the budget constraints bearing upon firms are soft, that is to say that firms must first realize their production plan, and then may obtain subsidies to increase their budgets and cover potential deficits.

In an economy with resources shortages, firms have a tendency to overevaluate their input needs so as to protect themselves from potential or real shortages. Their soft budget constraints incite them to act as such. This explains plan bargaining often described in the STE.

The rationing procedures of the planning center can be manipulated. Indeed, the latter never really comes to know the real demand of firms, be it for raw materials, semi-finished products, or labor. This is why the notion of excess demand or supply remains undetermined in the traditional, central planning system.

The economic analysis of employment and wages highlights first of all the phenomenon of shortage in the labor force. Historically, the total number of economically inactive persons (housewives) or underemployed persons (certain farmers) was absorbed by a system of production where the demand for labor had no strong financial constraint limiting hiring. The constraint on firms is expressed "in quantity," in so far as, in the majority of the STE, employment has reached its maximum level.

The purpose of wage rate planning is essentially to guarantee a continuous growth of the wage income which one attempts to adjust to the fluctuations in consumption.

To sum up, according to the shortage theory, the planning center strictly controls the average wage rate of each firm, but not the level of employment. This is why the constraint on the use of the labor force is deemed soft. It must be noted, however, that firms risk running into shortages, at least as far as certain skills are concerned.

The labor supply is largely determined by sociological factors: the status of workers in agriculture (presence or absence of individually owned farms) and the evolution of the social role of women.

Using certain anti-equilibrium analyses, Kornai maintains that the decisions of those in charge of planning and of firms are based not on an economic calculation of optimization, but on decision processes which are based on past experience and on socio-economic pressures. In matters of wages, the small percentage of the wages bill which is not allocated automatically to increases goes to categories of personnel or sectors whose demands have been unsatisfied for a long time.

Finally, Kornai proposes a new microeconomic approach to the STE. He tries to show that, once institutions are explicitly part of economic analysis, economic agents have multiple objectives and their behavior is subject to multiple constraints.

Kornai's critiques are institutional and sociological. In this way, they are close to Western institutionalist thinking which questions the competitive nature of the labor market.

In addition, the shortage, or in the terms of Kornai, the fact that firms are limited in their hiring, is somewhat related to the theory of excess demand (repressed inflation) on the labor market. Even if the coexistence of shortages and excesses introduces a bias in the aggregation procedures, Kornai recognizes that shortage is the dominant phenomenon. Consequently, one could argue that the labor shortage can be considered as a minimal evaluation of the constraint which weighs upon firms' hiring.

If we turn to the way in which individuals use their work time, it appears that their behavior is affected by the wage rate. Indeed, individuals react to pay differences between sectors and firms. If then the supply of labor, taken globally, is considered, in the shortage theory, as independent of the evolution of wages, it is because this theory implicitly assumes that the labor force is fully employed and that supply cannot be increased.

Why the population gives so much of its time, when the demand for certain consumer goods is rationed, remains to be explained. The secondary economy appears to be important. If official wages decrease, people work more in the secondary economy. In addition, income which, because of the shortages, cannot be spent on official markets can be spent on the great number of parallel markets.

The opposition between the theorists of disequilibrium and Kornai reflects the differences in regulation in the two systems. The former provide a model of regulation where the State relies on macroeconomic instruments, most of the time, in the manipulation of monetary variables.

State regulation in the shortage theory is decidedly different. Firms are little affected by the evolution of monetary variables. Rather they are subject to constraints "by quantity." There are certainly shortages, but also State controls which function down to the level of the firm.

How can one determine whether the dichotomy outlined between these systems is justified? In order to do so, we have chosen to present briefly the results of an econometric study which we carried out on the macroeconomic determinants of the wage rate in the two systems. (Redor (141), pp. 133–48, 175–85).

For the WS, the approach is classical: it consists in isolating the factors which provide the best model of the relation between the wage rate on the one hand, pressures on the labor market, the role of collective bargaining (by way of negotiated wages), and ultimately of the State (for example by means of the minimum wage in the same countries), on the other. For the STS, we shall seek to determine whether there are short-term determinants of the wage rate which can be either variations in the labour supply (captured by the level of employment in an economy where one assumes that there is an excess demand for labor), or variations in the labour demand (itself linked to the fluctuations in the investment cycle). If the results of these tests are negative for the STE, then the analysis of the shortage theory, according to which wages are essentially administratively regulated, will be strengthened.

2 MIXED REGULATION AND ADMINISTRATIVE REGULATION OF WAGES

1 Mixed regulation of wages in the Western system

The modeling of the evolution of the wage rate in industry in the WS is based on much theoretical and empirical research.

Short-term variations in the wage rate in the WS
The disequilibrium theory prompts us to seek determinants of the evolution of wages other than labor productivity and to focus our attention on economic policy. One must also mention works concerned with the relation between wages and unemployment. This relation is most commonly interpreted as follows: as on any other market, the price of labor increases when the excess supply decreases, that is to say when unemployment decreases and inversely.

The nominal wage rate is a function of unemployment and fluctuations in prices. Hence the problem of the study of the indexation of wages to prices and the feedback effects of the anticipated prices on the equilibrium of employment is raised (Friedman (77)).

For France during the period from 1960–80, the clearest result of estimations refers to the relation of wages, however defined, and whatever the category of wage-earners, to the prices of consumer goods, as well as the prices of industrial production and the prices of value added. This relation is all the more remarkable in so far as the corresponding regression coefficients, which represent the elasticity of wages compared to prices, do not differ significantly from 1 (Redor (141), p. 133.).

The introduction of the influence of consumer prices with a one year lag is rarely significant. This confirms empirical and econometric studies which evaluate the lag in the indexation of wages to prices at approximately one trimester.[5]

As for the relation between unemployment and pay, a Lipsey-type relation enabled us to show that unemployment influences manual workers' wages much more closely than other categories of wage-earners.

The determinants of workers' pay are all the more apparent if we consider that the hourly wage rate for workers is closely linked to variations in the minimum wage.

In France, the regulation of the wage rate in industry appears to result from two kinds of factors that are distinctly different.

First of all, State intervention by way of the minimum wage, but also by anticyclic economic policy, are important. It can be demonstrated that the wage rate and, more generally, the percentage of wages in national income, can be affected by "restriction plans" adopted to fight inflation and (or) international trade or State budget deficits.

But State action is not enough to eliminate short-term fluctuations, represented by unemployment. In addition, wages are indexed on prices, a practice which, to a large extent, is based on collective bargaining. This regulation is therefore mixed, half way between competitive regulation which depends principally on the state of the market, and regulation controlled by the State and a few employers' and workers' trade unions.

For the FRG, the estimations show a link between the wage rate and prices with a one year lag. This phenomenon is the result of collective wage bargaining which takes into account consumer prices of the preceding year. This is why this formula was also used in the ATLAS model (55).

The eventual impact of wage negotiations on the evolution of industrial earnings was tested according to the indications of Weigend (167); we used the negotiated wage rate of manual workers as the explanatory variable in the wage equations. The former comes from the agreement reached by the trade unions of I.G. Metal. The results of the econometric estimations are very important in so far as the actual hourly earnings of workers in industry as a whole are statistically linked to the average wage rate of metal and metallurgy manual workers. In addition, this is true for other categories of

5 For the three we studied, we followed the ATLAS model of Cellier, Le Berre, and Miquieu (55).

workers (clerks and managers). Thus two results are empirically proven.

First, wage agreements greatly influence earnings by way of negotiated wages and a *de facto* indexation to prices with a one year lag.

Second, wages increases in the metal and metallurgy sectors seem to be propagated toward other sectors, and from the manual worker category to other categories of personnel.

Finally, if there is little direct intervention by the State in wage determination, the mixed nature of wage regulation in the FRG is the consequence of two very different phenomena. First, there is collective wage bargaining, with a decided influence, which concerns large sectors of industry. It determines the negotiated wage rate for the coming year, and, according to our calculations, this is largely respected.

However, the econometric study showed that unemployment has a definite influence which is felt in two ways. First, it can influence the definition of the negotiated wage rate. The fact that unemployment appears more clearly in equations which do not include the negotiated wage rate reinforces this thesis. It is possible that the application of agreements is modulated according to short-term fluctuations in employment rate for the year under consideration.

As for the United Kingdom, the relation between production or consumption prices and nominal earnings is very close, as is the case in France and the FRG, and this is true when manual workers' earnings, or the average earnings of all categories of wage-earners, are considered. This relation is also confirmed with a lag of one year in prices. This conforms to the analyses carried out with the ATLAS model according to which there is a six month time lag in the indexation of wages to prices.

The evolution of workers' wages is weakly linked to that of unemployment. This link is strengthened and extends to all categories of personnel if we consider that the effects of unemployment are felt with a lag of one year. This delay can be explained both from a competitive as well as an institutional, theoretical framework. It is possible that the unemployment of one year weighs on the wage negotiations for the coming year. From a microeconomic perspective, one can argue that, when unemployment rises each firm acts to lower wages or to control their growth with a lag of adjustment of approximately one year.

We may take into account the role of collective wage bargaining, as for the FRG, by introducing into the wage equation, the negotiated wage rate of manual workers.[6] The results are important: this rate influences greatly and significantly the hourly earnings observed for manual workers, but also the earnings of wage-earners as a whole. The elasticity of hourly earnings compared to the negotiated wage rate is 0.64 and 0.60 respectively. In equations where the negotiated wage is taken into account, unemployment ceases to have any influence if we look at the category of wage-earners as a whole. It appears then, that just as in the FRG, unemployment and the negotiated wage rate are connected.

The role of the State in wage regulation must be underlined. Even if there is no active policy of a minimum wage, the State intervenes periodically, even by way of legislation, to limit the rise in wages. The cyclic movement of the economy is marked and very regular, taking on what is traditionally called a "stop and go" movement. In analyzing this phenomenon, one must take into account the trade balance and the distribution of income. In periods of expansion, there are great balance of trade deficits and inflation increases. Consequently, those in charge of the economy take restrictive measures such as raising taxes, cutting budgets, and increasing interest rates. This "stop" period is all the more accentuated by the fact that, despite restrictions, exports stagnate. During "stop" periods, there is a slow down, even a decrease in the real wage rate, and in the wage share in national income. Once there is a slackening in economic policy, the wage increases resume.

Given the fact that the legislative means of limiting the rise in wages directly affect wage agreements, the State has a very effective means of intervention at its disposal. Our estimates show that the wage rates that result from collective bargaining are largely applied.

However, as is the case for the FRG, there are good reasons to believe that the results of wage bargaining are effected by the unemployment rate. Here again the means of determining wages are mixed and not entirely independent of short-term fluctuations of the labor market, and, at the same time, depend on the intervention by trade unions which represent sometimes several hundred thousand individuals, as well as by the State.

---

[6] The negotiated wage rate of workers is that of manufacturing industries. It is a mean based on the sector wage rates negotiated in collective bargaining. The data corresponding to these works are published by the British Statistical Office (16) and (17).

In the United States, the indexation of wages to prices is rather slow and incomplete and the influence of unemployment is not negligible. The former may originate in collective wage bargaining which is carried out over relatively long periods and concerns a minority of wage-earners (Dunlop and Galenson (72)).

Finally, in Belgium, the indexation of the wage rate to prices is quasi-immediate and total. Unemployment also has a tremendous impact.

What is learned from the statistical study of mixed regulation

Thus, despite important national differences in wage regulation, there are certain dominant features common to all the WE. First of all, the unemployment rate has an impact, even if it was weakened during certain periods, notably the mid seventies. In this sense, the indicators which we mentioned should be taken as elements of a set of possibilities. An in depth model of the determining factors behind the evolution of wages might uncover, instead of or in addition to the indicators of unemployment, variables such as the fluctuations in the profit rate of firms or the use of production capacities.

For this reason, wage regulation in the WS cannot be taken as dependent solely on the State or organizations participating in collective bargaining, and whose decisions would ultimately adjust with a certain lag to the fluctuations of labor productivity.

Wage regulation, as it appears in light of our analyses, is half-way between a centralized and administrative regulation on the one hand, and a decentralized, competitive type regulation on the other hand. In this way it is mixed. It is the result of a complex interaction between economic policy, collective bargaining, and the state of the economy.

2 Administrative regulation of wages in the Soviet-type system

Short-term variations of the wage rate in the STS

A model of the wage rate in the STS must be based first of all on the aforementioned theoretical considerations concerning the theory of repressed inflation and the theory of shortage.

From this framework, we tested the relation between the wage rate and the level of employment in industry. Indeed, in an economy of permanent repressed inflation, firms are rationed in their demand for labor; there is an excess of demand on the market and the level of employment is determined by supply. If supply increases as a function of wages, there should be a positive relation between wages and employment.

One might also argue, as does the Hungarian economist, Bauer (41), that during the cycle, the wage rate is linked positively to, but slightly flattened by, fluctuations in investment. The rise in the average wage would be at its highest during a period of high employment. Pressure to decrease would be felt in the down phase of the cycle.

Although Bauer does not treat this question explicitly, one can interpret the phenomenon as being the effect of the increase in the demand for labor in the up phase of the cycle. In the theory of repressed inflation, one can conceive of a situation whereby firms are rationed particularly in their demand for labor in this state of the economy. In order to loosen the hold, it is possible that the planner gives up a little the control which weighs on the wage policy of firms. If in addition, we suppose that the supply of labor is increasing with wages, there is a positive relation between the variations in investment, in wages, and in employment.

Finally, one must pay particular attention to the relation between prices and wages. Indeed, the variations in prices are low, even very low in some STE, at least according to official statistics. Therefore, it is necessary to determine if fluctuations in nominal wages are independent of those of prices or if the planning center, within the framework of wage policy, indexes completely or partially one to the other.

We carried out the study for the period 1960–80, on a yearly basis, for Hungary, Poland, and the GDR (Redor (141), pp. 160–86). In Hungary, the only variable that is statistically linked to the nominal wage rate is the consumer price index, with a one year lag. The fact is that in Hungary, as in the other STE, consumer prices, according to official indexes, remained stable until the beginning of the seventies. Then they rose sharply, a rise which affected the wage rate.

No relation between the variations in the hourly or monthly earnings and the number of workers employed in industry was found. There was a high, negative correlation between the fluctuations in the number of employed workers and consumer prices.

From studying the statistics, it appears that prices began to rise rather quickly starting in 1970, whereas the number of people employed in industry fell. It is difficult to consider this fall as an indication of unemployment if one takes into account the state of Hungarian institutions. From an economic standpoint, the relation that was proven would mean that unemployment and prices fluctuate in the same direction, which makes little sense. If we consider that the decrease in the number of employees corresponds to a marked rationing in labor demand by firms, one should expect to witness, within the framework of the theory of repressed inflation, a decrease in real wages, which in fact does not come about until 1979.

Indeed it appears that shortages in the labor force brought about bottlenecks on the consumer goods market, which pushed the authorities to raise the prices of the goods which were most lacking.

For Poland, there is a strong correlation between certain explanatory variables of wage evolution. Variations in consumer prices are correlated first with those in investment, second with the numbers of employed, and third with labor productivity.

During the decade 1970–80, the investment cycle was quite different from that of the preceding decade as well as from that of Hungary and the GDR. Indeed, in Poland, this period was characterized by an economic policy, under, Gierek, with very high levels of investment over five years (1970–5) followed by massive reductions thereof. The investment cycle, which is usually five years long, was stretched out to ten years.

This led to a major upheaval in previous economic relations. Variations in investment, in wages, in labor productivity evolved in a curve which took the form of a parabola with a maximum in 1974 or 1975. Consumer prices, stable until 1973, rose sharply starting in 1974 and 1975, and increased steadily until 1980, continuing to rise after this date. The period of price rises corresponds to the descending phase of the investment cycle which explains the negative correlation observed between these two variables.

Until 1979, the authorities were able to maintain the former method of distributing national income despite major fluctuations in economic variables. The rise in prices in the years 1974 to 1979 insured that rises in real wages remained limited, as in the past. It is only from 1979 until 1980, that the rises in nominal wages won by social movements were not entirely compensated for by the fluctuations in consumer prices (Redor (140)).

If we introduce a one year lag in the wage equations, the correlation between explanatory variables is decidedly lower, and the quality of the econometric estimations better. The relation price/wages is high, as is the influence, with a one year lag, of variations in investment on industrial wages. This year perhaps represents the investment lag.

Can it be said that Bauer's theory is applicable to Poland? The answer is not at all a firm yes. Indeed, we have shown why the period 1970–81 is exceptional for Poland, and that the other STE do not share its characteristics. Real wages did, in fact, fluctuate in the same way as the principal economic indicators for the years 1970 to 1979. The years 1980 and 1981 are the only exceptions, since nominal and real wages continued to increase despite the very important decrease in these same indicators. The economic policy initiated in 1982 brings the Polish economy, and hence the wage regulation, close to the traditional model of the STE.

Applying the previous models to wage regulation in the GDR, gives poor results from an econometric point of view. There is no statistical relation between variations in the monthly or hourly earnings of workers, or in wages of all categories of workers on the one hand, and of the number employed or of investment on the other.

There is a difference between the GDR and other STE studied, if one considers that the rise in consumer prices was very slow over the entire period under study. Prices even decreased over several years. Hence the GDR is similar to the traditional Soviet model where variations in official prices are minimal,[7] and often negative.

We are now in a position to provide the first series of answers to the theoretical questions that have been posed so far throughout this book.

What is learned from the statistical study of administrative regulation
First of all, in the three STE, there appeared no statistical relation between fluctuations in earnings, whatever the unit of time or the category of wage-earners considered, and the number of employees.

Two conclusions may thus be drawn. The first is that, in light of these results, it is not necessarily invalid to analyze the STE in terms of disequilibrium. It can be argued that, during the period from 1960 to 1980, there were sub-periods characterized by an excess of supply, followed by sub-periods of an excess of demand on the labor

---

[7] On the necessary precautions for interpreting the official statistics, see Redor (141), pp. 104–5.

market. In this case, some of the points studied (the number of the employees) depend on the labor supply function, thought to be increasing, and some others depend on labour demand, thought to be decreasing. It is logical, therefore, that there be no increasing relation between the fluctuations in the number of employees and in earnings. The same is true if, given the general axiom of disequilibrium theory, the supply of labor is taken to be independent of earnings.

From a second point of view, the results of the tests suggested by Kornai confirm his analysis of the regulation of wages in economies dominated by shortage. Indeed, according to this conception, the very notion of a labor market is out of the question, supply and demand of labor not being directly related to wages.

It appears that our econometric results taken as a whole are in favor of the theory of shortage. Indeed, hourly and monthly earnings are largely disassociated from the short-term fluctuations in employment, which could have been supposed to exert "pressure" on the relations between wage-earners and firms, or between wage-earners and planners.

Bauer's hypothesis, that wage evolution is linked to the cycle of investment is dubious. Only in Poland is there a clear relation between these two factors, for reasons having to do with the particularities of the economic policy in this country during the years 1970 to 1981.

The aim of the planning process is, above all, to control the stability of the evolution of wages and, in so doing, of the spending of the population, so as not to further upset a consumer goods market afflicted with important shortages. From this point of view, the aim of the planner is not to realize equilibrium or reduce disequilibrium in a labor market, which in fact in traditional microeconomic terms does not exist. The planner maintains that the supply of labor is largely independent of wage fluctuations which remain, it must be noted, low. In the same way, firms are largely concerned with realizing their production plan.

Although no complete study of the USSR has been carried out, in all likelihood this country conforms to the model outlined above. In this country, like the GDR, the official price indexes report very low fluctuations since the Second World War. Even if the quality of these indexes is open to criticism, they must be taken into account in so far as most decisions in economic policy are based upon them. Parallel to this stability, one notes a regular growth in nominal and real wages.

Seurot ((152, p. 122–9) has shown how rises in wages remained steady from 1960 to 1980, despite important fluctuations in labor productivity throughout the period, and a net slow down beginning in 1975.

One must take into account the recent work of certain theoriticians such as Sapir (150) in order to apply the theory of shortage to the cycle observed in the Soviet economy.

For Sapir, an increase in employment in the production goods sector can only be realized by taking labor from agriculture (where the labor force abounds). Wage increases are differentiated by sector and make it possible to reallocate labor to sectors where the shortage is greatest.

However, the unsatisfied needs for agricultural goods result in a high increase in imports, and the deficit in foreign trade soon causes the planner to reduce investment. The global wage bill is proportionate to the mass of available consumer goods and the latter depends in turn on the share of investment and consumption in the national product which are defined at the central level.

The logic behind the model is that during a cycle there is a relation between employment and wages, at least in some sectors. This idea is close to that of Bauer who inspired Sapir. However, the relation between deviations from the trends of the growth of employment and of the growth of wages is low, as was the case for the three STE already studied. In order to make this relation more obvious, it might be necessary to go to finer levels of analysis.

Still it is possible to put forth yet another interpretation. Perhaps the central planner does not differentiate intersector differences in wages according to fluctuations in employment, and thus he controls the level of employment in certain sectors directly.

In so far as we have shown that the intersector wage differences are always high, even when differences in the levels of formal professional training among workers have been eliminated, this latter proposition is all the more plausible. Heavy industries have particular advantages in this respect. In addition, it must not be forgotten that in the USSR (and in this country alone) the administration has a tremendous power to control the mobility of agricultural workers who are obliged to obtain administrative authorization to leave the land. In fact, the planner need not vary the wage differentials in the short term when they are structurally higher in sectors of heavy industry. All that the planner has to do is to authorize agricultural workers to move to industry for certain periods.

The Soviet model is indeed based on fixed prices and a fixed wage rate or, more specifically, an inflexible wage structure, within which individuals attempt to move, given the administrative constraints which weigh upon them.

We propose the term administrative regulation to denote such a system.

Administrative regulation is based on the strict control of income distribution. The center for planning sees that the increase in the wages bill follows that of the production of consumer goods.

The second element of administrative regulation of wages is that wages are disconnected to a certain extent from other economic variables. Whereas investment and labor productivity fluctuate greatly, industrial wages for example fluctuate very little. It is certain that the stability of the evolution of pay is used by the central authorities as a fundamental means to control the economic system.

The GDR and the USSR are the best examples of administrative regulation of wages. Our analysis does not disclose a very clear relation between wages on the one hand and prices, labor productivity, the number of employees, and capital investment on the other hand. On the contrary, Poland and Hungary differ from the original model of administrative regulation of wages as there were substantial increases in consumer prices starting in the early seventies, increases which affected the nominal wages.

These results give credence to the hypothesis that the central authorities, within the framework of annual planning, establish a norm for the evolution of wages applicable to the economy as a whole. This norm then is modulated from sector to sector.

Two fundamental questions arise from this theoretical schema. First, on what criteria is the evolution of wages based? Second, does the analysis of the institutional processes of decision-making and control in matters of wages confirm these hypotheses? We will answer the second question in the last section of this chapter. As for the first, one may invoke two types of results.

First, it is necessary to refer to the theoretical analyses of Kornai (101) who maintains that fluctuations in the wage rate do not adjust the supply of and the demand for labor, at least at the macroeconomic level. Wage regulation conforms to another kind of logic entirely. It is one of the elements of adjustment between the supply and the demand of consumer goods, and of the control of monetary holdings of the population.

Secondly, it is necessary to refer to the analysis of the distribution of income compared to the rate of accumulation. Indeed, a study of the period from 1960 to 1981 shows a regular increase on the part of productive investment in the Net Material Product. This was made possible by the constant pressure that was exerted on the share of wages in national income (Redor (142)).

Nevertheless, until the end of the period, the authorities were able to guarantee a stable and moderate increase in real wages and in consumption. Wage policy consisted thus in fixing a wage increase of 2 percent or 3 percent approximately, at least in Hungary and Poland, independently of production fluctuations. Given that the period, up until 1975, was characterized by considerable expansion, it was possible to increase the share of surplus in the national income devoted to the accumulation of capital. This surplus appears then as a sort of residual in rapid expansion. The stability of the evolution of the wage rate compared to other economic variables is significant in this respect. The same analysis can be applied to Poland, apart from the fact that important growth in the years 1970 to 1975, followed by the depression, brought about greater variations in the average real wage than in other countries.

During the years 1975 to 1981, economic growth slowed down, bringing about a drop in the increase in the average real wage, and a more important drop in the rate of investment; this evolution continued during the five year period from 1981 to 1986 (Chavance (60)).

Moreover, the analysis of the differences between mixed regulation and administrative regulation of wages, incorporating institutional factors, that is to say the practical means of State intervention and collective bargaining in both systems, must be completed. Indeed, in analyzing the STS, the role of the "planner" is often mentioned, but his actual means of action remain unexplained. We will attempt to examine these means of action. Similarly, the question of the role played by official Unions in wage regulation will be addressed.

Finally, it is the relation between wage planning at the central level and its practical application in firms which is at stake.

With regard to the WS, certain institutional specifications are necessary. Collective wage bargaining from country to country must be examined. In addition, the question of the effects on wages of collective bargaining and union membership at the firm level will be raised.

This will mark the end of the study of mixed and administrative regulation of wages. In the remaining chapters, it will be necessary to answer a fundamental question: how can one explain the wage isomorphisms, even partial, evidenced in the two systems, when the processes of wage regulation are so different?

3 THE INSTITUTIONAL APPROACH TO MIXED REGULATION AND ADMINISTRATIVE REGULATION OF WAGES

By institutions, we mean all those legal rules which concern a given community and which public authority controls, or at least to which it applies. This concerns the exercise of the power of decision in a legal framework and its application, when necessary, by public law enforcement.

Certain research, comparative in perspective, underscores the universality of the existence of labor agreements in all industrialized countries, be they Western or Soviet.

The proportion of workers affected by such agreements is more often than not high. It exceeds 90 percent in the majority of STE as well as in the FRG and in Denmark, 70 percent in the United Kingdom, but only 25 percent in the United States (Cordova (61), Martinet (120)).

However, despite the diversity of the procedures and the areas where collective bargaining applies within each economic system, there is a definite systemic difference in collective wage bargaining.

The essential difference is that in the WS collective wage bargaining is not directly controlled by State intervention, whereas it is in the STS. In addition, in the latter, the State has at its disposal powerful administrative means to enforce decisions taken on wages down to the firm level.

1 Collective wage bargaining in the Western system

The degree to which negotiation between management and trade unions is decentralized varies from country to country. On the one hand, there are the German, Danish, and Belgian systems which are highly structured and where negotiations occur on a branch or even a national level. On the other hand, there are the British, American, and French systems which are less structured.

In the FRG, collective wage bargaining takes place at the level of sectors. The system is "dualist" in so far as the negotiations that take place within firms concern only the qualitative aspects of labor. Sector negotiations deal with the wage agreements (Muller-Jentsch (127)).

Statistical analysis clearly elucidated the determining role played by the sector unions, especially in the metal and metallurgy industries. This study showed that the concentration of wage bargaining at the level of the sectors did not mean that the evolution of wages was independent from fluctuations in employment, especially in consumer goods industries. In addition, analysis of the wage share in the national income implies that economic policy has little impact on wage regulation. The study of German institutions confirms this fact: the State is not involved in collective contract negotiations, not even indirectly (Leithauser (107)).

In Denmark, wage negotiations take place every two years at the national level between the Danish Federation of Unions (LO) and the Danish Federation of Employers. This agreement can be adapted in certain sectors. One of the usual terms of the agreement is the indexing of wages to prices.

In Belgium, up until the beginning of the eighties, the indexing of wages to prices was automatic, with a one month lag. Wage negotiation takes place at the national or sector level. However, since the beginning of the seventies, there has been a trend toward "autonomy" of wage negotiations which are more and more frequently carried out at the firm level.

The United Kingdom provides an entirely different example. Collective wage negotiation has been traditionally "voluntary," that is to say based on contractual agreements between representatives of employers and wage-earners. The major difference, however, is that negotiation and wage agreements are very decentralized. They are decided at the firm level, and the biggest ones at the establishment level.

The economic policy-makers, be they Conservative or Labour party members, have been concerned for a long time with the system of wage negotiation, sometimes considered anarchic, given the

multiplicity of negotiating procedures, and the difficulty in controlling such a system within the framework of economic policy.

In France, the State, by way of a minimum wage, plays an
important role. Econometric analysis (refuted in section 2 of this
chapter) confirmed the concrete influence of the minimum wage
on the evolution of workers' earnings. The weight of the public
sector provides particular impact on wage negotiation over other
sectors.

Wage increases are little subject to contracts. In fact, collective
labor agreements which, it must be noted, the State may impose on
an entire sector of activity, define the structure of earnings, but do
not determine wage increases. In practice, recommendations for
wage increases put forth by an employers' federation for a given
sector play an important role in determining wages. The frequency
of wage conflicts at the firm level may be explained by the weakness
of collective wage bargaining.

In the United States, wage negotiation is very decentralized: it
often takes place at the firm level. For example, in 1975 there were
50,000 collective wage agreements. However decentralized, this
system is highly controlled. The National Labor Relations Acts
prohibits employers from organizing in-house Unions, and from
making decisions on wages without consulting the Union concerned.
On the other hand, strikes for wage increases are permitted only if
they do not hamper the terms of the on-going agreements.

Before ending this rapid overview, it must be noted that the
principle of State non-intervention in collective wage negotiation
has been somewhat twisted in certain countries since the beginning
of the seventies. Indeed, the State has intervened to lower the rate of
increase of negotiated wage and sometimes even to impose a freeze.

In Denmark, this kind of intervention dates from 1975: the State
decided to slow down the rise in wages several times by law, as did
Belgium starting in 1982. In France, "stabilization plans" directly
concerned wages, notably the "Barre plan" in 1976 and the
"Delors–Mauroy" plan in 1982–3.

In the United Kingdom, the government imposed a norm for
the increase in wages during collective bargaining in 1967 and in
1972. In 1974, it signed a "social contract" with the Unions, the
aim of which was to reach a moderate progression in wages in
exchange for social benefits for workers. This policy failed, how-

ever, and was abandoned due to the pressure of Union demands and strikes. Austerity measures enforced by the Thatcher government starting in 1979 brought about decreases in real wages in 1980 and 1981.

Finally, only Germany and the United States remained faithful to the principle of non-interference of the State in wage negotiations. However, collective bargaining between employers' organizations and Unions remains a fundamental element in the "mixed" regulation of wages. Indeed, wage negotiation is of a "mixed" nature itself in so far as it is neither completely centralized nor decentralized. Still it must be pointed out that the level of collective bargaining varies considerably from country to country.

Finally, the institutional approach must not override the fact that economic forces, notably the state of employment, strongly influence the evolution of wages. In addition to the specific impact of unemployment, the general state of the economy is closely related to the results of wage negotiations.

2 Centralized setting of wages in the STE

The role of the wage fund in firms

In light of the comparative research of Hagelmayer (85) on the STE, it is clear that there are important differences in the means and procedures of collective bargaining between different countries. However, one thing is common to all of them. The fixing of increases in wages is, *de juro* and *de facto*, outside the field of labor agreements at the firm and the sector level, and is strictly reserved for the central economic planners.

The purpose of labor agreements in firms is: "to improve the efficiency of operation of the national economy in keeping with the national economic plans." These agreements concern, for example "the realization of the plan, the reinforcing of discipline at work, and improving vocational training."

Annual planning of wages (which does not derive from labor agreements) applies to the Administration, and also to all the activities in the State sector, that is to say, nearly all the industrial and tertiary firms, as well as State farms. Pay scales and the skills corresponding to each function are defined by the Labor Administration (Ministry of Labor), and result from decisions made at Cabinet meetings. These decisions come into effect after the Department of the Administration at a lower level and the Central Bureau of Unions have been consulted.

· The five year wage plan is defined by the Planning Commission, ratified by the Cabinet, after consulting the central Union bureau (Kabaj (91) and Lowit (109)).

Most Western analysts underscore the minimal autonomy of Unions *vis-à-vis* political and economic power. The possibility for Union officials, who are Party members to contest is limited. However, even if there is little opposition and even if counter-powers are little developed at this level, the wage policy is cautious in so far as the authorities maintain a relatively stable increase in real wages.

It is necessary to question how the wage plan is put into practice down to the level of the firms. In the general framework of economic planning, an annual percentage of variation of the average nominal wage is calculated. Next, the Ministries elaborate upon it, defining the objectives to be realized by each sector. At the firm level, wage planning results from the determination and the control of the "wage fund," and in the case of Hungary, of the average wage. Bonuses paid out of a specialized fund (Adam (26)) are added to the actual wage.

The notion of wage fund is of particular importance in wage regulation of the STE. This fund is in fact the wage bill that each firm is authorized to distribute, for a given period, following negotiations between the Director of the firm and the governing Administration.

In the system which operated in most countries until the end of the seventies (Adam (26), pp. 60–5), the wage fund is planned by the Center independently of any indicator of the performance of the firm. At the end of the planning period, the wage fund "realized" is recalculated according to the level of production achieved and employment by skill. It is obvious that this system does not incite the firm to minimize the cost of the labor force. On the contrary, it incites the firm to produce as much as possible (which is usually the principal determining factor behind bonuses); this, in turn, increases the wage fund which the firm is authorized to pay out. This is the origin of the softness of the budgetary constraint on the labor force used by each firm. It must not be forgotten that, if the Administration does not normally impose strict limits on the level of employment in firms, it does make sure that the average wage paid out is not above the planned norm. This is a strategic variable in the regulation of the whole economic system; for the firm, this is a parameter which, to a great extent, determines the internal regulation of pay.

The waste of human resources, brought on by the administrative determination of the wage fund, explains why the most important "reforms" sought to link the level of this fund to indicators of economic performance. Thus, the 1973 reform in Poland established an increase in the wage fund over the preceding year in proportion to the increase in realized added value.

The Hungarian reform of 1968 was even more innovative in that the Planning Center simply established the rules to determine the wage fund. Wage increases from one year to the next hinged upon the firm's profits. Nevertheless, these increases were cushioned by a very gradual tax upon the firm. From 1971 on the increase in the average wage was linked to that of the gross income per employee, in order to keep the interfirm wage differentials from increasing. Finally, even in Hungary, the Administration continued in the eighties to limit the power of firms to determine their wage funds.

This is also true for firms' special funds, which, in all STE, are used to pay bonuses. The funding usually comes from profits. In fact, the sum paid to each worker varies little from firm to firm, and, bonuses are automatically renewed each year (Rogulska (148), pp. 178–200, 325–33).

The global wage bill is strictly controlled at the firm level so as to avoid what certain theoreticians refer to as "inflation" (Adam (26)). More precisely, the Administration limits the increase in the average wage within firms by conforming to the objectives defined by the central authorities.

Since the end of the seventies, different kinds of collective pay systems where wages are linked to efficiency have become more and more common. The 1979 reform in the USSR introduced the system of "brigades under contract." A team set up as a brigade is paid according to the realization of a production contract negotiated with a firm. In 1986, such contracts concerned 25 percent of the labor force (Duchêne (71)).

In this same country, the new 1986 reform reduced the fixed percentage of wages, which is now only 50 percent or 70 percent of the total wage. The rest is made up of bonuses which depend on results, on difficulty, and on skill required.

Nevertheless, these reforms, which touched many STE in the eighties, are not different, in principle, from previous ones. The essential issue is whether firms will be able to increase significantly their autonomy so as to determine their wage fund and above all the average wage that they pay out.

Finally, analysis of the institutions and the rules upon which wage regulation is determined confirms the existence of administrative regulation. The Planning Center establishes the norms of wage variation and has the power to regulate wages down to the level of firms.

The limits of the administrative wage regulation
One should not assume, however, that the central planner controls in detail the wage rates per skill in each firm. Indeed, we will concentrate on this area of liberty that firms maintain in the internal management of the wage bill ascribed to them, in an attempt to explain the isomorphisms of the pay structures in the two systems.

The planning system, in the STE, is much more able to control the average wage rate at the macroeconomic level than it is the wage structure within the firm. Administrative regulation has proven to be efficient in limiting the rise in wages and keeping it under the growth of global production. When comparing the planned objectives of the average nominal wage growth, and the results achieved, one comes to the same conclusion (Adam (26), p. 47). Naturally, this analysis does not hold for certain exceptional periods, such as Poland in the years 1980 and 1981 when the central government lost control of the increase in wages.

It must not be forgotten that there is no collective wage bargaining, comparable to that in Western countries, between employers and the Unions. The role of the only Union organization is to justify and to apply, rather than to contest, the decisions taken by the central government on matters of pay. Union power does not seek to profit from a favorable employment situation in order to obtain important wage increases. Conversely, the central authority does not take advantage of a less favorable situation in order to lower wages. It is only inclined to practice such a policy in the event of a prolonged crisis, such as that which has been going on since the end of the seventies. In addition, it is all the more difficult to exert short-term pressure on the growth of wages when unemployment is not widespread. The authorities are, thus, robbed of an important means of influence on wages. In this way the administrative regulation of wages is decidedly different from that of the WS.

Finally, the two modes of wage regulation are distinctly different. Whereas the Western firm, in matters of wage management, is essentially subject to constraints imposed by the economic and social environment (notably by virtue of collective bargaining), the Soviet-type firm must face a third category of constraints: those coming from the Administration, which are multiform and ubiquitous.

From this moment on, the problem that we must face is clear. How can we explain the isomorphisms of the wage structures, which we exposed in the first part of this book, when the institutional contexts are so different? We will base our answer on the following aspects: the means of managing the labor force within firms in the two systems, the role of formal and professional training, and the division of labor.

CHAPTER 7

The structuring role of sectors and large firms in the two systems

The statistical analysis of the wage structures pointed to the role of sectors of activity in the two systems. When the impact of the differences in formal education and professional training of the labor force is left aside, wages in the various sectors remain very different. Moreover, the ranking of sector wages is very similar in the two systems, and the factors that differentiate them are identical. In addition, in the WE, sectors where wages are the highest are those that are the most protected from fluctuations in employment.

It does not suffice therefore, to study the aggregated demand for planned labor on the one hand, and the aggregated demand of firms subject to competition on the other.

Sectors of activity, and the firms operating therein, constitute a fundamental element in what must be referred to as different demands for labor. Indeed, in the two systems, where wage rates are differentiated according to the per capita capital stock and the concentration of firms, there are necessarily heterogeneous demands for labor. It is in this sense that firms act to structure wages.

We shall hereby attempt to explain this strategy using the theory of the internal labor market of firms and show the role that they play in the training of the labor force.

I THE SEGMENTATION OF THE LABOR MARKET IN THE TWO SYSTEMS

1 Some theoretical and empirical elements

The principal concepts
The movement behind the notion of segmentation of the labor market originated in the American institutionalist approach. The

first works have to do with the analysis of wage relations during the Second World War. These works attempt to explain why wage discrimination exists and why some social groups live in extreme poverty in the United States (Kerr (96)).

According to Doeringer and Piore ((68), pp. 1–2), the internal labor market is "an administrative unit, such as a manufacturing plant, within which the pricing and allocation of labor is governed by a set of rules and procedures." The ambiguity of the term "market" emerges from this definition which must be taken in its largest sense as "the set of means to assign workers to jobs" (Gambier, Vernières (80), p.7). The "internal market" designates the rules for managing the labor force applied at the level of the firm or the establishment.

Doeringer and Piore contrast this first term with that of the external labor market which, they maintain, fits the criteria of a traditional analysis; the assigning of the labor force to jobs and the determining of wages depends directly on the supply and demand of the market.

There are points where these two markets overlap. Indeed, certain jobs, located at particular points within the general organization of the firm are filled by external recruiting and not by internal promotion.

If the term "market" seems inadequate for designating the means of managing the labor force, the question as to the meaning of the dichotomous internal–external market must also be raised. Indeed, Doeringer and Piore (68) argue that, within a given firm, the rules for managing workers, technicians, and executives are very different, hence the proposal by Gambier and Vernières (80) to distinguish within a firm "internal sub-markets."

The most important thing that we learn from this approach, and which numerous empirical studies in the United States and Europe attest to, is that firms "structure" the management of their labor force by creating promotion lines, wage benefits linked to seniority, while guaranteeing stable employment to certain categories of wage-earners. This creates partitions or the "Balkanisation" of movements of the labor force within the firms, but also between the latter and the outside. Therefore, the analysis no longer focuses on the adjustments between supply and demand of labor, but concentrates on the determining factors behind the internal management of labor.

We will use the term *segmentation* to designate these phenomena. This implies that the partitions and the rules that determine the management of the labor force and the wage structures are much more complex than the simple dichotomy between internal and external market would lead one to believe.

When distinguishing primary from secondary labor markets, a distinction outlined by Doeringer and Piore (68), one encounters the same ambiguity. Indeed, when these two authors leave the firm and seek to analyze labor at the macroeconomic level, they use the notion of the duality of the market. Jobs in the primary market are characterized by higher wages, good working conditions, and important opportunities for promotion.

On the secondary market, first the labor force is mobile and temporarily employed (domestics, hotel employees). Next, there are other employees who are an integral part of the organization of the firm, but who are subject to inferior employment conditions (in terms of wages, autonomy), and to variations in activity.

Nevertheless, the notion of duality must be generalized to take into account the complexity of segmentation. We think that dualism crosses each segment or each sub-market. By this we mean "areas which are particularly propitious to the mobility of the labor force given the existence of a common stock of aptitudes." The dualism, even if it is accepted as such, does not override the fact that each primary and secondary market is itself formed by the juxtaposition of sub-markets defined by as many categories of workers. An applied analysis of this segmentation of the labor market is now going to be carried out.

The segmentation of the labor market in the STE
It is of particular interest to our comparative approach to note that the concepts and methods of the analysis of the segmentation of the labor market have been applied to Hungary.

In fact, several teams of Hungarian researchers have tried to characterize the segments of the labor market, at the national and regional levels, and have carried out studies within firms to discover how internal markets function.

Starting from statistical macroeconomic and macrosocial data on Hungary, Nagy and Sziraczki (128) carried out a factor analysis to determine whether there were elements which made it possible to individualize distinct and isolated groups of jobs. Four factors of

Table 7.1. *Segmentation of the labor market in Hungary*

Job types	Wage	Mobility	Job skill	Work time
1 Wage-earners in the machine and construction industries.	high	strong	high	average
2 Wage-earners in industries with difficult work conditions (mining, metal industry)	high	low	low	low
3 Wage-earners in predominantly male jobs in agriculture and transport	average	low	low	very high
4 Wage-earners in predominantly male unskilled jobs (laborers, etc.)	below average	strong	low	high
5 Wage-earners in predominantly female semi-qualified jobs	below average	average	low	low
6 Wage-earners in predominantly female unskilled jobs (agriculture, public service)	below average	low	low	low

Sources: A. Nagy and G. Sziraczki (128)

differentiation were uncovered, thanks to which it was possible to define six groups of jobs (table 7.1) for the Hungarian economy.

The results of other studies,[1] mostly field-work, are congruent with that of Nagy and Sziraczki. The former show that the male and female labor markets are different and that women are paid far less than men. In addition, the labor markets for skilled and non-skilled laborers are also distinct, with little mobility between the two (Galasi and Sik (79)).

The analysis of the internal segments of firms shows that the directors of Hungarian firms seek, just as in the WE, to keep certain categories of the labor force stable by building promotion lines based on seniority and the level of professional training. Other categories of employees, usually unskilled, are subject to a high rate of mobility and are paid little.

It should be pointed out that the studies which we have just cited confirm some of our results. Notably we find again pay differences between men and women and between priority and non-priority sectors (table 7.1). Important information on the mobility of workers must however be added.

Mobility between firms, such as analyzed by Nagy and Sziraczki, for example, occurs in segments where the least skilled labor force is

[1] The study of Nagy and Sziraczki (128) was published in English by the University of Budapest. The works of Revecz, K Fazekas, Kalasz, and Köllö were published by the Institute of Economics, Hungarian Academy of Sciences (144).

concentrated. The latter benefits very little from programs of vocational training, and has little opportunity for promotion and progression in the organization of the firm. On the contrary, mobility within the firm, towards jobs offering responsibility, is reserved for skilled employees who follow a distinct path, based notably on specific vocational training courses.

The question remains as to whether what has been learned about the labor market in Hungary is applicable to the other STE. Malle (116) carried out an institutional study for the USSR. The results show that the Soviet labor market is highly segmented. The author underscores the role of central planning in this phenomenon.

The particular characteristics of each country are such that, just as in Western countries, the nature and boundaries of segments vary. But our analyses, notably through statistics, have show that there are, in the countries studied, significant differences in pay between men and women, between priority and non-priority sectors, and between concentrated and non-concentrated sectors.

The Hungarian example proves that the primary–secondary duality needs to be more detailed, and that the mobility of the labor force is more complex than this distinction would have it. The existence of priority sectors in the STE, for example, introduce an additional dimension in the structuring of the labor market. The high wages paid in these sectors constitute a powerful pole of attraction for the labor force.

The fundamental questions remain. Are the structures of the labor market in the WS and the STS similar? What are the factors behind these structures in a regulation system which we have referred to as mixed on the one hand, and administrative, on the other? How does the structuring of the labor market determine the pay levels?

2 *The causes of the segmentation of the labor market*

The role of firms in the Western system
In reference to the WS, Doeringer and Piore have put forth two types of causes which could be the sources of segmentation ((68), p. 57). First of all the function of the structures which make up the internal market is to minimize the cost of professional training and labor turnover for the firm. The structuring of the internal market varies from firm to firm, as the factors which determine costs vary

themselves. Among these, we might mention the technological level of the equipment used, the volume and the variety of production, the characteristics of the external supply of labor. All these determine the level and the dispersion of the skill of the workers employed, and the possibility of substituting one worker for another.

If the level of formal education and professional training required is low, the hiring criteria are not stiff, and the cost of turnover for the firm is also low. This is also true if there are many possibilities to substitute different categories of skilled workers without a high cost of training. In the opposite case, firms tend to stabilize their labor force by setting up well-established lines of promotion, wage incentives linked to seniority, and systematic training programs. The internal market is heavily structured. Firms use all possible means to avoid the "uncertainties"[2] of the management of the labor force.

Certain categories of wage-earners find advantages in the stability of the internal market, which is often strengthened by Union actions.

In order to understand how firms structure the labor market, another element must be taken into account. Indeed, firms use existing social divisions; in other words, they are not faced with a homogeneous supply on the labor market, but with distinctly different groups. Piore ((138), p. 47–8) writes: "It is noteworthy that the labor force for secondary jobs tends to rely heavily, although not exclusively, upon preindustrial groups and classes ... It seems that the Capitalist system finds these groups but does not create them."

In this way Piore explains that firms employ a labor force in the secondary market, notably women and migrant workers (national and international), which pre-date, as social groups, the development of Western type firms. In this sense, firms only organize the segregation of employment. They use the members of these social groups as a reserve supply of labor according to the fluctuations in their activities. In other words the social groups that are found in the lower segments of the labor market are not created by the firms, but they are often moved about by firms. This is true of national and international migrants.

In conclusion, firms appear to play an active role in the structuring of the labor market in the WS. This structure can only be the

---

[2] One can consider on this subject the title of the article devoted to the segmentation of the labor market in France by Piore, "Dualism in the labor market: a response to uncertainty and flux: the case of France" (138).

result of powerful firms which are able to compete in certain segments of the labor market, but have a common interest in maintaining segmentation. These firms are part of what we have referred to as the mixed regulation of wages. In the framework of this kind of regulation, sectors play an important role in determining the evolution of wages through collective bargaining. Unions do not systematically oppose the structuring of the labor market, in so far as it serves to stabilize an important part of the labor force. In addition, if the role of the State is not negligible, notably by way of legislation concerning lay-offs, a great deal of leeway is left to firms to manage the labor force. The State intervenes very little in fixing wages, especially by category of laborers during "stabilization plans."

The segmentation of the market and the administrative regulation of wages
Compared to this analysis, what about the structuring of the labor market in the STE and the respective roles played by firms and the State therein? The point that we wish to make is that despite a distinctly different institutional context, represented theoretically by the concept of administrative regulation, for the management of labor certain analogies with the WS can be made. This is the reason why the general phenomenon of segmentation of the labor market exists in both systems.

These analogies reside in the fact that both the Soviet type and the Western firms must, in the terms of Piore, "respond to uncertainties" in their economic environments. Despite central planning, it is not an exaggeration to maintain that the director of a Soviet-type firm lives in a universe which is as uncertain as that of his Western homologue, especially if we consider the management of the labor force.

The existence of "shortages in the labor force" have been at times analyzed by economists from the Soviet bloc.

In a series of monographs comparing French and Hungarian firms, Dubois and Mako (69) point out that in Hungary all the firms and establishments studied have great difficulty in stabilizing and recruiting labor, especially skilled labor.

A great number of directors of firms seek to stabilize the labor force and, if this might seem paradoxical, to hold on to those workers beyond the number needed, in order to cope, as much as possible, with uncertainties caused by shortages in the labor force. Indeed, the cost for the firm of turnover in employees is all the higher since it is difficult to replace skilled employees, and that it can, as a result, be difficult to realize the production plan. Some workers are even less attached to their jobs in the State sector since they have a second job in the private "unofficial economy."

In light of this, it is not surprising that it is possible to analyze the Soviet-type firm in terms of segmentation. A firm's first objective is to ensure that the production function as well as the related services have the necessary resources (human material) to fulfil the plan. Hence the creation of lines of promotion the purpose of which is to keep within the firms those workers who have the most important jobs. These channels rely on an internal training program which is adapted to the needs of the firm as well as on wages which rise with the level of responsibility and seniority.

If it is clear that firms seek to stabilize the labor force, it remains to explain the existence of the external market or rather the segments that make it up, and the segregation of jobs that result. On this issue, an analogy can also be drawn with the way a Western firm operates.

The administrative regulation of wages has been defined as a set of rules by which the State foresees and controls the evolution of the wage bill in each firm.

As in this type of regulation, *de juro* or *de facto*, the rate of the average wage is more strictly controlled than the number of workers, the firm tends to hire as many employees as possible so as to realize its production plan. But, and this is of capital importance, in order not to go over the norm of the average pay rise, the firm must limit the pay of those individuals who do not occupy important positions within the organization. By this we mean wage-earners with little seniority and with little internal training, just as in Western firms.

The existence of shortages which oblige the firm to stabilize part of the labor force, especially skilled labor, and of the norm of the average wage which cannot be disregarded by the directors, incites the firm to minimize the wage cost of certain categories of workers, most often the least skilled. This practice is observed in Hungary for example. Certain firms which are subject to control of the average wage, hire skilled labor, they also hire cheap low-skilled labor, while maintaining the average planned wage (Dubois and Mako (69), p. 453).

It is in light of this that one can explain segregation in the employment of women, evidence of which has been provided by our own work as well as by the works of those analyzing segmentation in the labor market.

Like in the WE, the system of production does not structure the labor market *ex nihilo*. The structure is based on a given social context: the arrival of masses of women on to the labor market in the fifties and sixties, the division of labor on the basis of gender which is partly a function of culture. In the administrative regulation of wages it is in the best interest of firms to isolate women in underqualified and underpaid jobs. It must be added that, just like in the US, segregation is more rampant at the intersector rather than the firm level. Our analysis of intersector earnings differences brought this out. For this reason, wage discrimination is difficult to analyze. Sectors dominated by "a female labor force" or a "male labor force" are distinctly different and difficult to compare.

2 MANAGING WAGES IN FIRMS IN THE TWO SYSTEMS

It is interesting to formalize the concepts that we have just presented and to link the theory of the segmentation of the labor market to the economic calculations of firms.

1 The basis of the theory of the efficiency wage[3]

The theory of the efficiency wage is based on the idea that it may be of interest to firms to vary their wage rates, bearing in mind costs due to turnover, absenteeism, or poor morale among employees.

In other words, this theory is founded on the idea that an individual's productivity is not only determined by innate or acquired (professional training) characteristics, but that it also depends on how much he is paid.

In addition, when a worker must be replaced (because of turnover), the firm bears the costs of hiring and adaptation. These vary according to the type of activity in which the firm is engaged, its organization, and its position on the labor market.

[3] The principal contributors to this area of research are Ballot and Piatecki (38), Malcomson (114), Perrot Dormont (135), Vaneecloo (165), Yellen (171).

Vaneecloo (165) underlined the links between training within firms and the cost of turnover of the labor force. Major transformation concerns skills common to a group of jobs and minor transformation concerns acquiring knowledge (elements) specific to each job or each firm. The central hypothesis of this theory is that all jobs have a specific component of varying importance. Consequently, any movement on the labor market results in a minor transformation, and sometimes a major transformation when there is a change in a category of employment.

The cost of a major transformation (sometimes referred to as "a complement transformation" in so far as it completes the initial training) includes the time necessary to train the wage-earners, but also the use of machines, of space, and ultimately of the loss of raw materials and intermediate consumption necessary for on the job training. This cost varies from firm to firm depending upon the production processes used, the level of the per capita capital stock, and the organization of labor.

The minor transformation (also called the 'substitute transformation') takes place, most of the time, on the job, and also depends upon the technology used, the per capita capital stock, and beyond that, the goods market in which the firm operates. Indeed, the organization of labor must take into account the more or less fluctuating nature of the final demand (in level and in structure). The latter conditions the flexibility of the organization and the degree of polyvalence of the workers, hence the extent of their transformation.

In the hypothesis where the specificity of jobs is high, the cost of the turnover of the labor force is high. The firm guards against this mobility by offering substantial advantages to its wage-earners. Of course some of these advantages are in the form of wages, but others include the guarantee of stable employment, or even the chance for promotion. Contrary to this, if the costs of transformation for a firm are low, the firm can hire beginners and can tolerate a high level of turnover.

Each firm seeks to minimize the cost of its labor force, that is to say the wage rate and the cost of turnover of the labor force which is itself a function of this rate. Therefore, the wage rate is a variable which the firm manipulates so as to minimize labor costs.

2 *The efficiency wage and the segmentation of the labor market in the two systems*

In this section, we will present a very simplified model of the determination of the efficiency wage, and we will then apply this model to the management of wages in the two systems.

The program of economic calculation in firms (Perrot-Dormont (135), pp. 360–70).

We consider that each enterprise minimizes the cost of employing each worker for a given level of production. The corresponding program can be written:

$$\min w/e\,(w)$$
$$w \geqslant w_0$$

w is the wage rate paid by the firm

$e(w)$: the effort of each worker, this is an increasing function of the wage rate.

w_0 is the reservation wage of each worker: wage under which he refused to work.

If λ designates the multiplicator associated with constraint, the first-order conditions of Kuhn and Tucker so that the program contains a solution that is admissible to workers is:

$$\frac{e(w) - we'\,(w) + \lambda}{(e(w))^2} = 0$$

$$\lambda(w - w_0) = 0$$

Which gives finally:

$$\frac{\dfrac{de(w)}{e(w)}}{\dfrac{dw}{w}} = 1$$

The efficiency wage is such that the elasticity of individual effort as compared to the wage rate is equal to 1.

It must be remembered that the effort of each worker $(e(w))$ is an increasing function of the wage rate. The higher the wage, the fewer the disruptions caused by turnover of the labor force, by absenteeism for one reason or another or by the low morale of the workers, the higher will be labor productivity.

It is essential to note that the efficiency wage is independent of the level of employment. One can suppose that the firm maximizes its profits and fixes the level of its employment in such a way that the wage rate is equal to the marginal productivity of labor. The latter depends on the level of employment and on the effort of the workers (Perrot Dormont (135), pp. 364–6).

However, it is possible to imagine that the production of the firm is constrained by effective demand and that the firm sets its level of employment to satisfy this demand. This does not affect the level of the efficiency wage.

If the model is applied to the STS, one can argue that firms minimize their average wage which is tightly controlled by the central planners. At the same time, firms do not seek to rationalize the level of employment for which this control is minimal.

In the section that follows, we will examine more closely the contribution of the theory of the efficiency wage to the economic analysis of the labor market in each system.

The theory of the efficiency wage and the segmentation of the labor market in the WE.

The theory of the efficiency wage makes it possible to explain certain features of the functioning of the labor market in the WE.

First of all, this theory can explain the rigidity of wages. It implies that firms are impervious to variations in the supply of labor, at least in the short run. Pay is determined on the basis of parameters which are linked, in part, to the internal organization of firms. From this perspective, one can consider that their theory provides a microeconomic foundation for the notion of Keynesian unemployment (Yellen (171)).

In light of this theory, it is possible to interpret in a new way the existence of differentials of wage rates in different firms (the firm effect). Indeed, the level of the efficiency wage depends on the particular characteristics of each firm: the cost of turnover of the labor force, and the amount of per capita capital stock.

From this moment on, the notion of an internal market within the firm becomes meaningful. There is indeed a specific wage rate in this market which differs from that of other firms.

The rule of this market is not perfect mobility, but the creation of channels of promotion so as to control the movement of the labor force. It is in this sense that the internal market of the firm is structured.

Finally, the very different level of the cost of turnover of the labor force provides a logical foundation for the notion of segmentation. Firms where this cost is low do not provide wage benefits or other perks (stable employment, working conditions, social benefits) for their labor force. On the contrary, firms where the costs of labor turnover are high strive to stabilize their labor force by offering high wages and favorable working conditions.

On the other hand, the existence of different wage rates from firm to firm favors discrimination and segregation. Firms where wages are high are in a position to choose members of groups reputed to be the most productive.[4] Consequently, members of other groups can only be hired by firms or sectors which pay little.

Is it possible to apply these analyses to our observations on the STS? We shall attempt to prove that the answer to this question is affirmative, and that the source of the wage isomorphisms evidenced by our statistical analyses are to be found in the analogies in the internal management of the labor force in the two systems.

The efficiency wage in the STS

The level of employment is not a variable which enters into the optimization calculation of the firm. This proposition holds in the theory of repressed inflation where the level of employment is constrained by the supply of labor. If we consider the theory of shortage applied to the labor force, the firm is not able to hire enough labor to realize its plans.

One must add that, for institutional reasons, the control applicable to firms concerns more the level of average wage that the firm is allowed to pay than the level of employment (see above, chapter 6).

The firm, under pressure from the planning center, must minimize its average wage cost, given that the cost of turnover of the labor force is included therein.

There may be forces within the firm that are working to increase this cost, notably when the structure of skills rises, or when certain categories, or all categories of labor, demand raises.[5] This incites the directors of firms to rationalize their internal wage management.

The importance of shortages in the labor force in the STE raises the cost of turnover of the labor force. First of all, the costs of training

[4] We have shown the role played by imperfection in information in the existence of discrimination (part I, chapter 2).
[5] On wage bargaining in Hungarian firms, see Revesz, Fazekas, Kalasz, and Köllö (144).

in the firm are high given the shortages which hit skilled wage-earners particularly. In addition, when a worker leaves a firm, it can take a long time to replace him.

In order to face the shortages of labor and the forces within the firm which raise the average wage, the firm structures its labor market. To do so, the firm creates channels the purpose of which is to stabilize the workers for whom the time spent (and hence the cost of) recruiting and training are highest. In other words, the firm in the STS minimizes its average wage cost by taking into account the cost of labor turnover. This is of capital importance since the turnover of employees can compromise the realization of planned production objectives, on which hinge the bonuses paid both to the employees and to the Director of the firm.

The cost of labor turnover is not just monetary, it must also be analyzed primarily in terms of breaks and disruptions to production, that is to say of the realization of planned objectives.

In light of these analyses, we conclude that the determinants of the wage structures at the firm level are analogous in the STS and in the WS.

We can therefore justify, in the same way as in the WE, the high wage dispersion which exists within the same category of employees. This is also the case for the increasing relation observed between the level of wages and the per capita capital stock and for the existence of segregation in employment and wage discrimination.

In fact, as has already been pointed out, the importance of per capita capital is an element which is linked to the cost of the transformation of the labor force in firms. As for wage discrimination against women in the STS, it is associated with the pressure that the Administration exerts on the level of the average wage. It is all the easier to minimize this average wage when there is strong discrimination against certain groups of individuals. Naturally such behavior is especially common in firms where there are many unspecific jobs. There are many women in such firms; here again discrimination and segregation in employment go hand in hand.

This model implies that the firm is relatively autonomous in the internal management of its labor force. Indeed, if in the framework of administrative regulation, the planning center is attentive to the evolution of the average cost of labor, the firm should benefit from a certain autonomy in managing the shortages of labor according to the objectives of the plan ascribed to the firm, and the material resources allocated to it. Labor is a particular kind of resource. The flow of workers must be controlled by material incentives which are, in fact, the differentials offered for a same category of labor. That such differentials exist is logical in a system which admits that certain sectors have priority over others.

Just as in the WE, certain sectors or certain firms must operate with a stable labor force, which has benefited from specific and in depth professional and on the job training.

In the logic of this system, one might think that the planning center seeks to control rather than suppress the differentials in wages from sector to sector and firm to firm. The center may be led to push for the transformation and fixing of labor by assigning high wage funds to firms whose production is deemed to have priority (production of investment, military goods, and goods for export).

In conclusion, it is necessary to examine the relation between the internal labor market of the firm and the position held by it on the goods market in the two systems. Or, it remains to be seen how the management of wages is modified according to the more or less oligopolistic nature of firms.

3 MONOPOLIES AND OLIGOPOLIES IN MIXED REGULATION AND ADMINISTRATIVE REGULATION OF WAGES

Our previous estimations uncovered a strong link between the sector concentration of establishments and the level of pay in the two systems. We shall now examine to what extent this link complements the theory of the efficiency wage. However, it will be necessary to distinguish the role of the oligopoly and the monopoly in the two systems because of the different structures of the consumer and capital goods markets in each of them.

Before trying to explain the origin of "the sector effect" on wages in the two economic systems, it is necessary to adopt a critical view of the definition of these sectors. Indeed, rather than analyzing "priority sectors" or "pilot sectors", it would be preferable to study the role of dominant firms. The statistical grouping of sectors does not necessarily cover firms with homogeneous technical and economic characteristics. For this reason, we will concentrate more on the theoretical role of big firms, rather than on sectors. We will not entirely forego the logic of sectors. Indeed, the sector exists institutionally by way of collective bargaining in Western countries, and by way of sector Ministries in some STE. In addition, statistical studies, however imperfect, must be used in so far as they can indirectly take into consideration the role of big firms notably through industrial concentration.

1 Wage structures and oligopolies in the Western system

The structuring of the internal market of oligopolies
First of all, it must be considered that the concentration of establishments can be linked to other factors of wage structuring. This is true of Union participation, which it is clear, at least in theory, determines a relatively high level of wages.

If we interpret the increasing relation between the rate of wage and the concentration of firms, within the framework of the efficiency wage, industrial concentration should imply relatively high costs of hiring and training, and therefore of turnover.

Such a relation is all the more plausible given that the concentration of establishments, is usually linked to the level of per capita capital stock.

Large establishments, and ultimately complex equipment (with a high ratio of capital per worker), make the organization of work, as well as the specific training of the labor force costly. In the same way, the financial risks encountered when turnover is high are also heavy. It is thus possible to speak in terms of a risk of disorganization, which varies according to the size of the firm and its capital stock. It is in the interest of the firm and of the planning authorities to bear this cost in mind when defining its wage policy.

From this perspective, we can say that there are three elements which contribute to the cost of turnover of the labor force. In addition to the cost of hiring and training, there is an eventual cost of disorganization in the case of the uncontrolled departure of certain wage-earners. This cost is a function of the time it takes to replace the wage-earners who leave (the time it take to hire and to train) and of the eventual disturbance to the organization of the firm resulting from these departures. The more complex and large the organization of labor, the higher the cost. However, even if these arguments are convincing, there is a dimension that is missing in this analysis. One must not overlook the fact that traditional microeconomic theory, as well as empirical studies, show that oligopalistic and monopalistic firms have higher profits than small firms which are assumed to be in a situation of pure and perfect competition.

Why do oligopolies pay higher wages?
Our conception of imperfect competition can be summed up as follows: the oligopolistic firm originally invested a great deal to transform its labor force, and also other areas, such as capital accumulation or marketing, areas with which we are not directly concerned here. These are the principal determinants of the position of such firms on the goods market. To maintain its dominant position, the oligopoly must maintain its lead notably in matters of managing manpower. This is why the firm pays high wages to control the turnover of its employees, that is to have a return on its investments in job training.

However, an additional explanation of the increasing relation between profit and wages must be envisaged.

We must incorporate "Behavioral" models (Jenny and Weber (89)) into our analysis. Under this heading come a rather large number of proposals which try to explain why the high profits of oligopolies go to the capital holders, but also, in part, to the wage-earners, when, on this last point, microeconomic theory predicts the reverse.

Weiss (168) thinks, that when a firm has a high rate of profit, Unions realize their demands more easily. Other authors, such as Tobin (162), underline the inflationist behavior of oligopolies. Indeed, an increase in the productivity of labor can be followed either by a decrease in prices or by a rise in wages. If the goods market is non-competitive and the Unions are active, the second possibility is realized.

Nevertheless, it is certain that the increase in the wage differentials is not a never-ending process.

The internal market is never totally cut off from the outside and the oligopoly can recruit on this, when Union pressure is too strong, for example. Naturally, in so doing, the firm must bear an additional cost of hiring and training the new labor force. Its choice is guided by the aim of minimizing the average cost of its labor force.

Thus we can explain the heterogeneity of the wage structures in the mixed regulation, where the role of the State in matters of wages is limited, in part, by the power of the large firms, which are very unevenly distributed in different economic sectors. What is the situation in the STS where the role of the State is decidedly different in matters of fixing wages as well as in matters of prices?

2 Wage structures and oligopoles in the Soviet-type system

We would like to defend the idea that in the STE there is a heterogeneous structure of production which allows large firms to exercise considerable power over the Administration, notably regarding wages. In addition, the Administration seeks to maintain the control of the evolution of wages at the macroeconomic level, rather than trying to halt initiatives at the level of firms.

In an article entitled: "The oligopoly in planning," Lavigne (104) approaches the issue of the nature and the role of big firms in the STE.

Having covered the bases that underlie the analysis of firms in optimal planning, which are very close to a neoclassical micro-economy, she looks at the real behavior of firms faced with the planning center. These always adopt a strategy which consists of dissimulating part of the information they possess, for example concerning their production capacities. The result is bargaining between the firm and the planning center.

Within the context of this bargaining, firms are not equal given the kind of market they operate in or their size. However, the experience of Hungarian reform of 1968 shows that the search for a certain "decentralization" of economic mechanisms was carried out to the detriment of the powers of the Administration, but to the profit of big firms reinforcing the oligopolistic nature of Soviet type "markets."

There are two sources of oligopolistic markets. First of all, the high industrial concentration is inherited from the model of development which was followed just after Soviet-type Socialism was instituted. Next, in a number of markets, there are "shortages" which give suppliers power over consumers.

Although Lavigne does not supply these examples, one might also argue that the decentralization of the year 1973 in Poland was carried out for the benefit of the WOG (Big economic organiz-ations), and in the GDR the creation of the VVB (Unions of firms of the people) coincided with the reform of 1973.

In all cases, attempts to decentralize consisted in fact in taking certain prerogatives away from Ministries which controlled firms, and in giving them to firms. This strengthened the power of industrial conglomerates.

These large firms are an essential element in the economic system. They can influence the level of prices even though these are controlled by the Administration (Seurot (151), pp. 171–8).

In the aforementioned case of bargaining, firms may ask for financial advantages or supplementary deliveries, in order to realize a plan which they deemed too tight. If firms are able to increase the level of their production or of certain indicators of success such as profit, this could influence bonuses. But the inverse relation seems to be the more often verified. Certain firms try to obtain wage increases from the Administration in order to incite employees to reach the objectives of the plan.

If the power of oligopolies in the Administrative regulation of wages is important, it must not be overestimated. The results of the short-term analysis showed a strong correlation between the fluctuations in sector wages (Redor (141), pp. 174 ff.). In addition, it is certain that the role of "priority sectors" the importance of which has been previously discussed are themselves a product of the Administration. The latter, at the outset of the STS had an economic objective: to lay the foundations for a certain type of development. It sought also to improve the situation for the working classes who bore the most difficult working conditions.

Finally, despite two means of wage regulation where the State intervenes in very different ways in the STS and the WS, the role of sectors and large firms appears to be important in both systems. The structures of production are not fundamentally different. They are based on a high concentration of the means of production in "active units" which structure their economic and social environment and notably segment their demand for labor.

Their power is felt in the creation of channels, which are obstacles to the mobility of the labor force, and which are the origin of segregation in the employment of certain categories of workers.

3 The basis of wage isomorphisms in the two systems

These analyses explain the wage isomorphisms in the two systems. Indeed, wage management in the WS and the STS has the following features:

1 The wage policy consists in minimizing the cost of the labor force

for a given level of employment, given the costs of hiring, training, and disorganization which uncontrolled turnover of the labor force may bring about.

2 In both systems, oligopolies pay relatively high wages as they are in a position to modify the economic environment to their advantage.

3 The internal structuring of wages by firms in the East and in the West serves to explain the important dispersion of wages for the same category of wage-earners between firms, the increasing relation between the wage rate, on the one hand, and the per capita captial stock as well as the concentration of firms, on the other hand.

Our analysis lacks one dimension, that is, beyond the structures and rules of firm management, the study of the organization and of the division of labor. Indeed, the question must be raised as to the possible relationships between the organization of power and jobs on the one hand, and the pay structure on the other. In the pages that follow, we will pay close attention to the relationships between manual and non-manual workers whose relative pay we know to be different in the two systems.

CHAPTER 8

Pay and the division of labor between manual and non-manual workers

The transformation of the labor force by firms, which has just been described, is tightly linked to the initial system of formal education. One can present the hypothesis that, at the national level, as at the firm level, this transformation is all the greater when the initial education is not adapted to the quantitative and qualitative needs of firms in terms of labor.

If the costs of the transformation of the labor force, which have to complete and compensate for the initial system of education, are high, the wage policy of firms tends to privilege seniority and in-house training and experience. In addition, the division of labor is strictly between those, relatively few, who have acquired the training which satisfies the needs of the firm and the remaining employees.

On the contrary, if the initial formal education (including vocational and technical training) is closely linked to the needs of firms, the latter base the wage structure on the diploma of each wage-earner. Seniority plays much less of a role in determining the internal wage rate in such a schema. The organization of labor is much less rigid due to the uniform education acquired in the school system.

According to the comparative studies of Maurice, Sellier, and Silvestre (123), France follows the first model rather closely, while the FRG follows the second. These authors place the interdependence between the determination of wages, the organization of labor, and the structure of the system of professional training at the core of their analysis.

To undertake an exhaustive study of the systems of professional training in the WE and the STE and the relationship between these and the wage structures would bring us well beyond the scope of this study. Nevertheless, a collection of elements on this subject are summarized in the following: Gaszo (81), Gruson and

Markiewicz (84), Tanguy and Kieffer (160), Redor (141), chapters 2 and 3).

First of all, within the STS, as in the WS, the educational and training systems are rather heterogeneous. Vocational training is very highly developed compared to general education in the GDR, Czechoslovakia, and the USSR, and it is less so in Hungary where the system is comparable to that of France.

In the STE as a whole, the principal factor behind professional promotion is a diploma, be it from general or vocational training. In countries where vocational training is powerful (Czechoslovakia, the GDR), it is the steppingstone to highly qualified jobs. On the contrary, in countries where technical education is little developed (Hungary), degrees in general education provide the most easy access to highly qualified jobs in firms, including managerial positions.

If it were necessary to draw a parallel between the formal education systems in the two, we would be inclined to say that it is a factor determining the place held by workers in the division of labor, and professional promotion as well. At this level of generality, one cannot help but note the analogy between the promotion channels in the WE and the STE which is linked to the segmentation of employment. In both cases, formal education is an element which serves to delimit channels of mobility. These channels are those from manual jobs to non-manual ones, which was not necessarily expected, given the low differentiation in wages between manual and non-manual workers in the STS.

The logic of our theoretical approach is that, in both systems, formal education is the means by which firms select or filter personnel to be promoted. It is not simply a question of detecting those persons who will be the most productive. It is above all a question of recruiting and promoting those who will fit in the best, the fastest, in the internal organization of labor, that is to say eventually in the process of production, but also in the hierarchy, in the relation of competition and cooperation within a team, a workshop, a department.

It must be noted that taking into account the system of formal education does not make it possible to explain certain particularities in the wage structures of the STE. The high disperson of pay of manual workers cannot be explained by the disperson of the formal education of workers. The latter varies from country to country whereas the former is high in all the STE.

In addition, even if the level of formal education among workers is high in certain STE given the particular role of technical education, this alone cannot explain the small differential between the pay of manual and non-manual workers. We must look for other explanations. It is for this purpose that we will study the features of the organization of labor and power, as well as the forms of pay in the WE and the STE.

I FORMS AND DISPERSON OF WORKERS' PAY

We will argue that the form of wages should be linked, in the STS, to a specific type of organization of labor. In addition, payment by results, which remains common for workers, is the principal factor behind the important pay disperson.

1 A comparison of the forms of pay systems in the STS and in the WS

The system of payment by results is much more common in the STE than in the WE (table 8.1). In fact, the piece wage system is predominant in the former. In the industries in the WE, payment by results is rare in France (11.8 percent of workers are paid by results) and in Belgium (5.4 percent). However, it holds a significant place in Denmark (18.2 percent) and above all in the FRG (22.3 percent). In the STE, this rate is about 50 percent. This percentage is all the higher given that for certain jobs it is difficult, because of the nature of the work itself, to fix a piece wage system. This is true of jobs in maintenance and cleaning. If we look at the distribution of the wage systems by sector in the four WE cited, it apears that payment by results is most common in certain consumer industries (textiles, garments, shoes), in mining, in machine manufacturing, as well as in automobiles and aeronautics. Conversely, it is practically non-existant in oil refineries and the chemical and electronics industries.

This distribution confirms that, for the WE, payment by results is linked to a Taylorian organization of labor. On the contrary, in highly developed sectors, which are heavily automated, only an

Table 8.1. *Pay systems of manual workers in industry (as a % of the total)*

Country	Wage calculated on a time basis exclusively	Wage calculated on a time basis with regular bonus paid on a collective basis	Task wage with a guaranteed minimum and bonuses	Piece wage exclusively	Two or several systems during the period
Belgium (1978)	82.9	11.5	4.6	0.8	0.2
Denmark (1978)	51.6	12.7	8.3	9.9	17.4
France (1978)	70.3	13.6	10.3	1.5	4.3
FRG (1978)	74.8		22.3		
Hungary (1977	60.0		40.0		
Poland (1979)	51.0		12.1		
GDR (1977)	4.2	43.1	30.0	22.7	
USSR (1977)	1.3	42.4	44.2	12.1	

Sources: Belgium (3), table T109; Denmark (4), table T109; France (5), table T109;
FRG (13), pp. 6 and 29; Hungary, Poland, GDR, USSR: Leistungslohn in
West und Soteuropa (100) pp. 103–5 (106).

hourly wage is paid. The work paces imposed on workers are such
that the notion of individual production is meaningless. It is indeed
that evolution in the United States that Aglietta (28) described: "the
inability of workers to influence work pace destroys the individual
link between wage control and work production."

However, in most of the STE, payment by results plays an
important role in most sectors of industry.

The piecework wage system is based, first of all, on the definition
of norms. More precisely, they concern the time allotted to produce one piece, or to accomplish one task, for a given job. These
norms are determined according to a system of timing and of
analysis of gestures, which are the same in the West. This is
essential for our subject. The division of labor is clear between
those in charge of the "methods bureau," who design the organization of labor and decide how time is to be broken down, and the
workers.

But what is particular to the STE is that these norms are not all set
up by firms. The administration controls their level and evolution.
Indeed, the Administration maintains control over the wage fund,
and, in certain countries, tries to limit the volume of employment of
each firm. The control of the labor norms is designed to check a rise
in the wage fund, and to determine whether firms have too many

employees. It must be noted that State intervention in this area varies; in Hungary for example, there is little.

Finally, the extent of the piece wage system in the STE, makes it possible, in our opinion, to establish a link between the forms of organization of labor and pay dispersion of manual workers, which is particularly high in these economies (see above: chapter 3).

2 The organization of labor and the pay dispersion of workers

The reasons for the extension of payment by results in the STE
It remains to be known why, above and beyond official texts, the system of payment by results prevails in the STE, and to determine the consequences for pay dispersion.

First of all, there is a relation between Soviet type Taylorism and of pay system. The particularities of this type of organization of labor, which cannot be interpreted outside its socio-economic environment, have sometimes been referred to as "altered Taylorism" or "arythmical Taylorism" (Lowit (110) and Urgense (164)).

For our purpose, it suffices to consider that it is based on the same principles as those in the West. Coriat's definition of Taylorism ((62), pp. 337–9) can well be applied to the STE. Taylorism implies the separation of the conception and the execution of labor, and the breaking down of both management and execution tasks. Putting these principles in practice leads to a system of allotted times. These are based on the precise study of the movements needed to accomplish production tasks and used to control individual productivity, measured with time norms.

However, in the West, the original Taylorism was highly modified by the introduction of Fordism, that is to say by the arrival of integrated assembly lines and conveyor belts. Consequently allotted norms have been replaced by paces imposed by automated production processes. At the same time, job interdependence increases and the individual nature of work decreases.

Finally, the automation of production processes and the use of microelectronics on a large scale in the WE have moved workers' tasks toward the control and the regulation of the functioning of automated machinery. In all cases, firm efficiency depends on the technical performances of the production processes, and human intervention must be adapted to their pace.

The pay systems that correspond to this type of activity are hourly rates, associated with bonuses, usually collective, according to the global results of the team, workshop, factory, or firm. This tendency makes it possible to explain the slow, but steady decrease in the piece wage system in the WE for the period covering the years 1960–80.

How can one explain, from this perspective, the persistence of Taylorism in the STE and of its attribute, the piece wage system?

First of all, it is a result of the technological lag in the STE. The development of assembly lines with conveyor belts, and more importantly of automated production processes, is only just beginning, even in the most advanced countries. In addition, the paucity of interindustry exchanges obliges many firms to make their own replacement parts, or intermediate products, necessary to their production, and which they cannot get from other firms. Even if some products are made in a Ford like series, one finds within a given firm many auxilliary activities using rudimentary technologies.

But another factor explains the extent of the piece wage system in the STE. It does in fact introduce an element of flexibility into the organization of the internal labor market of firms. The flexibility makes it possible to balance out in part the administrative regulation of wages.

By manipulating the production norms, firms are in a position to modulate workers' pay according to the place that the former occupy in the production process, and more globally, in the internal market of the firm. This also allows firms to fix pay according to the specific cost of labor force turnover, and in so doing, to protect themselves, in a certain sense, against the effects of shortages.

In this way evidence is provided in support of the idea that the administrative regulation of wages brings with it global constraints on the wage bill of firms, but that they nevertheless have great internal autonomy. The planning center accepts this flexibility even if it can lead to dysfunctionings in the intersector distribution of the labor force and between firms.

From this point of view, periods when piece wage systems develop can be interpreted as experience of "decentralization" of the managing of pay at the firm level. On the contrary, when the piece wage system is very commonly practiced and the differentials between firms marked, the planning center limits the conditions where this wage system can be applied and lowers the percentage of individual bonuses which are added to the basic wage. In this way, the wage "reform" of 1958–60 in the USSR was interpreted as a recentralization of pay planning (Kirsch (97), pp. 23–5).

The origin of the great dispersion of workers' pays in the STS
These analyses have a very important consequence for the interpretation of one of our principal statistical results. Indeed, the pattern of labor organization which prevails in the STE, as well as the pay systems, are powerful factors behind wage differentiation. They explain why the pay dispersion among manual workers is significantly higher in the STS than in the WS.

This phenomenon illustrates the principle "to each according to his work." This principle leads logically to differentiation in pay of manual workers, based on performances which vary considerably from one firm or sector to the other.

On the contrary, in the WS, the less individual nature of pay, influenced by new forms of labor organization, limit the range of workers' pay. One can also argue that pay based on a piece wage system follows the heterogeniety in the systems of production, that is to say that the unequal allocation of production goods in firms. It is also linked to the relation of the firms directors with the planning authorities and to the power of the former to negotiate the annual amount of their wage fund. The study of the intersector differentials in wages solidly backs this view. In addition, pay differentials between firms are also the result of the social and political preferences of the planning center which operate through the institutional framework of administrative regulation.

Among the particularities of the wage structures in the STE, our statistical analysis brought out the minimal difference in the pay of manual and non-manual workers. This phenomenon, which we are about to study, is also linked to the socio-political structure of the STE.

2 MANUAL WORKERS' AND NON-MANUAL WORKERS' WAGES

1 The paradox of Soviet-type economies

First of all, it has been shown that the organization of labor in firms in the STS is very fragmented. This division is the origin of the important dispersion of the pay of manual workers. In addition, for the category non-manual workers, this dispersion is of the same level as in the WE. Within each category, there is a strict division between tasks (managing and execution tasks), and this is reflected in the differentiation in pay.

The paradox comes from the fact that, on average, the wages of manual workers are very close to those of non-manual workers. Indeed, manual workers occupy a position in the social division of labor which is not very different from that of their Western counterparts. Still their position in the global structure of pay is much more favorable.

It is not possible to explain this paradox by referring to the system of pay of manual workers, founded for the most part on individual criteria. Indeed, one could easily imagine an important differential between the pay of manual and non-manual workers as going together with payment by results for the former.

It can be argued (see the beginning of this chapter) that the education system, especially in the technical field, is an important factor behind professional mobility, which brings together the levels of formal education and training of the manual and non-manual workers in the STS. Is it possible to say that this system is responsible for the small differentials between these two categories? We think not.

The comparison with the FRG may elucidate our answer. Indeed, in this country, where the system of formal education provides workers with a high level of technical training and great possibilities of promotion to non-manual jobs, the pay differential between the two categories of workers is much higher than in the STE. The parallel with the FRG (wages for non-manual workers is 135 if the manual workers is 100) and the GRD (105 for 100) shows that above and beyond historical affinities, cultures, and an education system, there is a systemic difference on this point.

To sum up, Soviet-type regimes did not revolutionize task hierarchies and the social division of labor between manual and non-manual workers. The important change that came about in pay relative to these two categories of workers since the origin of the STS is such that we are obliged to focus our analysis on another area of the social system: the socio-political relations which dominate in this system.

2 The role of socio-political transformations

The valorization of manual labor in the STE

The slight difference observed between the wages of manual and non-manual workers in the STE, is a result, first of all, of the political options chosen by the leaders in these countries.

The constitution of the USSR (1977) stipulates in article 19: "the State contributes to reinforcing the social homogeneity of Society, to abolishing class differences, essential differences which exist between the country and the city, between intellectual and manual labor" (Lavigne (105), p. 561).

The "leading function of the working class" is often evoked. According to this conception, the working class is at the head of Soviet society. This is explained, first of all, by the position it occupies in the economic system. Workers have a predominant social role because they work in industry, which, unlike agriculture, is almost totally State controled. Workers epitomize, therefore, a society in which all private ownership of the means of production will have disappeared (Kniazeff (98), p. 561).

Of course, these are declarations of principles. In reality, a strong division of labor between manual workers and managers has been shown to exist. Our analysis and reflection have shown that the position of workers in the social division of labor is not fundamentally different in the STS from the WS. It must be added that a number of sociological studies carried out in Poland and Hungary conclude that the socio-cultural status of manual workers remains very different from that of managers, as do the school achievements of children from working class backgrounds.[1]

In the area of wages, however, political leaders have in fact improved the position of manual workers. Our statistical analyses prove this beyond a doubt. One could think, however, that the leveling of wages between manual and non-manual workers contradicts this, maintaining of a net division between high and low positions in the firm's hierarchy. But one must consider that this hierarchy is preserved as the pay of managers higher than that of

---

[1] Among the numerous works published in Hungary and Poland on this subject, we can cite: Andorka and Zagorski (32), Gazso (81), pp. 378–81, as well as an entire work devoted to Stratification and Inequality, edited by Andorka and Kolosi (31); in French, one can consult the contributions of Strmiska (156) and Markiewicz (118).

workers. It is in fact the category of unskilled white-collar workers who are paid relatively little. This fact is confirmed by a comparative study carried out on a representative sample of workers in industry in the GDR, Czechoslovakia, Poland, Hungary, and Bulgaria (Askentievics (29), pp. 405–49).

There are also more strictly economic reasons which explain the high wages of manual workers.

First of all, working conditions are almost always systematically taken into account in designing wage scales. It is not unlikely that the high wages in priority sectors are paid partly because of the working conditions in the mining and metal processing industries which are particularly arduous.

In addition, the distinction between productive and non-productive workers may have favored workers in a system which claims to be Marxist. It should be pointed out, however, that, following Marx, in a Capitalist society or any society where there is an extensive division of labor, the notion of the productive worker does not only concern he who works directly in production: "To be productive, it is not necessary for one to be a laborer; it suffices that one be a member of collective labor or that one occupy any function in the latter" (Marx (121), vol. II, p. 183).

If productive labor "fecundates capital," it is because productive labor is the source of surplus-value; the former has the particular property of being able to create new value.

Indeed on this point, the Marxist analysis of the Capitalist system was transposed to the Soviet-type Socialist system. It must be remembered that the concept of national product, for example, only concerns the "material sphere" which is assimilated, with a certain ambiguity, to the sphere of productive labor. The dominant conception is that only productive labor is the source of economic surplus which makes the accumulation of technical capital and the development of services, notably collective ones, possible.

The depreciation of service activities in the STE

It is significant, in this respect, that in the service sectors, which have the reputation of being non-productive, wages are relatively low in the STE (table 8.2). This is especially true of Poland and the USSR.

Finally, even if, in theory, manual workers' labor is not to be assimilated with productive labor, many statistical classifications and research studies assimilate productive employees and "persons

Table 8.2. *Average earnings in some service sectors compared to industry (index 100)*

Branch	Trade	Education	Health	Banking and financial institutions
France (1978)	99.0	105.0	95.6	117.7
FRG (1978)	85.8	n.a.	n.a.	105.5
UK (1980)	80.8	110.4	86.8	99.4
Hungary (1980)	87.9	n.a.	96.5	n.a.
Poland (1980)	76.3	78.7	76.3	77.6
Czechoslovakia (1980)	—	92.8	93.2	93.8
USSR (1980)	74.5	73.3	68.4	87.5

Note: n.a. = not available
Sources: France: OSCE (5), pp. 30, 168, 308, 382
　　　　FRG: Statistiches Bundesamt (13), volume 1, pp. 90 & 732, vol. 2, pp. 58, 117, 121, 123
　　　　UK: Statistical Office (18), part C, table 54
　　　　Hungary: Statistical Office (20), 1981, p. 59
　　　　Poland: Statistical Office (21), 1982, p. 121
　　　　Czechoslovakia: Statistical Office (23), 1982, p. 213
　　　　USSR: Central Department for Statistics (24), 1980, pp. 364–5

working directly in production." It is noteworthy, from this perspective, that the abundant literature on poor incentives or mobilization at work concerns manual workers almost exclusively. This is also the case for reflections on the forms of pay which are supposed to provide incentives. The prevailing notion is that economic growth depends above all on the efforts of those who work directly in production, a notion which, it must be pointed out, goes along with that of "the leading role of the working class."

Economic conceptions converge with political objectives here. For all these reasons, the political power, through the administrative regulation of wages, raised the level of wages of manual workers as opposed to non-manual.

The situation is entirely different in the WS. First of all, these countries have not experienced social upheaval which has modified the relations between social classes as in the STE. From this perspective, the wage differentials between manual and non-manual workers which exist in France for example, can be taken as the fruition of a long evolution which goes back to the beginning of Capitalism.

Thus there appears a systemic difference between the wages of manual and non-manual workers. This is based on the socio-political choices of each system, and beyond that on the social structures thereof.

The question must be raised as to whether or not we have explored totally the area of systemic differences. Indeed, the study, notably the statistical one, which we carried out concerned pay in the strict sense of the term: we only took into account monetary earnings linked to the primary activity of each individual.

It is necessary to study, from this perspective, how our judgment on pay dispersion and on the factors that influence it in the two systems changes if we take into account benefits in kind and income from secondary (legal or illegal) activities: such factors influence the behavior of workers and notably their incentive to work.

CHAPTER 9

The dispersion of disposable incomes of households in the two systems

Up until now, we have focused our attention on monetary earnings in the strict sense. This is to say the direct pay of wage-earners which corresponds to their principal employment.

In so doing, we have followed the example of most theoreticians of the West and the East, who separate professional activities, and distinguish wages from other forms of income and deductions which are indirectly linked to work. Among the latter, we might list benefits in kind, social transfers, and taxes.

Such an approach is necessary. It is in fact logical to begin by circumscribing the area of study of official wages so as to better dissect and explain the structures thereof, and, secondly, to open up the analysis of indirect and unofficial pay.

In addition, pay, such as we have defined it, constitutes the largest part of direct and indirect labor income after taxes in both systems.[1] Numerous studies of the WS have shown that taxes and social transfers have a relatively small impact on the earnings dispersions of individuals.

Nevertheless, in an intersystemic comparison, we cannot be content with these results alone. Indeed, we might maintain, at least hypothetically, that certain characteristics of the STS, for example the important number of secondary jobs, benefits in kind, low income tax rates, weaken the analysis that we carried out on the dispersion of income from work, and, beyond that, on the determinants of the supply of labor.

The activities that each individual may have outside his principal job modify the quantity and the quality of his work. Therefore, income from secondary jobs legal or illegal (moonlighting) cannot be left aside.

[1] For a comparative approach to this problem, see our data (Redor (141)) in the appendix, pp. 2 to 21 on the components of the "social wage cost."

In addition, unemployment, and the decrease in income which results, strongly influences the behavior of workers. At the same time it introduces a new dimension to the analysis of the income dispersion of the active population. One has every reason to think that unemployment has a different impact on this dispersion in the two systems.

Our study will be based on the following two points:

1 We will estimate the influence of secondary activities and benefits in kind on wage dispersion in the STS. We will seek to determine whether the importance thereof demands that we reconsider our judgment of pay dispersion in the STS as opposed to the WS.

2 We will analyze the indicators of the dispersion and the concentration of the disposable incomes of households after taxes. The indicators are the products of numerous factors not all of which can be individualized. However, we will link the earnings dispersion initially conceived, to that of the disposable income. The scope and the validity of the results of the first part of this volume will thus be specified.

I PAY FROM SECONDARY ACTIVITIES AND BENEFITS IN KIND

1 The area of secondary activities

We will turn our attention first to the STS. We will seek to incorporate into our analysis forms of activity, and therefore income, that have no direct equivalent in the WS. At the end of this section, we will show how, compared to our previous analyses, taking them into account brings together or widens the distance between the structure of pay in the two systems.

A group of very diverse activities and sources of income in the STS
First of all, the secondary economy is made up of a group of activities which are outside the "Socialist sphere." The latter refers to the State operated firms and cooperatives which are controlled directly by the planning center. The secondary economy, therefore, refers to those private activities which subsist within the STE.

But the content and the status of secondary activities vary considerably from country to country. These include legal activities in agriculture (the farming of individual plots) or in small firms, especially commercial, trade or building activities. But this also covers illegal activities. These are close to the "black economy" in the WS. Such activities are outside all fiscal control, or concern the selling of stolen goods or goods which are normally prohibited in an official market such as alcohol. In this case we will speak of parallel activities. These are a sub-category of secondary activities.

Generally, secondary activities flourish in areas where the State activities are most lacking. These include the production or the commercialization of goods and services for which there are major shortages. Jobs therein are particularly numerous in construction and related services, health, auto repairs, etc.

Rules for fixing pay for this kind of activity escape all State control. Individuals who have specialities which are lacking in the State sectors are paid very highly compared to the average official wage.

Indeed, complements to pay that individuals earn, outside what is officially registered in statistics, are numerous and varied. For reasons of clarity, we propose to group them into three categories:

1 First of all there is that coming from a second job in the private economy. In the STE, second jobs are very common. In addition to their jobs in the State sector, wage-earners find a complement to their incomes by working in the secondary economy, legally or illegally.

This phenomenon is the direct result of the shortage of labor which is rampant in the STE. Given this shortage, private activities can only develop by employing wage-earners from the State sector on a part-time basis. Kornai (101) underlines the importance of secondary jobs and the interactions that these create between the two economies. For example, if pay in the State sector decreases or stagnates, workers then devote a major part of their time to the secondary economy (Galasi (79), pp. 179–80).

2 Furthermore, certain individuals receive additional pay, which does not figure in the official statistics, and which is paid by their principal employer, firm, or State administration. These are benefits in kind to the leaders of the administration, of the Economy, or of political circles. These benefits are numerous and particularly interesting in so far as they often concern goods that are in short supply.

For example, these leaders may have free access, or cut rates, on housing and cars. They may also have access to special stores where fine quality goods are sold at lower prices.

3 These benefits in kind which are not made public, are nevertheless paid by the employer. They must be distinguished from side benefits which certain wage-earners get from their jobs. The corresponding income is anything from tips to corruption.

For example, it is not uncommon for employees in State-run shops to resell subsidized goods at high prices. In the same manner, health workers or doctors may receive "gifts" from patients to shorten the delays or for special treatments. This practice is all the more common given that doctors are poorly paid. The personnel of State service firms – maintenance and housing repairs, car repairs – are also in a favorable position for exploiting shortages.

Some intersystemic comparisons of the income from secondary activities
It is interesting to compare this typology of secondary and side income in the STS with that of the WS.

1 Doubtless the individuals that have activities outside the official sector in the WS are very different from the people in the secondary economy in the STS. In the former, side jobs are held essentially by the unemployed. The wages from these activities are lower than those of the official labor market, but constitute nevertheless a subsistence income for those who are unable to find another job. Thus the analysis is the opposite of that which we have just carried out for the STS.

2 Benefits in kind linked to certain administrative functions, economic or political, are also important in the West. However, they have less of an impact on high incomes than in the STS.

The main reason is that, in the STS, shortages of consumer durables and non-durables make befits in kind very attractive and hence the price (theoretical) that economic agents are ready to pay for them.

3 Finally what about side income (bribes ...) earned within an official job? Here again, it is most likely that these are higher in the STS than in the WS. In the latter the limited extent of shortages means that few individuals are in a position to monopolize the production or the distribution of certain goods and services. It is significant that side benefits are usually paid to people in very

particular positions in the Administration: those, for example, who have the power to allot public contracts.

This overview suggests that the secondary incomes of working people are higher in the STS than in the WS. The theoretical basis of this difference is clear. In the STS, administrative regulation of the economy pushes into the unofficial sphere a very important number of activities which in the WS are part of the "market economy." In the WS, the area of the unofficial economy covers only the production or the commercialization of illegal goods (drugs, arms, etc.) or activities which violate labor laws.

It is significant that in the STS, among secondary activities, private illicit activities must be distinguished from licit ones. The former include a much wider area than the side economy in the WS, given the Administrative regulation of the economy which prohibits many activities which are legal in the WS. As for the latter, they are part of the market relations in the mixed economies of the WS.

It has often been said, and rightly so, that secondary activities constitute an element of flexibility which is necessary to the STE. It must also be pointed out that certain economic reforms, especially the Hungarian reform, were designed primarily to incorporate certain secondary activities into the official economy, by ascribing a judicial status thereto (Galasi (79), p. 171).

We must examine one last fundamental point. Does the high level of unofficial income of workers in the STS modify significantly our analysis of the global dispersion of pay? Within the pay scale, is the relative position occupied by different categories of workers modified?

We will now attend to the analysis of the income of parallel (illegal) activities. In the next section the other elements of the income of households will be brought up.

2 *The influence of incomes from parallel activities*

The great difficulty is that in the East, like in the West, there are no official statistics concerning parallel incomes. Those who profit therefrom are reluctant to provide information about activities which for the most part, are not taxed.

In a study Duchêne ((70), pp. 77–82) tries to spot the parallel economy and the inequalities of incomes the categories of wage-earners profiting from parallel incomes in the distribution of official pay that we studied in the preceding chapters. He points out that these categories are in fact dispersed evenly throughout.

Consequently, the hypothesis is put forward that taking into account unofficial incomes in the STE does not change significantly the general dispersion of pay. However, it modifies the relative position of certain categories of wage-earners who are able to profit from the parallel economy.

From this point of view, the study of Ofer and Vinokur (130) is of particular interest. They analyzed in detail the individual official and unofficial incomes of a sample of the Soviet population. This sample is made up of Soviets who left the USSR to settle in the West in 1974 and 1975. According to the estimates of Ofer and Vinokur, it is representative of the urban population of the European part of the USSR.

For the active population studied, the Gini coefficient corresponding to the official pay is 0.239. For all incomes, including unofficial ones, it is 0.251. The increase in the dispersion taking into account the parallel economy is very low. This study confirms that the corresponding incomes concern mostly the two extremes of the distribution. All the upper percentiles increase, as do the lowest ones. It appears that the impact of parallel incomes is felt slightly more in the lower percentiles. Taking them into account lowers the ratio of the upper vintile to the lower vintile from 5.4 to 5.1.

The conclusions of this quantitative research, which are of course to be confirmed using other samples and referring to other STE, join the remarks made at the beginning of this section. Taking the parallel incomes into account only increases slightly the pay dispersion. The main reason is that these incomes constitute an important input for the wage-earners at the bottom of the distribution. Nevertheless, it modifies the ranking of the different categories of wage-earners.

It is striking that this change brings the income distribution of the STS nearer to that of the WS. Indeed, the sectors and functions that profit the most from parallel incomes in the STS are those which, according to official statistics, are relatively privileged in the WS.

These include first of all the upper administrative, economic, and political leaders of the STS. It has been shown that they profit from considerable benefits in kind. This reinforces their position relative to their Western counterparts, whereas their official pay is, at least in certain countries, lower if in each system it is compared to the average wage.

At the bottom of the pay distribution in the STS, the wage-earners of certain services come close, within the distribution of total income, to the position of the same wage-earners in the WS. This is true of employees in trade if we take into account their parallel pay. It is even possible that their position is superior to that of the West if we refer to the intersector analysis of official earnings (chapter 6, section 4.1). It is also noteworthy that doctors who occupy a very inferior position relative to their Western counterparts, come much closer thereto if their parallel pay is integrated into the analysis.

We will now undertake a global approach, taking taxation into account. It will enable us to attempt a comparative summary of the elements which constitute the disposable income in the two systems.

2 THE DISPERSION OF DISPOSABLE INCOME

"Disposable income of households," usually refers to primary incomes (before redistribution) to which must be added social transfers in cash and from which must be subtracted direct taxes and social insurance contributions. To understand the dispersion in the WS and in the STS, we will present certain results obtained by Morrisson ((125) and (126)). This author uses surveys on household incomes published in the WE and in most of the STE. In addition, he has tried to correct the data for the STE using a hypothetical calculation of the benefits in kind of executive-directors which are not mentioned in official surveys.

1 The elements which make up the disposable income of households in both systems

In part 1, we studied in depth the structure of official pay and its dispersion in the two systems. The present analysis is based on these results and seeks to place the dispersion of disposable income of households relative to that of pay. We will then present the statistical results of Morrisson.

First of all, taking into account households rather than individuals

Table 9.1 *Ratio between the average amount of social benefits perceived by wage-earners and the average wage (in %)*

France (1981)	FRG (1981)	UK (1981)	Hungary (1981)	Poland (1981)	GDR (1981)
31.5	36.2	24.5	18.5	16.9	17.6

Sources: D. Redor (141)
Documents in annex; tables 1B, 1D, 1F, 1I, 1L, 1N

increases the income dispersion: the average number of persons per household increases with income. This is true for both the STE and the WE; however, it must be pointed out that in so far as the distribution of households by size varies from one country to another, a bias is introduced into the comparison.

Let us look at the way the elements that make it possible to go from the pay distribution to the disposable income distribution and let us study the way they influence the dispersion of the latter.

The level of direct taxes in the STS is low compared to the WS. For example, in Hungary and Poland, wage-earners' pay is not taxed. In most of the other countries, the income tax rates are low. This is the case in the USSR where each category of income is taxed separately and where the rates on the taxable brackets never go above 20 percent. It is therefore not surprising that taxation does not have redistribution effects in the STE (McAuley (112), pp. 292–5).

There is therefore an important difference with the WS. Taking into account direct taxes therefore lowers pay disperson in the WS as compared to the STS.

The social benefits paid to wage-earners, that is to say family allowances, health, invalidity, and maternity insurance are, compared to the average wage, higher in the WS than in the STS. This appears to be the case for retirement benefits as well.

However, these average data do not enlighten us as to the redistributive effect of these benefits. Given the similarity of the social insurance systems, we can emit the hypothesis that the effect is proportionate to the volume of benefits perceived. If this hypothesis is confirmed, the volume is greater in the WS and taking social benefits into account lowers the pay dispersion in the WS relative to the STS.[2]

Income from private, legal activities in the STE is taken into account most of the time in surveys on household budgets. For the WS, one must mention income from stocks, shares, and real estate which are very unequally distributed over households. This income has practically no equivalent in the STS. It is certain that the effect thereof is to increase income disperison in the WS relative to that of the STS.

We have shown why benefits in kind of executives and people at the head of the administration, the economy, and politics are higher in the STE than in the WE. In the WS, the price of benefits in kind is easy to estimate; they are declared by firms who grant them and by the individuals who profit from them to the taxation authorities, at least in theory. This is not the case for the STS where there are no official statistics published on this subject. Above all, the price thereof is little known or totally unknown when these benefits in kind include, what is often the case, products or services which are lacking on the official market.

In order to get around this problem, Morrisson ((125), pp. 227–30) provides the following corrections. First of all, he estimates the number of people who receive benefits in kind by virtue of the position they hold in the power hierarchy. He roughly estimates the number as 1.5 percent of the wage-earners at the top end of the distribution scale. Secondly, he estimates the amount of benefits received based on monographic studies carried out in the STE. It appears that these would double the income of the receivers. He does no further correction in order to take into account the other forms of parallel income in the two systems, and notably income from black market and illegal trafficking. Here one might see a bias introduced into the comparison, except if one maintains that the impact of illegal activities on the income dispersion is the same in the two systems. At the present time, we are not in a position to know if this condition is met.

Finally, the author presents two series of indicators of the disper-

---

[2] Kende ((94), pp. 108–22) defends this point of view using precise, statistical data concerning Hungary, Poland, and Czechoslovakia.

sion of income of households in the STE. The first series uses official statistics, the second corrects the official statistics by taking into account the benefits in kind of the elite of the STS, using the aforementioned corrections.

The last element which differentiates the distribution of disposable income for households and that of pay and which must be included in our study, is non-working adults, either unemployed or inactive for different reasons (homemakers, retired).[3]

The levels of activity are considerably higher in the STS than in the WS. This is an additional element which increases the dispersion of the income of households in the WS relative to the STS. Indeed, if there is little difference between households in the rate of activity in the STS, this difference is significant in the WS.

The very high number of unemployed in the WE compared to the STE also has an impact on income dispersion. In the WS, unemployment benefits decrease the loss of wage income. Nevertheless, unemployment is a powerful source of differentiation when it touches more than 10 percent of the active population, and when its average duration is over one year.

Finally, the different elements considered function in opposite ways and the result of going from the dispersion of pay to the dispersion of disposable income is unpredictable. To determine this result, it would be necessary to know the intensity of each force at work. However, we do not have at our disposal sufficiently detailed data to be able to calculate this intensity. Nevertheless, we can calculate their results. To do so, it is necessary to calculate the dispersion of disposable income for households in the two systems.

2 There is no systemic difference in the dispersion of disposable income for households

The principal results

We will account for the work of Morrisson ((125) and (126)) whose sources and hypotheses we have just outlined. He calculated several indicators of the distribution of disposable income for households for seven WE and seven STE. The Gini coefficient and the Theil coefficient were used. In addition, the income distribution was

---

3   The case of the retired was raised during the study of social insurance benefits.

broken up into ten brackets of equal size, and the income relative to each bracket was divided by the mean.

If benefits in kind are not taken into account in the STE and, if official data are used, the ranking by decreasing order of the concentration of disposable income of households does not allow one to differentiate the WE from the STE. The United Kingdom, for example, is very close to Poland, the USSR and Hungary, and Denmark is close to the GDR.

If we integrate the weight of benefits in kind in the STE into the analysis, according to the hypotheses outlined previously, we obtain the following ranking based on the indicators of Gini and Theil: (1) the United States, (2) France, (3) FRG, (4) USSR, (5) Poland and Hungary, (7) the United Kingdom, (8) and GDR, (9) Denmark, (10) Sweden, (11) Romania and Bulgaria, (13) Czechoslovakia.

This ranking shows that the distribution of disposable income for households is not more egalitarian in the STS than in the WS. In addition, in each system, it is possible to distinguish two categories of countries based on the concentration of disposable incomes. The category with a low concentration of incomes in the WS includes the Scandinavian countries and the United Kingdom, and in the STS, the GDR, Romania, Bulgaria, and Czechoslovakia. Countries with a high concentration of income include the United States, France, and the FRG for the WS, and the USSR, Poland, and Hungary for the STS.

Morrisson considers the different brackets within each income distribution and distinguishes the two systems. The income available to the tenth bracket of households in the distribution (it must not be forgotten that the distribution is broken up into ten classes having an equal number of individuals numbered from one to ten starting from the bottom of the distribution) relative to the mean does not differ significantly in the two systems. This is not the case for the bracket at the bottom of the distribution where the disposable income, relative to the mean, is higher in the STS than in the WS. However, the relative situation of the seventh and eighth classes of the distribution is less favorable in the STS than in the WS.

The author concludes that the two sets of Lorenz curves of the concentration of incomes intersect, and that, as a result, it is not possible to state that the distribution of income is less egalitarian in one system than the other.

The dispersion of pay and the dispersion of income in the two systems
The question arises as to how to situate the results of Morrisson relative to those that we obtained for the dispersion and the concentration of pay.

First of all, there is no systemic difference in the dispersion and the concentration of disposable income of households, as well as in the dispersion of pay. The elements that make it possible to go from the latter notion to the former balance each other out, this is an important result. However, before arriving at any conclusion, we would like to turn once again to the ranking of the countries in our study, based on the dispersion of individual pay or based on disposable income.

In both cases, France and the United States come first. But for income dispersion, the FRG occupies a much higher position than for pay dispersion. The United Kingdom occupies a lower position. For the latter, the weight of income tax must be brought up, as until the beginning of the eighties it was high in the United Kingdom. As for the progression of the FRG relative to certain STE when going from the dispersion of pay to that of income, this could be explained by the inegalitarian character of income from capital and property holdings. In addition, within the WS, the weight of direct taxes is less in the FRG than in the United Kingdom or the Scandinavian countries.

Within the STS, Hungary goes up the hierarchy and Czechoslovakia falls behind. It is the country with the lowest dispersion of disposable income of households. It is probable that this change in rank is due to the important development of secondary and private activities in Hungary, which are legal and therefore appear in official statistics. In the group where the dispersion of disposable income is low, these activities are not widespread. However, this in no way makes it possible to state the extent of illegal activities in this group of countries.

Finally, one must ask why the income of the lowest bracket is higher in the STS than in the WS.

There are two possible interpretations. Either social benefits in favor of the poorest classes are more important in the STE than in the WE, or the integration of the population as a whole in our analysis, and in particular of the unemployed, results in lowering the relative income of certain households in the WS.

We think that the second interpretation should be considered. Indeed, it has been shown (table 8.3) that, relative to the average wage, the volume of social benefits was lower in the STE than in the WS. Given that the rules governing these are similar in the two systems, their redistributive power is not greater and might even be lower in the STE. This is why, even though at the present time there is no statistical element to defend this point of view, we are led to uphold the hypothesis that the relatively low income available to households at the bottom of the distribution in the WS can be explained by mass unemployment.

3 What is learned from the comparison of the dispersion of disposable income

The main conclusion is that, if the indicators of concentration and dispersion increase when we go from the notion of individual pay to that of disposable incomes of households, the increase is of the same magnitude in the two systems. Naturally, there are certain rerankings observed within each system. Nevertheless, we verified the absence of a systemic difference in the dispersion and the concentration of disposable income as well as pay.

However, the elements which play a major role in moving from one notion to another are usually different. First of all, we will disregard those that are responsible for a rise in the distribution of disposable income.

For the WE, it is important to bear in mind the role of the income from real estate. However, the fact that the classes at the top of the distribution compared to the mean are not in a more favorable position relative to those of the STE may come as some surprise. We can explain this in two ways. First of all, direct taxation has a leveling effect which does not exist in the STE. It must be pointed out that the WS countries where the pay dispersion is the lowest are also those where taxation is the highest and inversely. This is why the Scandinavian countries are at the bottom of the ranking of pay dispersion as well as of disposable incomes. On the contrary, the United States and France are at the head of both rankings. The FRG is an exception to this rule in so far as it has one of the lowest pay dispersions in the WS, and has a higher rank for the dispersion and the concentration of disposable income.

The second explanation has to do with benefits in kind which, in the STS, add considerably to the income of people at the top of the distribution.

It is tempting to seek a parallel between the income from real estate in the WS and that from benefits in kind of executives in the

STS. In both cases, it is a question of income highly concentrated at the top of the distribution. Even if these incomes have different sources, they are linked, in both cases, to the exercise of economic, or even political power. It is possible to extend the parallel by comparing property rights in the WS, to the rights available to the governing elite in the STS on the State budget. The latter are the sources benefits in kind.

Another element which increases pay dispersion in the WS, and which has no equivalent in the STS, is unemployment. The impact thereof on the bottom of the distribution is clear.

Nevertheless, social benefits influence the distribution of income in the same manner. The redistributive effect of social benefits in cash is important in the STS as Kende (94) has shown for Hungary, Poland, and Czechoslovakia. It is certainly not greater than in the WS. We might add that the share of social benefits in kind (education, health, transport, housing) in the consumption of households differs little between the two systems. In addition, the redistributive power of this kind of benefit, unlike the aforementioned, is very little (Kende (94), pp. 114–19).

The tax system and social benefits are close to the equality criterion. Okun ((132), p. 150) maintains that the tax system and social benefits are the only means of reducing inequalities in the WS. Let it be said that from this point of view taxes which weigh on wage-earners play an ambiguous role. If the structure of pay corresponds to an efficiency criterion, taxing them questions this criterion.

But Okun contests the neo-classical analysis of wages and the fact that individuals are in fact paid at their level of marginal productivity. The purpose of taxes, from this point of view is to remedy the inequalities linked to the imperfections of the wage structure (presence of monopolies, of oligopsonies, etc.).

Social benefits have the same function in both systems: providing individuals at the extreme end or outside the wage-earning population with a means of subsistence. These individuals include the handicapped, invalids, the retired, people unable temporarilly or indefinitely to work.

There remains the question of evaluating all the results that we have uncovered since the beginning of this study. This implies that we interpret the isomorphisms, but also the systemic differences of the first part, and that we place them in the general framework of the socio-economic relations of the two systems.

CHAPTER 10

A tentative synthesis

Following our statistical research, we arrived at some initial conclusions, answering some of the questions raised in our introduction. Now we would like to regroup the statistical and the theoretical results. Indeed, we have come to know the wage structures in the two systems and their determining factors and we are now in a position to evaluate definitively the existence of wage isomorphisms and systemic effects.

I WAGE ISOMORPHISMS AND THE LABOR FORCE IN BOTH SYSTEMS

We will summarize our results in the form of a table. Next we will present wage management in firms and the place and role of the labor force in the two systems as the principal sources of isomorphisms outlined throughout this study.

1 A summary of the principal results

Tables 10.1 and 10.2 summarize the results obtained in all the previous chapters of both parts of this volume. Each table corresponds to a step in the approach described at the beginning of this work.

The first step consists in comparing the elements that constitute each structure. The purpose is to decide if the wage structures of the two economies, one being taken in the WS and the other in the STS, differ significantly (in the statistical sense of this term). If this difference appears for all of the pairs so formed, then there is a systemic difference relative to the parameter studied.

Thus we have given up the idea that the systemic effect has one single impact on wage structures, which would in fact give too great

Table 10.1. *Summary of statistical studies of systemic effects on wages*

Indicator, parameter or characteristic	Significant systemic studied difference
Lognormality of the earnings distribution	No
Total dispersion of earnings	No
Dispersion of earnings of manual workers	Yes
Dispersion of earnings of non-manual workers	No
Difference between earnings of manual and non-manual workers	Yes
Difference in earnings according to level of education and training	No
Impact of the concentration of firms on the dispersion of wages	No
Difference in earnings between men and women	No

Table 10.2. *Summary of the study of the structuring factors of wages*

Factors considered	Are the factors structuring wages qualitatively different in the two systems?
Role of the State and of collective wage bargaining	Yes
Social structures	Yes
Education and training system	No
Structuring role of large firms	No
Division of labor: managers and workers	No
Forms of pay	Yes

an importance to the determining powers of the system. In fact, the systemic effect is multidimensional or, more precisely, to each parameter considered a systemic effect corresponds if the statistical tests disclose a significant difference.

The next step, the study of the factors behind the structuring of wages, relies on another logic entirely. The statistical results serve as a basis for the qualitative analysis of the role of institutions, systems of formal education and training, the division of labor and power in firms, and social relations.

In addition, for an isomorphism, even partial, to exist, not only must the indicator or parameter selected not be significantly different from one system to the next, but also the factor or factors which determine it or them must be the same in both systems.

Tables 10.1 and 10.2 show that the isomorphisms found originate in the wage and labor force management in the firms of both systems, as well as in labor organization.

2 Managing wages and the organization of labor

The analysis of the short-term evolution of wages, the role of the State and of institutions, notably collective wage bargaining, led us to distinguish mixed regulation in the WS on the one hand, and administrative regulation in the STS on the other. Thus firms in the two systems are faced with a number of variables and external constraints which are different.

Nevertheless, by studying the formal education and professional training of wage-earners and the managing of the labor force within the first, we were able to uncover substantial common ground between the two systems.

Wage policy and segmentation of the labor market by firms

Our analysis show that firms structure the internal labor market in the same way in the two systems. More precisely, the same internal variables and constraints determine the morphology of these markets. This depends on the size of firms considered, the methods of organizing labor, the general and specific level of formal education and professional training of the work force employed, and on the cost of turnover.

In both systems, firms seek to minimize the wage cost. They include the cost of sacking, of hiring, and of training, that is to say the cost of manpower turnover. The differences of these costs explain in part the differences in wages, for the same level of formal education and professional training, which exist between firms and sectors.

In the administrative regulation of wages in the STS, the State plays a fundamental role and determines the environment of firms. It does not control the level of employment of each firm, but the average wage that these are authorized to pay. Administrative authorities are very particular about this variable: it is the key to the system of accumulating capital and equilibrium, forever precarious, on the consumer goods market.

Firms attempt to reach, or even to surpass, the production objectives assigned, while keeping the average wage cost of their labor force down to a minimum. The wage cost, like in the WS, includes the cost of turnover of the labor force which is a function of analogous parameters.

The most striking illustration of these analyses concerns the intersector wage structure. We showed that this structure, if we leave aside the mining industry, is isomorphic. This isomorphism comes from the fact that the factors determining sector wages are themselves distributed in the same way in sectors in the two systems. They include the concentration of firms and establishments, the capital stock per worker used, the level of formal education and professional training of manpower, and the percentage of women employed in the sector.

More fundamentally, this reflects the similarity behind the conceptions of the organization of labor and power in firms.

The division of labor and power in firms
The wage distributions, with a few exceptions that we have already explained, can be considered to be lognormal. This result shows that the pattern of wage progression within organizations, and notably firms, is the same. Theoretically this pattern provides incentives: the higher the wages on the pay scale, the greater the absolute differentials between the two levels.

This is one of the reasons why those who are at the top of the wage distribution, and particularly executives, do not appear to be at a disadvantage in the STS as compared to the WS.

This kind of wage differentiation in the two systems goes together with a strict division of labor between managers and directors, on the one hand, and workers or employees on the other. This division is based on an organization of labor which we have called Taylorian, in the most general sense of the word.

We could certainly prove that there is a lag between the evolution of the two, and show that even the most advanced STE are significantly behind their Western counterparts in the conception of labor organization and in the application of science to production processes. But this is not our purpose.

The division and the organization of labor are based on the same logic and on the same conception of power in the firm in both cases. The movements and the division of workers, for example, are a function of time norms calculated and allotted by bureaucratic methods using organizational techniques which are similar in the East and the West.

But beyond this brief analysis of wage relations within firms, one must ask more generally what the role and the status of the wage-earning population are in the two systems.

3 Role and status of the wage-earners

Mobility of work and unemployment

In the STS, the active population is presently free to move in the absence of administrative constraints. This historical evolution is important if we consider that this has not always been the case, especially in the USSR. In this country until the end of the fifties, and until the beginning of the eighties for the agricultural population, changes of firm or Kolkhoz were subject to administrative authorization.

We are witnessing in the STE the emergence of great poles of activity which benefit from an important movement of manpower. The high level of wages is the principal factor behind this movement. It is true that these poles of activity are to be found in industries and sectors where wages are higher than average.

In addition, the lack of large-scale unemployment in the STE must be taken into account. This is an important difference between the two systems. Indeed, we have shown, following Kornai (101) that this phenomenon is based on the centralized allocation of production resources, including human resources. The budget constraints concerning the use of these resources are "soft." It must be remembered that in saying this we are referring to the number of individuals employed and not to the average wage. This explains the importance of manpower shortages in the STE.

But this question has important socio-political implications. The absence of unemployment and layoffs on a large scale is an element which gives a particular aspect to the wage-earning populations in the STE. Nevertheless, in the future, the economic and political leaders may seek to introduce certain kinds of unemployment for several reasons.

First of all, the question of the restructuring of old activities remains unanswered in the STS. The fact that firms are not able to lay-off is one of the factors contributing to great rigidity in economic structures. It is often difficult to create new firms given the shortage of manpower, and the suppression of obsolete production and activities is very slow.

Certain leaders maintain that unemployment is necessary as a means of putting pressure upon, or even of stimulating effort on the part of wage-earners, and of increasing their mobility. Monographs carried out in firms in the STS point to the very low mobility of industrial managers (Granick (83), pp. 484–5).

But it is not unlikely that were unemployment to be introduced in the STE, even progressively, it would run up against important political obstacles in a system where unemployment has always been held to be a specifically Capitalist affliction.

The role of secondary markets and parallel incomes

Secondary and parallel markets and incomes help to bring the wage structure in the STS closer to their Western counterparts.

First of all, in the STS, secondary and parallel activities and production correspond to a part of the labor market where there is no State regulation, and most of the time, no legislation. Workers' turnover and wage flexibility prevail in this area. In so far as having two jobs is common, a large number of wage-earners from the State sector are also in a competitive position.

In addition, we have shown that the income from parallel and secondary activities makes the position of wage-earners in the pay hierarchy in the STE and the WE comparable. It must not be forgotten that among the principal beneficiaries of this kind of income are the wage-earners in the services.

Moreover, the disposable income of the ruling elite is considerably increased when their benefits in kind are taken into account. If we consider these benefits, the percentage of disposable income of individuals at the top of the distribution, which is not significantly different in the STS and in the WS, confirms this statement.

Finally, the existence of private, official markets and parallel consumer goods and services markets strengthen the monetary constraint which weighs on the wage-earners of the STE.

Wage-earning, which is largely responsible for the isomorphisms that we have outlined all along in this study, is closely interconnected with economic and social relations in the West as in the East.

However, these analyses must not lead us to forget that we

uncovered important systemic differences throughout the course of our study.

2 SYSTEMIC EFFECT AND SOCIETAL EFFECT

The wage structures of a given economy are subject to two influences. First, this economy is a part of a system, and, in this way, the economy has certain properties of the system. We will summarize, first of all, our analyses of the systemic effects on wage structures. These concern the role of the State and the socio-political structures of one system and the other.

But the wage structures cannot be dissociated from social and cultural relations, from organizational practices typical to each society and which constitute the "societal effects." Secondly, we will underline the importance of the societal effects in each system, and we will examine to what extent these effects override the opposition between WS and STS.

1 The role of the State and of socio-political structures

The theoretical developments of part I led us to reconsider the traditional opposition between the market and planning theories and to substitute the distinction between mixed regulation and administrative regulation of wages. The essential difference lies in the fact that the State, in administrative regulation, intervenes directly in controlling the evolution of wages. This intervention takes place both at the macroeconomic level by fixing the norms of wage progression, and at the level of the firm by controlling the evolution of the average wage. This gives a distinctly different profile to the short-term evolution of the wage rate in the STS and in the WS: in the STS the latter is independent of the fluctuations of employment and of the investment cycle.

Historically, the emergence of a new ruling class in the STS drastically reduced pay dispersion. In a like manner, the promotion of the working class, the principal anchor of Soviet-type regimes, was accompanied by a sharp progression of the position of manual workers in the general distribution of pay. Nevertheless, their place and their role in the social division of labor and in the power structure of the firm has scarcely been modified compared to that of their Western counterparts.

Among white-collar workers, unskilled workers are in as unfavorable a position in the STS as in the WS. The promotion of manual workers was done to their detriment. They are at the bottom of the power hierarchy in firms, where they occupy jobs that are reputed to be unproductive, which from an ideological point of view, may serve to justify their low pay.

Comparing the positions of executives in both systems necessitates a more complex study. First of all, Western analysts do not entirely agree as to the criteria of selection and promotion of executives in the STS. Some underline the importance of the educational system and its "meritocratic" nature, which brings its function close to that in the WS (Markiewicz-Lagneau (118), pp. 410–37). Others, on the contrary (Lowit (110)), maintain that access to executive positions, especially upper executive positions, is a function of political criteria. In any case, the studies done in the STE as well as the monographs done on Soviet-type firms by certain Western researchers show that if higher education and training, usually at a university level, is not a sufficient condition to reach an executive position, it is nevertheless, at the present time, a necessary condition (Granick (83), chapter 14).

In addition, when comparing the pay of executives (divided by the average pay of all wage-earners), especially when taking into account benefits in kind, we uncovered no systemic difference. However, we must add several complements and restrictions to this result.

First of all, the category of executive covers a vast and heterogeneous group of activities. This brings up the problem of pay dispersion among executives, and more generally of pay dispersion within each category of wage-earner in the WS and in the STS.

We have shown that pay dispersion among manual workers is higher in the STS than in the WS. We explained this fact by a greater individualization in the organization of labor.

But this phenomenon appears to hold true for all categories of wage-earners. Indeed, whereas total pay dispersion remained stable for the years from 1960 to 1980 (see part I, chapter 4), the intercategorical differentials decreased. This evolution is particularly noticeable in the USSR. More and more, therefore, the general wage dispersion depends on intracategorical wage differentials.

Among executives, differentials are all the more significant in so far as the benefits in kind of leaders concern a small margin of the group of wage-earners (1 percent or 2 percent depending upon the estimations). Therein lies the source of a new systemic difference, for, if this evolution continues, the categories which serve to classify wage-earners in the WS will no longer be applicable to the analysis of the STS. It will become necessary to establish new classifications based on criteria which have as yet to be defined. Among these, we might expect to find the sector of activity (priority or non-priority), the position of firms and of their managers in relation to the administration (ministries, planning commissions). This position can, in fact, influence the outcome of wage bargaining between directors of firms and the Administration upon which they depend.

Nevertheless, such an evolution is not inevitable. We have learned from the past that "wage reforms" have sometimes taken significant steps backward. The aim of these reforms is to "recentralize" and unify the process of establishing wages, which results in an important decrease in intracategory differentials. An example of this appears in the Soviet reform of 1958.

2 The place of societal effects within each system

Our analyses have shown that, within each system, if we refer to all the parameters and factors studied, there are important differences in the wage structures of the countries studied. A systemic analysis tends to consider, in fact, that each system is made up of a group of economies whose characteristics, to begin with, are not distinct from each other. Presently, we will group the elements of such a societal study.

In the Western system
The first rift that appears in the Western system concerns the United States on the one hand and the West European economies on the other.

Although we have little, notably statistical, information available on which to base our comparison, there appears to be a clear difference between this country and the others.

First of all, the pay dispersion in this country is much higher than in the other economies. This is also the case for the disposable income of households. Next, the differentiation factors are more marked in the United States. This is the case, for example, of wage differences based on gender. These two phenomena are linked. The part of the variability "explained" by the differences in wages based on gender is the same as in other countries (see part I, chapter 3). The high differential between men's and women's wages in the United States is in fact just one of the aspects of the American societal effect which is characterized by greater wage inequalities than in other countries, whatever the factor or the type of population studied. The importance of these inequalities cannot be attributed solely to the diversity of the American population and activities.

It is not our purpose to analyze the origin of this societal effect. We will limit our remarks on this subject to possible axes of research. On the institutional level, collective wage bargaining, which is carried out at the level of firms or groups of firms, is more decentralized than in Western European countries. In addition, the State never intervenes in negotiations and allows auto-regulatory mechanisms to operate, which might explain the important short-term fluctuations in the wage rates.

It must not be forgotten that studies on the structuring of the labor market originated and were first applied in the United States. Thus, we cannot conclude that the American labor market answers the criteria of pure and perfect competition. This market is made up of segments influenced by the labor demand of firms based on a theory which we have tried to explain (part II, chapter 7).

Moreover, the weight of ideological and cultural factors must not be neglected. We must not forget that the importance of pay dispersion comes from the particularly favorable position of wage-earners at the top of the distribution, on the one hand, and, from the particularly unfavorable position of those at the bottom of the distribution. In order to explain the former, it must be pointed out that the wages of upper executives are more flexible than anywhere else and are a function of the results of the firm.

The situation of the wage-earners at the bottom of the distribution may be explained by the lack of any national minimum wage, and more generally by the dominating individualist ideology in American society. The latter remains reserved when faced with the possibility of any socialization of individual costs and risks.

Finally, the particular nature of the American model leads one to question whether there are not two sub-systems within the WS, one American and one Western European.

Within Western Europe, the principal difference appears between Denmark and the other countries studied. It is true that a French societal effect appeared in our analyses, concerning the general dispersion of earnings and wage differentials between manual and non-manual workers. In addition, France stood out against the FRG thanks to the works of Maurice, Sellier, and Silvestre (123), which are presented briefly in the introduction to chapter 8.

Nevertheless, the case of Denmark is noteworthy as being the opposite of the American one. Whatever the population considered, the general dispersion of pay and income is very low, and the factors behind the differentiation are weaker than in other countries. There is therefore here a societal coherence between the general distribution of wages and the factors differentiating them.

We are not in a position to elucidate this coherence. We can however trace a few possible paths.

We have shown the important role played by the main Danish Union in negotiating mechanisms that reduce the inequalities of wages, between men and women, for example, and in imposing a minimum wage. These Union actions often succeeded, with the help, or at least the approval of the Social Democratic governments that have been in power.

This is one of many examples of the existence of a Scandinavian model in the distribution of income and social welfare. Sweden is of course part of this model and, according to the estimations of Morrisson (126) is close to Denmark.

In the Soviet-type system
According to our statistical results national differences are less important in the STS than in the WS. We might add that it is possible to distinguish two categories of countries if we consider the dispersion of disposable income. Indeed, this dispersion is relatively high in the USSR, Poland, and Hungary, whereas it is low in the GDR, Bulgaria, Romania, and Czechoslovakia. However, this distinction is not quite so clear for pay dispersion (table 3.3).

These minimal national differences, at least on a general level, are difficult to interpret. We can point, in the case of Poland, to the important place occupied by the mining industry which traditionally has priority, and where pay is high. For Hungary, we must underline the less centralized nature of economic mechanisms and above all the development of secondary activities which can compete with the State sector.

To explain the weak dispersion of pay and the high social mobility in Czechoslovakia, Strmiska (156) evokes a deep egalitarian feeling that is part of the history of this country. This argument does not appear sufficient to our way of thinking, and it would be necessary to at least show how this feeling is translated into contemporary socio-economic reality.

3 Concluding remarks on the relations between systemic and societal effects

The systemic and societal effects are closely tied even if we have sought, for the sake of our analysis, to dissociate them. In fact, one must think that the systemic effect overdetermines the societal effect.

Let us take the example of the FRG and the GDR. During the course of our study, it came out that these two countries are very close in a number of areas, such as the system of formal education and professional training, the organization of labor, and the inter-sector wage structure. Nevertheless, membership in the STS has marked the wage structure of the GDR as compared to the FRG's in certain particular ways. This corresponds to the systemic effects which we outlined during our analysis. Manual workers are paid relatively more in the GDR as opposed to the FRG, the short-term evolution of the wage rate is more regular in the GDR, which is the mark of strict State control.

Finally, the wage structures of a given country are the product of a large number of influences: those which hinge on its social and political history, those which hinge on its economic functioning, and those which touch upon the institutions, themselves the result of its belonging to a given economic system.

Conclusion

The purpose of this conclusion is not to go over the broad lines of our comparison of the wage structures in the WS and the STS, as this was done in the final chapter of part II. The purpose is to answer two questions. The first has been brought up throughout our analyses. It concerns which criteria and which instruments are relevant in comparing the wage structures and their dynamics. We will present the results of our investigations on this point.

The second is a new objective. It concerns integrating the political and economic changes, that occurred in certain countries in the East in 1989 and 1990, into a broader prospective overview of labor and pay in Europe.

What criteria and what instruments are to be used in evaluating the dynamics of the wage structures?

Let us begin by taking the equality and efficiency criteria of pay defined by the market and planning theories that we presented in our introduction.

Is it possible to maintain that the equality criterion is better respected in one system than another? The answer is no: this criterion is not met in either the East or the West. Moreover, wage discrimination against women, wage differences between sectors of activity, excluding wage-earner skill differences and which are related to the structure of markets in which firms operate, or to the structure of the means of production, have the same impact on the total pay dispersion in the two systems.

Thus, the criterion of equality of pay appears to be an ideal state toward which each system may aspire, but which neither ever attains. The socio-economic dynamic emerged throughout our developments as a continuous movement of structuring and destructuring (Bartoli (40), pp. 361–75), that is to say as a movement which creates and destroys inequalities.

Is it possible to distinguish the wage structures in the WS and in the STS on the basis of the efficiency criterion? The answer to this question remains inderterminate. In fact, the logical chain which links in theory the level of formal education and professional training, to individual productivity and wages is very loose in the two systems. It must not be forgotten that the level of formal education and professional training is just one of many determinants of the dispersion of individual wages in the WS and in the STS. In addition, the test of the relation between labor productivity and the wage rate, on a yearly basis and at the macroeconomic level, turned out to be negative in both cases.

The search for and the analysis of the efficiency of pay structures calls for a finer and more diversified approach than that offered by the two theories, as well as a revision of the notion of individual labor productivity. In this respect, it is necessary to introduce the factors that certain authors in the West as in the East refer to as "pay incentives." The idea is sometimes put forth that the higher the pay dispersion, the more pay structures provide incentives. We think this idea can be criticized.

First of all, the essence of this question lies in the evaluation of the performances of individuals and groups of individuals. The general mechanisms of the economy play a fundamental role here. Many economists from the STE underline that the wage structure does not push workers to maximize their efforts in the STS as it does in the Western system. Our statistical results show that the dispersion of pay does not explain this systemic difference. We must seek the cause of this phenomenon in the methods of evaluating labor. These depend on a large group of parameters such as labor norms, and above all prices, the incoherences of which have often been described by the leaders of the STE themselves.

In addition work incentives are linked to social factors such as the forms of labor organization and the exercise of power in firms, as well as the adherence of economic agents to the objectives and ideals of the system to which they belong.

Finally, the limits of the efficiency and equality criteria are clear. They correspond to a strictly economic approach to wage structures, which, however necessary, is insufficient. We have shown this by introducing societal effects and systemic effects which link the economic system to the other elements of the system as a whole.

Here we may refer to the notion of "exogenous variables of

propagation" or "propogators" defined by Bartoli ((40), p. 365.). The introduction of propagators corresponds to the notion whereby the evolution of the economic system cannot be understood solely through the dynamics of prices and quantities. Possible interactions with variables external to the economic system must be added. In the case which is of interest to us, the wage structure can be represented by a vector corresponding to the wages of different categories of workers. Each element of this vector is in relation to certain economic variables of the system. But, each element also interacts with other factors, which we have pointed out throughout our study, and which may be qualified as political, administrative, or catalytic (depending on the degree of concentration of sectors) propagators, as propagators reflecting the division of society into classes, as cultural propagators, as propagators of the social division and organization of labor, as demographic and Union propagators.

It is certain that the wealth of this approach has not been fully exploited yet. Indeed, this approach has remained more qualitative than quantitative. The intensity of the force represented by each propagator, and the role thereof in the dynamics of the wage structures, has only been estimated for certain ones, and very globally at that.

It should be pointed out that we have built a precise and uniform model of the role of the concentration of activities on the intersection wage differences for each economy. In addition, the impact of the political propagator has appeared as a determinant of the small wage differences between manual and non-manual workers in the STS. Also, the administrative propagator determines a type of wage regulation which is specific to the STS.

In so far as propagators are fundamental determinants of the dynamics of the wage structures, but also of the economic system as a whole, they are at the heart of reflections on the perspectives of the two systems.

Perspectives for the beginning of the twenty-first century

In chapter 5, we showed that the two economic systems have had stable wage structures (at least for the global dispersion of earnings) since the fifties. We explained this phenomenon by an institutional, social and political stability in both systems up until the mid eighties.

From this point of view, there was a fundamental break at the end of the eighties and the beginning of the nineties during the political and social changes in Eastern Europe. The case of the USSR must be distinguished from that of other Eastern European countries.

For the Soviet Union, if only because of its size, economic transformations will be slow. In addition, this country made little progress toward reforms in the seventies and eighties. Theoretical and applied reflections on the future economic changes remain at an embryonic stage (Aganbeguian (27)).

The structural evolutions necessary to bring the USSR close to the WE are tremendous. In the case of employment alone, one has only to consider that at the end of the eighties almost one fifth of the active population (evaluated at 125 million people) was employed in agriculture. Finally, there are enormous political obstacles to realizing such transformations. This is why the labor economy (the means of allocating human resources and the managing thereof within organizations) is bound to evolve slowly during the nineties. As for the wage structures, sectors with relatively high wages (mining and steel) will be slow to lose hold of the particular position they occupy in the USSR.

The movement toward decentralization and the autonomy of firms might bring about an increase in the general dispersion of wages and income. Political decentralization and the independence of some Republics might have the same effect. But the evolution will be gradual given resistances to change which are inevitable in this area, and given the ever possible about-turns.

For the Eastern European countries that are the most advanced in their move toward transformation of the economic system (Hungary, Poland, Czechoslovakia, and the GDR, now part of unified Germany), the perspectives are different. It is clear that they have opted for a market oriented economy. Our results tend to prove that in *matters of the labor economy and the wage structures*, change towards a Western model will be facilitated by the isomorphisms which we have previously underlined.

Indeed the upheavals at the end of the eighties were preceded by a slow decentralization of the labor force and wage management at the organization level (especially in Hungary and to a lesser degree in Poland). This should make it easier to move toward a Western model.

In many areas such as the financial and monetary system, the place and the role of the States' economic policy, institutions and mechanisms will take a long time to set up. On the other hand, human resources are an advantage in favor of the transition. First of all, the level of formal education and professional training of the labor force is relatively high and in certain areas as high as in the WE (Gazso (81), Gruson and Markiewicz (84), Tanguy and Kieffer (160)). In addition, the principles of the organization of labor, the rules regarding promotion, the model for establishing pay within organizations are close. This makes it possible to assume that the labor force has the capacity to adapt to changes that are taking place or that will happen.

One should, nevertheless, not underestimate the breadth of future changes. They will cause massive unemployment, initially at least. Structural changes are inexorable. They will bring about the disappearance or the decrease in the numbers of employees in big State firms or in heavy industry in favor of light industry and services. To this structural unemployment, which will make it necessary to bring about worker retraining programs, one must add unemployment due to systemic change. By this we mean that the change in economic regulation will bring about the suppression of less profitable activities which in the former State system were heavily subsidized.

In the more particular area of wage structures, the general dispersion of pay will not evolve on a large scale if we consider that, during the eighties, there was no systemic difference in this area. However, the relative position of certain qualifications or socio-professional categories may vary according to new social priorities (promotion of commercial and financial functions in firms, for example).

As for Western Europe, the nineties will be marked by the economic integration of the EC countries. Our study showed that in fact in the five EC countries studied, the wage structures (general dispersion of pay, wage differentials between qualifications) varied considerably from one economy to the next in the mid-eighties. It appears that the period of "Common Market" was initially built on an area of free trade, but did not succeed in making working conditions or pay homogeneous as foreseen by the treaty of Rome. The economic integration of productive systems, which should progress during the nineties, may help to achieve the objectives set up by the treaty[1]

[1] See Hellier, J. and Redor, B.: *Le travail en Europe aujourd'hui et demain*, Masson, 1991.

Finally, one cannot rule out the hypothesis of the creation of a large economic confederation which, in the long run, will regroup the European economies in the East and West. In this perspective, the factors that bring them together, that is to say the isomorphisms, that we pointed to throughout our study, may be considered as the first elements which might serve as the foundations of an economic union on a continental scale.

Appendix

The following tables sum up the main statistical sources used in the book.

Western economies

	Belgium, Denmark, France	FRG	United Kingdom	United States
Name of the survey and publication containing this survey	*Structure of earnings 1978–79* Vol. 2: France Vol. 3: Belgium Vol. 5: Denmark	*Gehalt und Lohnstruktur-erhebung 1978*	*New Earnings Survey 1980*	*Money income of house-holds in the USA,* Current population reports series, p. 60 US Department of Commerce 1985, 1981
	Statistical Office of the European Community 1983, 1984 (EURO-STAT)	Statistische Bundes Amt 1982	Central Statistical Office 1981	
Statistical methodology	Sample survey. In industry the sampling ratio varies between 10% and 12% according to the countries.	Sample survey. Methodology is harmonized with EUROSTAT	Sample survey. The sampling ratio is 1%	Sample survey. In 1985 57,000 households were surveyed
Periodicity	Irregular	Irregular	Yearly	Yearly
Sectors surveyed	Industry. Building and civil engineering, trade insurance	Industry. Building and civil engineering trade insurance	All sectors (including public administration)	All sectors, except armed forces (including public administration)

Western economies (cont.)

	Belgium, Denmark, France	FRG	United Kingdom	United States
Units surveyed	Establishments of more than 10 wage-earners	Establishments of more than 10 wage-earners	Households	Households
Wage-earners surveyed	All wage-earners full-time employed	All wage-earners full-time employed	Men: more than 20 years old, Women: more than 17 years full-time employed	All wage-earners full-time employed
Type of payment surveyed	Hourly earnings (manual workers) Monthly earnings (all workers) before income taxes	Hourly earnings (manual workers) Monthly earnings (all workers) before incomes taxes	Hourly earnings Weekly earnings before income taxes	Yearly earnings before income taxes

Soviet-type economies

	Hungary	Poland	GDR	Czechoslovakia	USSR
Name of the survey, and publication containing this survey	*Foglalkoztatotsag es Kereti Aranyok* (yearbook on employment and wages) Hungarian Statistical Office	*Rocznik Slatystyczny* (statistical yearbook) Polish Statistical Office	*Statistisches Jarhbuch der Deutschen Republik* (statistical yearbook) Statistical Office of the GDR	*Statisticka Rocenka* (statistical yearbook) Czechoslovakian Statistical Office	*Otchet* (Census on wages March of each year). This census is not published by TSU. Data can be found in (146) and (147) of our bibliography

Soviet-type economies (cont.)

	Hungary	Poland	GDR	Czechoslovakia	USSR
Statistical methodology	Exhaustive census	Exhaustive census	Exhaustive census	Exhaustive census	Exhaustive census
Periodicity	Yearly	Yearly	Yearly	Yearly	Every two or three years
Sectors surveyed	All sectors (including public administration) except armed forces	All sectors (including public administration) except armed forces	All sectors (including public administration) except armed forces	All sectors (including public administration) except armed forces	All sectors (including public administration) except armed forces
Units surveyed	All firms and organizations of the state sector	All firms and organizations of the state sector	All firms and organizations of the state sector	All firms and organizations of the state sector	All firms and organizations of the state sector
Wage-earners surveyed	All wage-earners full-time employed	All wage-earners full-time employed	All wage-earners full-time employed	All wage-earners full-time employed	All wage-earners full-time employed
Type of payment surveyed	Monthly earnings before tax	Monthly wages before taxes	Monthly earnings before taxes	Monthly wages before taxes	Monthly earnings before taxes

Glossary of principal terms used on the subject of wage inequalities

Concepts concerning the description and the analysis of wage inequalities are not strictly determined, and they may vary in use from author to author. It is for this reason that we will present here the exact meaning as used in this work. Given the small number of terms, we will present them in logical and not alphabetical order.

Wage inequalities: This term is used in the most general sense to signify the differences or differentiation in wages for individuals or groups of individuals whatever the causes.

Disparities: Differences in wages of individuals who do the same job with the same intensity.

Discriminations: Wage disparities effecting certain individuals or groups thereof on the basis of their personal characteristics such as religion, culture, gender, age, social background.

Wage hierarchy: Ordinate series of *n* prices relative to *n* categories of wage-earners, devoid of wage disparities.

Wage structure: The group of relations which determine the differences in wages for individuals and groups of individuals. One goes from the notion of hierarchy to that of structure by taking disparities into account.

Wage distribution: Frequency of a population of wage-earners distributed according to the increasing level of wages.

Dispersion: Indicator of the measure of the individual or group wage differentials relative to the average of the population considered. The main indicators of dispersion used in this work are standard deviation, the coefficient of variation, and variance.

Statistical sources and bibliography

STATISTICAL SOURCES

SOURCES: STATISTICAL OFFICES OF THE EUROPEAN COMMUNITIES

(1) OSCE: *Education et formation*, Eurostat, 1980.
(2) OSCE: *Investissements annuels en actifs fixes dans les enterprises industrielles des Communautés Européenes*: 1977–1982
(3) OSCE: *Structure des salaires en Belgique 1978–1979*, vol. 3, Eurostat, 1984.
(4) OSCE: *Structure des salaires au Danemark 1978–1979*, vol. 5, Eurostat, 1984.
(5) OSCE: *Structure des salaires en France 1978–1979*, vol. 2, Eurostat, 1983.
(6) OSCE: *Structure des salaires au Royaume Uni 1978–1979*, vol. 10, Eurostat, 1986.

AMERICAN SOURCES

(7) US Department of Commerce: *Money income of households, families and persons in the United States*, Reports series P. 60, 1981 and 1985.

FRENCH SOURCES

(8) Baudelot, C. and Lebeaupin, A., *Les salaires de 1950 à 1975*, département population et ménages, division revenu, INSEE, 1978.
(9) INSEE, *Rapport sur les comptes de la nation*, série C, 1983 and 1984.
(10) INSEE, *La Structure des salaires dans l'industrie et les services en 1978*, Série M nᵒ 90–91, March 1981.
(11) INSEE, *Les salaires dans l'industrie, le commerce et les services en 1980*, Série M, nᵒ 113, July 1985.

WEST GERMAN SOURCES

(12) Statistisches Bundesamt: *Gehalts und Lohnstrukturerhebung: Arbeiter und Angelstelltenverdienste in Produzierenden Gewerbe im Brof und Einzelhandel bei Kreditinstituten und Versicherungsgewerbe 1978,* Faschersie 16, 1980.

(13) Statistiches Bundesamt: *Gehalts und Lohnstrukturerhebung 1978: Arbeiter und Angelstelltenverdienste in Produzierenden Gewerbe im Grof und Einzelhandel bei Kreditinstituten und Versicherungsgewerbe,* 1982.

(14) Statisches Bundesamt: *Statistiches Jahrbuche für die Bundersrepublik Deutschland,* 1982 and 1983.

(15) Statistiches Bundesamt: *Volkwirtschaftliche Gesamtrechnungen* Fascherie 18, Reihe 1, Konten und Standardtabellen, 1981.

BRITISH SOURCES

(16) Statistical Office: *Annual Abstract of Statistics,* 1983 and 1984.

(17) Statistical Office: *Employment Gazette,* 1983 and 1984.

(18) Statistical Office: New Earnings Survey, 1980.

HUNGARIAN SOURCES

(19) Hungarian National Office of Statistics: *Foglalkoztattsag es kereseti aranyok* 1980 (yearbook of employment and wages in 1980).

(20) Hungarian National Office of Statistics: *Statisztikai evkőnyu* (statistical yearbook), 1980 and 1984.

POLISH SOURCES

(21) Polish Office of Statistics: *Roznik Statystyczny* (statistical yearbook), 1962, 1981, and 1984.

EAST GERMAN SOURCES

(22) Staatliche Zentralverwaltung fur Statisstik: statistisches Jarbuch der Deutchen Demokratischen Republik, 1968 and 1982.

CZECH SOURCES

(23) Czechoslovak Office of Statistics: *Statisticka Rocenka* (Statistical yearbook), 1971, 1980, and 1982.

SOVIET SOURCES

(24) Central Office of Statistics: *Narodnoe khozjaistvo SSSR* (The Soviet national economy), 1980 and 1984.

BIBLIOGRAPHY

(25) Abdel, Fadil M., *La planification des prix en Union Soviétique*, Presses Universitaires de France, 1975.

(26) Adam, J., *Wage Control and Inflation in the Soviet Block Countries*, Macmillan, 1979.

(27) Aganbeguian, A.G., *Perestroîka, le double défi soviétique*, Economica, 1987.

(28) Aglietta, M., *Régulation et crise du capitalisme, l'expérience des Etats Unis*, Calmann-Lévy, 1976.

(29) Aksentievics, G., "International comparative survey on the situation of industrial workers," in Bohm, A. and Kolosi, T., *Social Structure and Stratification in Hungary*, Budapest institute for Social Sciences, 1982, pp. 405–31.

(30) Aleksandrova, E. and Fedorovskaja, E., "The mechanisms behind the formation and the elevation of consumption," *Voprosy ekonomiki*, 1, January 1984, pp. 15–25 (in Russian).

(31) Andorka, R. and Kolosi, T., (eds.), *Stratification and Inequality*, Budapest Institute for Social Sciences, 1984.

(32) Andorka, R. and Zagorski, K., "Structural factors of social mobility in Hungary and Poland," *The Polish Sociological Bulletin*, 2, 1979, pp. 128–38.

(33) Archembault, E. and Greffe, X. (under the direction of), *Les économies non officielles*, La Découverte, 1984.

(34) Arrow, K. J., "The theory of discrimination," in Ashenfelter, O. and Rees, A., *Discrimination in Labor Markets*, Princeton University Press, 1973, pp. 3–13.

(35) Askanas, B. and Levcik, F., *The Dispersion of Wages in the CMEA Countries*, The Vienna Institute for Comparative Economic Studies, reprint series 70, December 1983.

(36) Asselain, J.C., "La répartition des revenus dans les pays du Centre-Est européen," in Kende, P. and Strmiska, Z. (95), pp. 33–77.

(37) Atkinson, A.B., *The Economics of Inequality*, Oxford University Press, 1975.

(38) Ballot, G. and Piatecki, C., "Turnover, productivité et hiérarchie dans le marché du travail," *Revue Economique*, 2, March 1986, pp. 285–306.

(39) Barro, R.J. and Grossman, H.I., *Money, Employment and Inflation*, Cambridge University Press, 1976.

(40) Bartoli, H., *Economie et création collective*, Presses Universitaires de France, 1977.

(41) Bauer, T., "Investment cycles in planned economies," *Acta Oeconomica*, 3, 1978, pp. 243–60.

(42) Becker, G.S., *Human Capital*, National Bureau of Economic Research, 1964.

(43) Becker, G.S., *The Economics of Discrimination*, University of Chicago, 1971.

(44) Benassy, J.P., *Macroéconomie et théorie du déséquilibre*, Dunod, 1984.

(45) Benassy, J.P., Boyer R., and Gelpi R.M., "Régulation des économies capitalistes et inflation," *Revue économique*, May 1979, pp. 397–441.

(46) Bergson, A., *The Structure of Soviet Wages*, Harvard University Press, 1954.

(47) Bergson, A., "Comparative productivity and efficiency in the Soviet Union and the United States," in Eckstein, A., *Comparison of Economic Systems: Theoretical and Methodological Approaches*, University of California, 1971, pp. 161–218.

(48) Bergson, A., *Productivity and the Social System in the USSR and the West*, Harvard University Press, 1978.

(49) Bergson, A., "Income inequality under Soviet socialism," *Journal of Economic Literature*, 22, September 1984, pp, 1052–99.

(50) Boncoeur, J., "Le traitement du travail dans quelques modèles théoriques de planification de la production en économie socialiste," in Lavigne, M. (ed.), *Travail et monnaie en système socialiste*, Economica, 1985, pp. 205–32.

(51) Borc, L., "La répartition selon le travail" in *Work Pays under Socialism*, Ekonomika, 1977, pp. 129–45 (in Russian).

(52) Boyer, R., "Les salaires en longue période", *Economie et Statistique*, September 1978, pp. 27–57.

(53) Boyer, R. (under the direction of), *La flexibilité du travail en europe: une étude comparative des transformations du rapport salarial en Europe dans sept pays de 1973 à 1984*, La découverte, 1986.

(54) Cayatte, J.L., *Qualifications et hiérarchies des salaires*, Economica, 1983.

(55) Cellier, F., Le Berre, R., and Miquieu, D., "Le modèle multinational Atlas: première partie, les modèles par pays," *Economie et Prévision*, 62, 1984, pp. 1–61.

(56) CERC, *Dispersion et disparités de salaires en France au cours des vingt dernières années*, La Documentation français, 25–26, 1st and 2nd trimesters 1975.

(57) CERC, *Dispersion et disparités de salaires à l'étranger: Etats-Unis, Grande Bretagne, Allemagne Fédérale; Comparaison avec la France*, La Documentation française, 29–30, 1st and 2nd trimesters 1976.

(58) CERC, *L'évolution des salaires en France au cours des trente dernières années*, La Documentation français, 97, 1985.

(59) Chapman, J., "Soviet wages under Socialism," in Abouchar, A., *The Socialist Price Mechanism*, North Carolina, Duke University, 1977, pp. 246–81.

(60)   Chavance, B. (under the direction of), *Régulation, cycle et crises dans les économis socialistes*, EHESS, 1987.

(61)   Cordova E., "La négociation collective dans les pays industrialisé, un aperçu comparatif," *Revue International du Travail*, July-August 1978, pp. 459–75.

(62)   Coriat, B., "Du système de Taylor à l'atelier de série robotisé: Quel Taylorisme demain?" in de Montmillin, M. and Pastre, O., *Le Taylorisme*, La Découverte, 1983, pp. 335–50.

(63)   Csikos Nagy, B., "Productivity and Wage Policy in the Socialist Countries," *Est, Revue du CESES*, September 1978, pp. 117–28.

(64)   Dancet, G., *Contractualisation salariale et compétivité: la Belgique*, in Boyer, R. (53), pp. 105–31.

(65)   Daubigny, J.P., Fizaine, F., and Silvestre, J.J., "Les différences de salaire entre entreprises, étude microéconomique," *Revue économique*, 2, 1971, pp. 214–45.

(66)   Denis, H. and Lavigne, M., *Le problème des prix en Union Soviétique*, Cujas, 1965.

(67)   Depardieu, D. and Payen, J.F., "Disparités de salaries dans l'industrie en France et en Allemagne: des ressemblances frappantes," *Economie et Statistique*, May 1986, pp. 23–34.

(68)   Doeringer, P.B. and Piore, M.J., *Internal Labor Markets and Manpower Analysis*, Heath Lexington Books, 1979.

(69)   Dubois, P. and Mako, C., *La division du travail dans l'industrie: étude du cas hongrois et français*, CNRS, University Paris VII, Groupe de Sociologie de travail, 1980.

(70)   Duchêne, G., "Economie parallèle et inégalités de revenus," in Kende, P. and Strimska, Z. (95), pp. 77–83.

(71)   Duchêne, G., *L'économie de l'URSS*, La Découverte, 1987.

(72)   Dunlop, J.J. and Galenson, W., *Labor in the Twentieth century*, Harcourt Brace, 1978.

(73)   Ehrlich, E., Kramarics, G. and Tüü, L., *Enterprise and Establishment Size in Industry in East and West, Collected Statistics*. Wiener Institut für Internationale Wirtsschaftsvergleiche, 61, 1980.

(74)   Engels, F., *Anti-Duhring*. Editions sociales, 1971.

(75)   Fisher, I., *The Theory of Interest*, Macmillan, 1930.

(76)   Flakiersky, H., "Economic reform and income distribution: study of Hungary and Poland," *Eastern European Economics*, 24 (1–2), Winter 85–6, pp. 1–165.

(77)   Fiedman, M., "The role of Monetary Policy," *American Economic Review*, 58, 1968, pp. 1–17.

(78)   Galasi, P., "L'économie non officielle hongroise," in Archambault and Greffe X. (33), pp. 171–82.

(79)   Galasi, P. and Sik, "A study of the position of firms on the labor market," *Szocialista Vallat*, 1979 (in Hungarian).

(80) Gambier, D. and Vernières, M., *Le marché du travail*, Economica, second edition, 1985.

(81) Gazso, F., "Social mobility of young workers in some Socialist countries," in Böhm, A. and Kolosi, T., *Social Structure and Stratification in Hungary*, Budapest Institute for Social Sciences, 1982, pp. 363–403.

(82) Granick, D., *Le chef d'enterprise soviétique*, Edition de l'enterprise moderne, 1963.

(83) Granick, D., *Enterprise Guidance in Eastern Europe*, Princeton University Press, 1975.

(84) Gruson, P. and Markiewicz, Lagneau J., "L'enseignement supérieur et son efficacité: France, Etats Unis, URSS, Pologne", *Notes et études documentaaires*, 4713–14, April 1983, pp. 1–174.

(85) Hagelmayer, I., "Agreements by collective bargaining in the Socialist countries," *Acta Juridica Acadmiae Scientiarum Hungaricae*, K Tome 15, 3–4, pp. 399–416.

(86) Hensen, V., *Wage Differences, Wage Policy and Employment in the 1970's*, The Danish National Institute of Social Research (in Danish with a summary in English, pp. 157–75), 1980.

(87) Howard, D.H., "The disequilibrium model in a controlled economy: an empirical test of the Barro-Grossman model," *American Economic Review*, December 1976, pp. 861–79.

(88) Howard, D.H., *The Disequilibrium Model in a Controlled Economy*, Lexington Books, 1979.

(89) Jenny, F. and Weber, A.P., "Concentration, syndicalisation et rémunération salariale dans l'industrie manufacturière française," *Revue économique*, July 1975, pp. 622–54.

(90) Jurisse, A., *Statistiques harmonisées des gains: description et proposition d'aménagement*. Rapport présenté à l'Office statistique des communautés européennes, Eurostat, E2, 83108, November 1983.

(91) Kabaj, M., *Payment by Results and Job Evaluation in Poland and in Other Selected Socialist Countries*. Institute of Labor and Social Studies. Roneotyped document, Warsaw, September 1979.

(92) Kalecki, M., "On the Gibrat Distribution," *Econometrica*, 1945, pp. 161–70.

(93) Kantorovitch, L.V., *Calcul économique et utilisation des ressources*, Dunod, 1983.

(94) Kende, P., "Le partage des ressources au niveau de la consommation," in Kende, P. and Strmiska, Z. (95), pp. 86–124.

(95) Kende, P. and Strminska, Z., *Egalité et inégalités en Europe de l'Est*, Presses de la Fondation nationale des Sciences Politiques, 1984.

(96) Kerr, C., *Labor Markets and Wage Determination, the Balkanisation of Labor Markets and Other Essays*. University of California Press, 1977.

(97) Kirsch, L.J. *Soviet Wages: Changes in Structure and Administration since 1956*, MIT University Press, 1972.

(98) Kniazeff, I., "Le travail et les sociétés socialistes," *Annuaire de l'URSS et des pays socialistes européens*, Librairie Istra, 1977, pp. 540–77.

(99) Koopmans, T.C. and Montias, J.M., "On the description and comparison of economic systems," in Eckstein, A., *Comparison of Economic Systems: Theoretical and Methodological Approaches*, University of California, 1971, pp. 30–74.

(100) Kornai, J., *Anti-equilibrium*, North-Holland, 1971.

(101) Kornai J., *Economics of shortage*, North-Holland, 2 volumes, 1980. translation used: *Socialisme et économie de la pénurie*, Economica, 1984.

(102) Krencik, W., *The Fundamental Problems of Wages and the Economic Reform*. Institute of Labor and Social Affairs, Warsaw, 1982 (in Polish).

(103) Lange, O., *Leçons d'économétrie*. Gauthier-Villars, 1970.

(104) Lavigne, M., "L'oligopole dans la planification," *Economie et Société*, *Cahiers de l'ISMEA*, série G, September 1977, pp. 991–1036.

(105) Lavigne, P. and M., *Regards sur la constitution soviétique de 1977*, Economica, 1979.

(106) *Leistungslohn in West und Osteuropa*, Institute für angewandte Arbeitswissenschaft, April 1982.

(107) Leithauser, G., *Des flexibilités et pourtant une crise: la République Fédérale allemande*, in Boyer R. (53), pp. 181–207.

(108) Lévy-Garboua, L., "Education, origine sociale et distribution des gains," in Eicher, J.C., and Lévy-Garboua, L. (eds.), *Economie de l'éducation*, Economica, 1979, pp. 29–48.

(109) Lowit, T., *Le Syndicalisme de type soviétique*, A. Colin, 1971.

(110) Lowit, T., *Autorité, encadrement et organisation du travail dans les industries des pays de l'Est européen*. Laboratoire de sociologie du travail et des relations professionnelles du CNAM, May 1980.

(111) Lydall, H., *The Structure of Earnings*, Clarendon Press, Oxford, 1968.

(112) McAuley, A., *Economic Welfare in the Soviet Union*, Allen and Unwin, 1979.

(113) McAuley, A., *Women's work and wages in the Soviet Union*. Allen and Unwin, 1981.

(114) Malcomson, J.M., "Unemployment and the efficiency wage hypothesis", *Economic Journal*, 91, December 1981, pp. 848–66.

(115) Malinvaud, E., *Réexamen de la théorie du chômage*, Calmann-Lévy, 1980.

(116) Malle, LS., "Heterogeneity of the Soviet labor market as a limit to a more efficient utilisation of manpower," in Lane, D. (ed.), *Labour and Employment in the USSR*, Harvester Press, 1986, pp. 122–44.

(117) Marchal, J. and Lecaillon, J., *La répartition du revenu national*, vol. I, *Les salariés*, M. Th. Génin, 1958.

(118) Markiewicz, Lagneau J., *Le système scolaire et l'éthos méritocratique*, in Kende, P. and Strminska, Z. (95), pp. 410–37.

(119) Marsden, D. and Saunders, C., *Pay Inequalities in the European Communities*, Butterworths: European Studies, 1981.

(120) Martinet, G., *Sept syndicalismes*, Le seuil, 1979.

(121) Marx, K., *Le Capital*, Editions sociales, 3 volumes, 1970.

(122) Marx, K. and Engels, F., *Critiques du programme de Gotha et d'Erfurt*, Editions Sociales, 1972.

(123) Maurice, M., Sellier, F., and Silvestre, J.J., *Politique d'éducation et organisation industrielle en France et e Allemagne*. Presses Universitaires de France, 1982.

(124) Moroney, J.R., "Do Women Earn Less Under Capitalism?" *Economic Journal*, September 1979, pp. 601–13.

(125) Morrisson, C., "Distribution des revenus et des droits dans les pays de l'Ouest et de l'Est," in Kende, P. and Strmiska, Z. (95), pp. 218–56.

(126) Morrisson, C., "Income distribution in East European and Western countries," *Journal of Comparative Economics*, 8, 1984, pp. 121–38.

(127) Müller-Jentsch W., "Nouvelles formes de conflits et stabilité institutionnelles en R.F.A.," *Sociologie du travail*, 2, April–June, 1980, pp. 152–68.

(128) Nagy, A. and Sziraczki, G., "Labour market segmentation in the mid 1970's in Hungary," Roneotyped document, Budapest University, November 1981.

(129) Oaxaca, L., "Sex discrimination in wages," in Ashenfelter, O. and Rees, A., *Discrimination in Labor Markets*, Princeton University, 1973, pp. 124–51.

(130) Ofer, G. and Vinokur, A., *Private Sources of Income of the Soviet Urban Household*, Contribution to the World Congress of Soviet Studies of Garmisch (1980).

(131) Ofer, G. and Vinokur, A., *The Distribution of Income of the Urban Population in the Soviet Union*, contribution at the World Congress of Soviet Students of Garmisch, 1980.

(132) Okun, A.M., *Equality and Efficiency – The Big Tradeoff*, Brookings Institution, French translation used: *Egalité et efficacité. Comment trouver l'équilibre?* Economica, 1982.

(133) Pareto, W., *Cours d'économie politique*. Librairie Droz (new edition by G.H. Bousquet and G. Busino), 1964, (2 volumes).

(134) Pavlevski, J., *Le niveau de vie en URSS*, Economica, 1975.

(135) Perrot, Dormont A., *Information, incitation et contrats: des fondements microéconomiques pour une dynamique du marché du travail*, Thèse de Doctorat d'Etat, University of Paris I, 1986.

(136) Perroux, F., *Unités actives et mathématiques nouvelles*, Dunod, 1975.

(137) Piaget, J., *Biologie et connaissance*, Gallimard, Idées, 1967.

(138) Piore, M.J., "Dualism in the labor market: a response to incertainty

and flux: the case of France," *Revue économique*, 1, January 1978, pp. 26–48.

(139) Pryor, F., *Property and Industrial Organization in Communist and Capitalist Nations*. Indiana University Press, 1973.

(140) Redor, D., "Quand Etat et salariés s'affrontent sur le partage du revenu national," *Economie et humanisme*, 278, July-August 1984, pp. 42–50.

(141) Redor, D., *Salaire et système économique: un essai de comparison*, Thèse de Doctorat d'Etat, University of Paris I, 1985.

(142) Redor, D., "Régulation de la part salariale en système socialiste," in Lavigne, M. and Andreff, W. (under the direction of), *La réalité du socialisme, contrainte, adaptation, progrès*, Economica, 1985, pp. 143–68.

(143) Redor, D., "L'approche quantitative de la comparaison des systèmes économiques," *Revue d'études comparatives Est-Ouest*, 4, December 1986, pp. 27–48.

(144) Revecz, G., Fazekas, K., Kalasz, I., and Köllö, J., *Wage Bargaining in Hungarian Firms* (2 volumes). Hungarian Academy of Sciences, Institute of Economics, Studies 23 and 24, 1984.

(145) Riboud, J., *Accumulation du capital humain*, Economica, 1978.

(146) Rimachevskaja, N.M. and Rabkina, N.E., *The bases of the differentiation of wages and incomes of the population*, Ekonomica, 1972 (in Russian).

(147) Rimachevskaja, N.M. and Rabkina, N.E., "The income of households as an indicator of well-being," in *Besoins, revenus et consommation*, Nauka, 1979, pp, 84–107 (in Russian).

(148) Rogulska, B., "La structure d'incitation au travail en système socialiste," Thesis for the Doctorat d'Etat, University of Paris I, 1982.

(149) Roy, A.D., "The distribution of earnings and of individual output," *Economic Journal*, 1950, pp. 489–505.

(150) Sapir, J., "Mouvements cycliques dans l'économie soviétique: un modèle investissement, productivité, emploi," in Chavanne B. (60), pp. 159–92.

(151) Seurot, F., "Formes de marché et politique des prix en économie soviétique," in Lavigne M. (ed.), *Travail et monnaie en système socialiste*, Economica, 1981, pp. 148–78.

(152) Seurot, F., *Inflation et emploi dans les pays socialistes*, Presses Universitaires de France, 1983.

(153) Silvestre, J.J. *Les salaires ouvriers dans l'industrie française*, Bordas, 1983.

(154) Simon, H.A., *Models of Man*, Wiley, 1957.

(155) Sofer, C., *La division du travail entre les hommes et les femmes*, Economica, 1985.

(156) Strmiska, Z., "La mobilité sociale des sociétés de type soviétique dans une perspective comparative," in Kende, P. and Strmiska, Z. (95), pp. 159–217.

(157) Strumilin, S.G., "On the determination of value and its application in the conditions of socialism," *Voprosy ekonomiki*, 8, August 1959, pp. 92–92 (in Russian).

(158) Strumilin, S.G., *The Problems of Socialism and of Communism in the Soviet Union*, Nauka, 1961 (in Russian).

(159) Strumilin, S.G., *Problems of the Economy of Labor*, Nauka, 1964 (in Russian).

(160) Tanguy, L. and Kieffer, A. "L'école et l'enterprise, l'expérience des deux Allemagnes," *Notes et études documentaires*, 4669–4670, May 1982, pp. 1–159.

(161) Taubman, P., *Sources of Inequality in Earnings*, North-Holland, 1975.

(162) Tobin, J., "Inflation and unemployment", *American Economic Review*, March 1972, pp. 141–52.

(163) Turner, H.A. and Jackson, D.A.S., "On the stability of wage differences and productivity," *British Journal of Industrial Relations*, March 1969, pp. 3–15.

(164) Urgense, "Le taylorisme arithmétique dans les économies planifiées du centre," *Critique de l'économie politique*, 19, April–June 1982.

(165) Vaneecloo, N., *Théorie de la transformation de la main d'oeuvre*, Economica, 1982.

(166) Ward, T., "De la crise rampante à la rupture," in Boyer R. (53), pp. 65–88.

(167) Weigend, A., *Lohndynamik und Arbeitsmarktstruktur*, Campus, 1981.

(168) Weiss, L.W., "Concentration and labor earnings," *American Economic Review*, March 1966.

(169) Wiles, P.J.D., *Distribution of Income: East and West*, North-Holland, 1974.

(170) Wiles, P.J.D. and Markowski., "Income and distribution under communism and capitalism: some facts about Poland, the UK, the USA, the USSR," *Soviet Studies*, 4, April 1971, pp. 487–510.

(171) Yellen, J.L., "Efficiency wage models of unemployment," *American Economic Review*, 74 (2), May 1974, pp. 200.

(172) Zvolesnky, V., *Socio-economic Aspects of Wage Structure in Czechoslovakia*, Internation Social Science Council, Internal Workshop on Wage and Payment Systems, Siofolk (Hungary), September 1986.

Index